Vladimir VYSOTSKY:

Hamlet with a Guitar

Vladimir
VYSOTSKY:

Hamlet with a Guitar

PROGRESS PUBLISHERS · MOSCOW

Translated from the Russian by *Sergei Roy*

Designed by *Boris Kazachkov*

Compiled by *Yuri Andreyev, Iosif Boguslavsky*

Владимир Высоцкий. **Человек. Поэт. Актер**

На английском языке

Printed in the Union of Soviet Socialist Republics

$$B \frac{4702010200\text{-}284}{014(01)\text{-}90} 58\text{-}90$$

ISBN 5—01—001125-5

CONTENTS

Page

Translator's Note 9
Vladimir Vysotsky in His Lifetime and after Death 14

I. SELECTED POEMS AND SONGS (50 OUT OF THE
TOTAL 700) 29

From the War Songs
   Братские могилы 30
   Common Graves 31
   Он не вернулся из боя 30
   He Was Shot Down in Yesterday's Fighting . . . 31
   Мы вращаем Землю 32
   We Turn the World 33

For the Sea Cycle
   «Корабли постоят — и ложатся на курс...» 36
   "Anchored Ships Lie in Port..." 37
   Белое безмолвие 38
   The White Silence 39
   «Штормит весь вечер, и пока...» 40
   "The Storm Is Raging All the Night..." 41
   Баллада о брошенном корабле 42
   The Ballad of an Abandoned Ship 43

Sketches of Everyday Life
   Песня завистника 48
   Song of a Begrudger 49
   Смотрины 50
   A Bride-Show 51
   Маски 54
   Masks 55
   Товарищи ученые 56
   Comrade Scientists 57

From the Sports Cycle
   Песня о друге 62
   Friendship 63

Songs of the Fairytale Cycle
   Про дикого вепря 66
   A Song about a Wild Boar 67

A Poet and His Work

О фатальных датах и цифрах 70
On Fatal Dates and Figures 71
Натянутый канат 72
The Tightrope 73
  I. Певец у микрофона 76
  I. A Singer at the Microphone 77
 II. Песнь микрофона 78
 II. Song of a Microphone 79
Чужая колея 82
Someone Else's Rut 83
Бег иноходца 86
The Pacer's Race 87
Я из дела ушел 88
I Have Quit My Old Job 89
Мой Гамлет 90
My Hamlet 91

The People and Times

Баллада о детстве 96
The Ballad of Childhood 97
Банька по-белому 104
Bath-hut 105
Песня о времени 108
A Song about Time 109
Баллада о борьбе 110
Ballad about Struggle 111
Расстрел горного эха 114
The Shooting of the Mountain Echo 115

"It's My Fate..."

Две судьбы 116
Two Fates 117
«Мне судьба — до последней черты, до креста...» . . . 120
"It's My Fate, to Fight on to the End, to the Cross..." 121
Охота на волков 124
Wolf Hunt 125
Песня о судьбе 126
A Song about My Fate 127
«Дурацкий сон, как кистенём...» 130
"A Stupid Dream Lambasted Me..." 131

"It's All Wrong, Boys..."

Я не люблю 134
How I Detest 135
Очи черные 136
Those Big Dark Eyes 137
  I. Погоня 136
  I. The Chase 137
 II. Старый дом 140
 II. The Old House 141
Моя цыганская 142
My Gypsy Song 143
Купола 146

The Domes 147
Разбойничья 148
Highwayman's Song 149
Прерванный полёт 150
Stopped Mid Flight 151
Песня конченого человека 154
The Song of a Goner 155
«Мы все живем как будто, но...» . . . 158
"We All Seem to Be Living, but..." . . . 159
Притча о Правде и Лжи 160
A Parable of Truth and Lie 161
«Я бодрствую, но вещий сон мне снится...» . . 164
"I Am Awake, yet Dream Prophetic Verses..." . . 165

From Dedications to Friends
Памяти Василия Шукшина 166
Im Memory of Vasily Shukshin 167

"I Am Sure I Will Die..."
Кони привередливые 170
Unruly Horses 171
Памятник 172
The Memorial 173
Райские яблоки 176
Apples of Paradise 177
«Когда я отпою и отыграю...» 178
"How I Will End When I Have Sung My Fill..." . . 179

I Love You Here and Now
Баллада о любви 182
A Ballad about Love 183
«Люблю тебя *сейчас*...» 184
"I Love You *Here and Now*..." 185

From the Last Poems ....
«И снизу лед, и сверху — маюсь между...» 188
"Ice Down Below, Ice Up Above — I Freeze Between..." 189

II. VYSOTSKY ON HIS WORK 191

From a 1970 Questionnaire 192
From an Interview to the *Literaturnaya Rossiya*
Newspaper (1974) 197
From an Interview Granted to the Pyatigorsk TV
Studios (1979) 199
Speeches at Concerts: a Mosaic
On My Song Writing 201
My Parts in the Theatre 212
On Work in the Cinema 214
On Popularity 216

III. POETS SPEAK OF A POET 219

Vladimir Beekman. The Runner 220
Pyotr Vegin. The Dream of a Centaur 221

Andrei Voznesensky. The Poet 222
Alexander Gorodnitsky. "The Poet's Dead. Thus Hamlet Died
    Once, Tested..." 224
Andrei Dementyev. The Black Swan 225
Yevgeny Yevtushenko. The Song Sellers 226
Lyubomir Levchev. Requiem 228
Bulat Okudzhava. "Of Volodya Vysotsky I Wanted to Make Up
    a Song..." 230

IV. REMINISCENCES . . . . : . 231

N. M. Vysotskaya. Kindness Was His Main Character Trait . . . 232
S. V. Vysotsky. That's What My Son Was Like 239
Iza Vysotskaya. Life Was Wonderful When Volodya Was Alive 243
The Father Through the Eyes of the Son. (An Interview
    with *N. Vysotsky)* 247
Marina Vlady. I'm Living Thanks to You... 251
Vladimir Akimov. Volodya (The Years of His Youth) 264
Igor Kokhanovsky. The Beginning 290
Vadim Tumanov. Life Without Lying 301
Mikhail Shemyakin. About Volodya (The Last Years) . . . 315
Bella Akhmadulina. A Word about Vysotsky 322
Mikhail Ulyanov. He Lived Like He Sang... 324
Alla Demidova. He Wrote the Way He Lived 327
Valery Zolotukhin. It Was Like I Said, or a Study in an
    Unstable Vowel 339
Yuri Trifonov. A Few Lines about Vladimir Vysotsky 344
David Samoilov. My Acquaintanceship with Vysotsky 349
Gennady Poloka. He Quickly Shook Off the Burden of Each
    Defeat... 354
Joseph Heifitz. Two Films with Vysotsky 368
The Vainer Brothers. Notes about Vladimir Vysotsky 376

Brief Notes on the Authors 419
Notes 421

Any translation of Vysotsky's song-poems must in all honesty be preceded by an exercise in apologetic self-abasement or attempt to explain away the gulf between the sparkle and magic power of the original and the, shall we say, colourlessness of the translation. Unfortunately for the translator, the colour of Vysotsky's songs is almost totally local colour, his work being one seven-hundred-song-long play on words, their sound, meaning, associations, connotations, evocations, and what not, all idiosyncratic, all virtually incomprehensible outside a Russian context. When he writes, and sings,

> *Plennykh gonyat — chego zh my drozhim?*
> *"The prisoners of war are driven — why are we afraid?"*

his audiences have an instant picture in their minds of endless columns of captured Germans being marched through the streets of Moscow, silent crowds of Russians lining the streets watching their would-be conquerors in — anger? hatred? triumph? puzzlement? A moment of history in just two words, half a line, the equivalent of which is not to be found in any language: there just weren't any such scenes in London or New York. Or you take this:

> *I zhit khorosho! I zhizn khorosha!*
> *"Life is fine, and it's fine to live!"*

It is a line from Mayakovsky (later echoed in Stalin's "Life has become better, life has become merrier!"). For decades it was the slogan of official optimism running in counterpoint to the gloom and doom of the mass reprisals. Placed in a hilarious skit about, presumably, sports, the line is mercilessly guyed, becoming an ironic comment on the all-too-familiar reality.

One could (and indeed should) write a footnote on

nearly each of Vysotsky's lines, to make the Vysotsky phenomenon comprehensible to the public abroad. The reader will find a few such comments on the translations below — where an item of allusive Russian must be kept in the translation if Vysotsky's point is to be made at all. Other such comments are scattered throughout the reminiscences, for example, V. Zolotukhin's piece on *Bath-hut*. Needless to say, these are merely the first steps of an undertaking that might do for Vysotsky what Nabokov did for Pushkin.

A few words are in order here on some aspects of Vysotsky's language. Vysotsky was a linguistic genuis, apart from all the other kinds of genius that he was. His idiolect is a fantastic mixture of Standard and Substandard Russian, slang of all kinds, dialect words, etc., their use impeccably controlled by the Nekrasov formula: "style in keeping with theme". Being tied to a definite time, place, and milieu, these lexical items (and, for that matter, syntactic patterns) do not easily lend themselves to transplantation onto a different linguistic soil. Take a line like:

Tolkovishchu veli do krovyanki
"They argued till blood was drawn".

It would be difficult to translate this into Standard Russian, let alone English — if the aim was to keep the force of the line intact. That's gutter talk. If you find an equivalent of it, it will smack of the gutters of Chicago or London or Liverpool, and we can't have that, we know it's the gutters of Moscow speaking. Thus there is a loss in expressiveness — an inevitable one, one would like to think; that is, not due to the translator's ineptitude but to the nature of the material. There are many songs written entirely in that language (happily not so many in the present collection), and I honestly believe they are better left untranslated.

A few words about Vysotsky's technical skills as a versifier. There are those who speak of his guitar-poetry as not quite a literary phenomenon — something from the domain of mass culture, perhaps. Surely, Vysotsky's poetry had an effect on the masses. Even looking at it from the purely linguistic angle, for nearly two decades the Vysotsky language was the most prominent feature of the linguistic scene in the USSR; his texts, though unprinted, were the most frequently reproduced and memorised; his punchlines, turns of phrase, and so on, are common linguistic currency, authorless by now, the very fabric of the prevalent mode of expression. The "Vysotsky craze", though, has a solid base not only in the topicality of his themes but also in the poetic texture of his work, the aptness of the lines and rhythms and images. When he put his mind to it, Vysotsky could always find *the* word or phrase to catch the spirit of the thing he sang of and the audience's imagination — and what more could a poet wish? But this is not an apologia for Vysotsky the poet — rather an apology for the translations' failure to do justice to Vysotsky's poetics. In sheer ebullience of genius, he could write a longish song-poem with one or two rhymes only — an impossibility in English, if one does not want to bore the reader into the ground. Vysotsky used an incredible number of rhyming schemes, some of which he invented. Rhyme has outlived its usefulness, people say; the proposition more likely applies to poets who cannot find any more fresh rhymes in Russian — and Vysotsky was not one of these. Among a host of other devices, he could rhyme one word with three : *postupyu — po stu pyu*, producing an identical rhyme — and one more headache for the translator's bag of worries. Or else he would rhyme a whole word with part of another: *obrusevshiye — sevshiye* "Russified — thrown into prison", working in, apart from the rhyme, a paronymic effect (see below). Needless to say, all these innovative types of rhyme are much harder to come by in English than in Russian, with its highly developed system of morphological endings.

And as for internal rhyme! He would use it either occasionally or systematically throughout a poem, so that there would be double the number of lines in it, if you stopped at the caesura. As one tries to do the same in English, one is reminded, say, of the contortions Byron went through in writing *Don Juan*.

Then there is patronymic writing — probably the most remarkable feature of contemporary Russian poetics, and the least translatable: two like-sounding words are placed next to each other so that a contextual relationship is established between their normally unconnected meanings: cf. *trusíl i trúsil* "jogged along and feared", *zalatayu zolotymi ya zaplatami* "I will patch it up with gold patches", *ni pozhit, ni vyzhit* "you can neither live nor survive". Vysotsky revelled in this type of writing, as in all word play.

Ah, it's no use. One could write a treatise about Vysotsky's poetic innovations and then hit on a poem like *My Gypsy Song* (nothing Gypsy about it, except the tune) consisting almost entirely of colloquial and folklore clichés of vague or no meaning, loosely and incoherently strung together yet affecting the very depth of the Russian soul:

>*Net, rebyata, vsyo ne tak...*
>"*No, boys, nothing's the way it should be...*"

No textual analysis would serve here, the text being minimal and the subtext, pure mood. Characteristically, the printed text of the song omits the refrain borrowed from the source song — emotionally, the most moving part of the piece — simply because this refrain is a repetition of and variation on a senseless phrase: "Ah, once, and once more, and many-many times more", etc. On the whole, one is left with the impression that Vysotsky could do anything he pleased with the Russian poetic language, his power over words — and us — being such that whatever he wrote and sang *became* poetic language, even if he slipped into what appeared to be asemantic doggerel. Like I said, just a genius playing a bead game with words and melodies and hearts.

One last technical detail. English words are shorter than most Russian ones, so there are more words to a line in the English version than in the Russian — and this runs counter to Vysotsky's feeling for the subtext, for the innuendo, for the avoidance of the explicit. As these are songs, one cannot adopt a different, shorter metrical scheme. Hence a fair amount of padding, which weakened still more the punch of the original.

One can only hope that this, and the other shortcomings of the translations, will dwindle into insignificance when a sufficiently gifted English-speaking singer or singers try to relive Vysotsky before live audiences. After all, the Swedes have done it, they took the Taganka by storm in the autumn of 1988. Apparently we are here faced with a difficulty that no printed translation, annotated or not, can overcome: the moment a Russian (or a Daghestani or Kazakh or anyone in the Soviet Union, for that matter) reads a line of Vysotsky, that powerful voice starts rumbling in his head, and the printed text becomes a mere prop for memory. Some have complained even, on first seeing the poem-songs in print, that reading them without hearing the voice was a bit like smelling a rose while wearing a gas-mask. Not a very inspiring image to leave a reader with, but realistic — if that is any consolation.

I would like to express my heartfelt gratitude to Mark Buser for editing the translations of the poems. *

S. R.

---

* All poetic translations in this book are mine ; all exceptions are indicated.— *Tr.*

VLADIMIR VYSOTSKY IN HIS LIFETIME AND AFTER DEATH

1

When Vladimir Vysotsky's 50th anniversary was marked in January 1988, it seems there was not a single publication in this country, local, regional or national, which did not go into raptures over the work of the remarkable poet, singer and citizen. A four-part serial was shown on the Central TV network, preceded by a two-part film broadcast by the same studios, and accompanied by one-part films broadcast by the various local networks. The regular bulletins of the All-Union Council of Amateur Songs recorded a peak of publications on the scale of a solar prominence. There was more stuff printed, said and shown about Vysotsky in the anniversary weeks and months than in all the previous years. Vysotsky memorial meetings were held in many cities and towns; some of them were broadcast on TV; scholars also arranged official occasions. Interesting books appeared both in Moscow (from the Kniga, Sovetsky Pisatel, Fizkultura i Sport, and Muzyka publishers) and in several other cities. Several other books are soon due to appear. Speaking as editor-in-chief of The Poet's Library, I can assure the reader that Vysotsky will be amply represented in the *Author's Song* collection prepared by our editors.

Whatever our attitude to Vysotsky, we cannot but see that this upsurge in the whole people's interest in the poet's life and fate is an almost unprecedented phenomenon. True, the anniversary merely emphasised and showed clearly the love for Vysotsky which had also been obvious before and manifested itself, say, in millions of people turning out for his funeral, and the mass processions converging on his tomb, after.

Right now, though, I would like to draw attention

to a very morbid and, I would say, all-pervading feature of both the public opinion as a whole and of art criticism in particular, as far as Vysotsky is concerned. Basically, this feature is an uncontrolled swinging of public opinion from one extreme to the other. Each of us must have seen a heavy cannonball on a steel cable used for knocking down ramshackle buildings. The cannonball swings far from the normal level and then swings back, heading for the wall, it goes bang! and a gap appears in the wall, another bang, and the gap is wider, then a third, and the bricks come down in an avalanche, the job is done, you can call in the lorries to pick up the rubble.

It is an extremely useful operation in knocking down decrepit structures, including social ones! What happens, though, when the cannonball, directed by not very scholarly or even sober minds, is used to knock down beautiful and solid buildings?

In the past, certain indefatigable folks pulled the cannonball very far to one side: all avant-garde was bad! So do we have to declare now, in our infinite wisdom, that all things realistic are bad? Swing it wide, brother, we live but once!

In this context, let me say this about Vysotsky. I hate both the unrestrained worshipping of Vysotsky (the cannonball swinging left) and contemptuous disregard for him (the ball swinging right), as well as all sorts of turbid swirlings round his name. The truth, and nothing but the truth in its entirety—that is how it should be.

The incense so lavishly burned in the anniversary weeks of 1988 has already produced ironic grins on all sides at all those individuals whose efforts too obviously indicated either a fanatic anguish or a desire to assert their significance, so far unrecognised, in the poet's fate. Let us not bother with the nonprofessionals who kowtowed in those anniversary weeks so hard that they hurt both themselves and their idol. As for Vysotsky himself, all his public appearances, beginning with the first concert before the Leningrad club called Vostok in January 1967, were constructed as many-sided versatile shows touching on all the strings of the human nature, from easy responsiveness to a joke, to an ability to think

15

deeply about the problem of universal evil or one's personal guilt for the disorderliness of the world we live in. But let's forget them, those "players on one string — the bass string" (although it must be noted that their inflexibility put many people off Vysotsky in those days). And I wish it were *those days* only: alas, we still encounter this sort of "methodology" of analysis today.

In this book, the reader will find, among other highly interesting reminiscences by relatives, friends and colleagues, the remarkable contribution by artist Mikhail Shemyakin who speaks, incidentally, about the causes of Vysotsky's alcoholic breakdowns. Unlike those, regrettably numerous, persons who refer so contemptuously or slightingly to the subject, Shemyakin writes of the incredible overstrain that demanded an escape from the daily routine in any way whatever — if only for a short period. I am not speaking of this in order to justify these "escapes" but only to explain the complexity of the situation. I was at Vysotsky's side in periods of absolute sobriety, and I can state definitely that he implacably refused all invitations from friends and admirers "to have a few". The causes that were at work here lay really deep.

2

Let me repeat that literally hundreds of excellent publications have appeared in connection with Vysotsky's 50th anniversary. There is so much material of varying scope and type that we are certainly ready to publish a fundamental *Vladimir Vysotsky Encyclopedia,* like those that academics have published on Mikhail Lermontov or Taras Shevchenko. I have no doubt that such a work will be prepared for publication and see light, for data on Vysotsky's life and work are collected enthusiastically and continually all over the country. But we also need a kind of filters here, to protect the analysis of the poet's fate from all sorts of underhand speculation and queer games started after his death by various individuals. We must, in short, winnow the chaff away, keep the seeds and sow a good crop. The point is that there are now a great many people eager to make some capital on the wave of Vysotsky's popularity and so constructing one-sided theories with Vysotsky's songs as their material, vigorously exploiting that in Vysotsky's heritage which suits them, and ignoring the rest. After all, there are only 32 letters in the Russian alphabet, and all Russian words consist of these letters, providing, in their turn, building material for the whole of the great Russian literature. Compared with this, the possibilities of arbitrary constructions out of Vysotsky's 700 songs comprising the whole of man's world are truly unlimited: such an "alphabet" can yield a million articles and books none of which will repeat the others.

Without a thought for censorship or pleasing the authorities, Vysotsky criticised what blocked the course of life right there and then, not after the event! It is easy to imagine what Vysotsky would sing of in these days. I can picture myself a song from the "chess cycle", with a brilliant move by the black King (two exclamation marks here) — the introduction of limitations on subscription to newspapers and magazines, so that *glasnost* was curtailed and the public's attention diverted from other serious problems. I believe that he would have ridiculed all that ballyhoo about the construction of the Baikal-Amur Railway, he would have called to account the people who wasted all those funds and manpower on a useless project. I have no doubt that he would subject to close scrutiny those who deliberately distort *perestroika,* adapting the old command-and-administer system to the new conditions. Knowing him, we would of course expect him to denounce in his songs all kinds of nationalists warming their hands at the fire of the people's grief, the hucksters jacking up prices, in short, everything that is of such concern to us — without awaiting any explanations from the top on who is personally responsible for what, on who has been relieved of his post and is therefore no longer dangerous. I believe that Vysotsky would be unable to pass in silence over the depravity universally expressed in the refusal to work and in dislike for those who work hard. At the same time I am quite sure that he would sing with warmth, humour and love of those whose broad backs have always been the basis of the might of this great land. Vysotsky spoke the whole truth about his times (and he would

17

speak the truth about ours) as a true creator of the people's life, and it would be dishonest to pull his creative heritage apart, adapting it to all kinds of speculative goals.

3

A real poet is a man who knows reality as thoroughly as he knows his own work — from within, in all its deep inner interconnections and laws of its development. That is why there is so much truth in his fairytales: he wrote them to please his own soul, which was so wide open to human life and human beliefs. There are countless proofs of Vysotsky's democratic spirit and of the national character of his art.

Vladimir Vysotsky was a songsmith; his poems were basically oriented towards the listeners' living perception. In this tape-recorder era, songs spread on a mass scale, in unlimited numbers. What is recorded on a spool of tape or cassette by one listener can spread like wildfire among thousands of other owners of tape-recorders. This lucky coincidence of the author's individuality (composer of "author's songs") and the new technology for the spreading of culture must be taken into account in the analysis of both the popularity and the specificity of Vysotsky's poetics.

All this may be as it is, but there are hundreds and even thousands of authors singing for vast audiences, it's just a sign of these tape-recorder times, but only the songs of a select few remain recorded on tapes and spread among the people in a geometrical progression. Why is that so? What were the essential needs of the times that Vysotsky's songs satisfied? Should we begin pedantically analysing hundreds of his poetic texts (and some of the verses have up to seven and even twelve variants, as established by Andrei Krylov), we shall hardly be able to isolate, with mathematic clarity and in chemically pure form, that element which constitutes the "exclusive property of ... works", as critic Vissarion Belinsky put it. This element is composite, and it is only possible to define it by considering Vysotsky's work in all its parameters. The songs of *Nerve,* the first Vysotsky collection published in this country, appeared under ten headings. Apart from this, about a couple dozen other headings may be discovered in the incomparably more complete collections of his works in type-written volumes compiled by Vysotsky's admirers. The question may be asked as to which poem or heading comprises the formula we are looking for? The only possible answer to this query is, in all the headings at once.

Could it be that the meaning of Vysotsky's work is expressed in these lines from *A Singer at the Microphone*?

> *I'm bathed in light, before the crowd, alone;*
> *I'm here to give my darling public pleasure.*
> *It's like an icon-stand, this microphone...*
> *But — no! Tonight, it's more like an embrasure.*

Of course, these words express his responsibility before himself and the people. But they do not exhaust Vysotsky's work, not by a long chalk!

Or take these lines from a song that has become a classic already — *He Was Shot Down in Yesterday's Fighting:*

> *There was plenty of room for us in the dugout,*
> *Even time flew for both of us lightly...*
> *I'm alone now, and I am beginning to doubt:*
> *Wasn't I downed in yesterday's fighting?*

Again we can say that this is Vysotsky — but is this the whole of Vysotsky?

Or you may choose these lines from the well-known song about mountain climbers:

> *If a chum*
> > *begins acting rum,*
> *Not a friend, not a foe,*
> > *but so...*
> *And if suddenly you can't tell*
> *If he means ill or well,*
> *Take him off mountaineering —*
> > *dare!*
> *But don't let him stray*
> > *away!*

> *When he's roped on one rope*
> *with you*
> *You'll find out if he's true.*

This is, of course, a very important facet of Vysotsky, but it is only one aspect. Consider yet another song:

> *I'll no more smash shop windows or punch holes*
> *In human faces, man, I tell you straight.*
> *The two disjointed halves of my sick soul*
> *From this day on I'm going to unite.*

Again, this is merely a small fragment of the great mirror that reflects the world of Vysotsky.

Then there is *The Tightrope*; *The Pacer's Race*; *How I Detest...*; and *Unruly Horses*. Yes, all this is Vysotsky but not the whole of Vysotsky. Considered separately, none of them explain the causes of the poet's popularity throughout the country.

In the article "In the Mirror of His Work (V. Vysotsky as a Phenomenon of Culture)" written by Valentin Tolstykh, Dr. Sc. (Philosophy), we read these remarkable words: "At present, there is no shortage of courageous, fearless descriptions and evaluations of the contradictions and shortcomings in the national economy, moral defects and losses, lack of consciousness, spirituality and culture. But this 'authorised' courage, so to speak, however sincere and full of civic spirit (as distinct from critique rooted in social demagoguery, of which we have a great number of past masters), evokes a sense of annoyance... Let us refrain from asking the sacramental and tactless question, 'Where were you yesterday? Why didn't you say so earlier?' Let us simply recall, or remind some people, that there were also those who were not silent, who spoke of things which an artist cannot pass over in silence under any circumstances, without waiting for better times or 'authorisation' to speak of these things... One of these artists was Vladimir Vysotsky, who realised in his work, without high-flown declarations or promises, the principal obligation of a real artist and citizen — the obligation to speak the truth about the times and himself." * The author points to

---

* *Voprosy filosofii*, 1986, No. 7, p. 112.

a number of writers (a small number, it must be said) who endeavoured to speak the truth and nothing but the truth regardless of the circumstances; it will only be just to note, though, that Vysotsky's fearlessness distinguished him even in this small group of glorious names, although essentially V. Tolstykh is, of course, quite right.

The discrepancy between words and deeds which had such a devastating effect on our society's economy and morality in the past and is still not overcome, inevitably evoked protest among people. We all felt the need for drastic changes in our social life, and we perceived Vladimir Vysotsky precisely in this serious social context.

For me, just as for the other admirers of Vysotsky, the civic core of his creative work was his truthfulness, the acuteness of his reactions to the issues that concerned the public — an acuteness that was signally lacking in the abysmal vacuity of "popular" songs. Considered on this plane, Vysotsky's work was normal utterances of normal people strange to any duplicity (to seeing one thing and saying another), utterances elevated by the splendid artistic gifts and talent for sincerity to the level of high art belonging to the people. Those were the roots of his popularity.

It would be absurd to insist, and no one seems to insist, that all his songs are equally perfect. Of course not. Some of his songs are of average quality only, others lack in balanced composition, still others were written expressly for a certain occasion — a friend's birthday or a party of close friends. All that is so. And still, *Bath-hut* is a narrative of the tragic fate of a man who went through the slaughter-house of Stalin's labour camps. *Someone Else's Rut* is a parable of the perniciousness of movement by inertia, without thought. *At the Restaurant Yesterday Night* is a biting satire on the impudent thieves and hucksters who have usurped the top rungs of the social ladder and are now prospering. *The Penal Battalions,* now—I can't think of another treatment of this tragic subject in all our literature on war. *By Our Reckoning We Hadn't Had Too Much:* Vysotsky spoke of alcoholism, laughing through tears, long before the government bethought itself and decided to take some measures against it.

At the same time Vysotsky was, and still is, loved not

only for being harshly truthful. Vysotsky was richly endowed with a sense of humour, and he wrote whole cycles of sly and funny songs at the same time as he composed the tragic ones. Of course, there are a great many songs in which the only worthy character is, properly speaking, the author himself; but there are also a great many pieces expressing his sincere admiration for strong, kind-hearted and courageous men retaining their human qualities under the most difficult and sometimes fatally dangerous circumstances.

The song *My Finish Line Is the Horison* is dedicated precisely to the people whose lives are inspired by dreams and an eternal quest, not by vodka and finery.

One could compile a whole anthology of Vysotsky's songs about men worthy of the name of man. But that would be just as one-sided as an attempt to select only the dramatic, dark and gloomy songs, the songs of discontent. Dismembering Vysotsky's poetry would mean murdering it! A real man, he was not one of those who do nothing but complain about the imperfection of the world we live in, watching from the sidelines. He has a very biting poem, with this refrain:

> *I'm sorry for the dead, at heart,*
> *But take good care to keep apart.*

In his *Memorial*, he protested vehemently against being "reduced" after death. He defined the essence and the meaning of his work with absolute precision, much better than any critics: "I write songs on various subjects. I have series, or rather cycles, of songs on the war theme, on sporting life, fairytale songs, lyrical songs. But there is in fact only one theme in my songs, the theme of life. There's just this one theme: we must live better; and the form might vary, from comedy to fairytale, to humour." *

He pursued that theme with truthfulness and goodwill towards people, trying to help all of us to the full extent of his giant's strength and fierce temperament; that is why the people's hearts lay open to him.

---

* *Literaturnaya Rossiya*, August 8, 1986, p. 10.

It seems that Vysotsky died only recently, that black day seems to be close at hand, but the children who were born that year already go to school. Time rushes impetuously forward, like a river full of rapids, and reality around us changes constantly. The problems that have worried us so agonisingly, which pierced our hearts, will inevitably be solved, sooner or later. The agonies and worries of our times will disappear, giving way to others. So, how will Vladimir Vysotsky's work be seen in a few years, given the crazy tempo of our life? Won't it recede into the background?

To this, we can say "no" quite definitely, although foreign readers and listeners either do not know of or are not too interested in the purely internal processes to which the strings of his guitar responded so resonantly. The people abroad had their own lives to live and difficulties to overcome. And yet, books on Vysotsky's life and work are published abroad much more promptly than in this country (although incredible errors sometimes creep into those books); collections of his songs published there are much more representative than here (although Vysotsky is sometimes ascribed songs he never wrote); records are produced in countless numbers, and as for cassettes, they are sold at dumping prices, to corner the market (while here only small cooperatives produce them). Supply is the child of demand, and, judging by the variety of forms in which Vysotsky is supplied, the demand abroad is really great. Now, what are the causes of his fame there? And what will determine his popularity here when the journalistic topicality of his work, so important for us, his contemporaries, wears off?

The question is all the more important since the true scope of Vysotsky as an artist belonging to the whole people and, moreover, as a phenomenon of world culture, becomes apparent.

Vladimir Vysotsky's work has analogues in folk art. Why is that so? The fact is that the characteristic features of both are a great variety of aspects, corresponding to the many-sidedness of life itself; the absence of any controls or regulations stipulating what can be written about and what cannot; an optimistic view of the world, despite the tragedies with which this world abounds.

Vysotsky's works helped, fearlessly and fiercely, to solve the topical social and artistic problems of his times, and that is the first and the most important secret of Vysotsky's fame, his behest to men of art. At the same time his songs reach into the depths of human morality, raising to the surface the eternal subjects of humanity's concern and reflexion; this is the second, and just as important, secret of the people's love for Vysotsky, and another of his behests to the workers of culture.

Since times immemorial, the people's perception of art is primarily ethical and only secondarily aesthetic, the ethical evaluation determining the aesthetic one. This should be accepted as a given, one that permits us to see the causes of Vysotsky's vast popularity. His songs represent the entire range of human emotions, thoughts and acts without any exception; any incompleteness of the reflexion of the human world is one of the causes of potential fragility and short life of a work of art. We know that man is a being capable not only of feeling but also of thought, action, and goal-directed decision-making. Folk art is precisely a proof that man has a great many aspects, and that all these aspects can be expressed through suitably many-sided means. From this angle, Vysotsky's work is truly many-sided, and thus has roots and parallels in folk art. One would be hard put to it to name a single basic human value, an archetypal value, that would not be expressed, with purity and dignity, in his songs.

A man's strength and reliability, his loyalty to the duty of defending children, women, the Motherland, his own convictions. It is these intransient human values that are asserted in his war cycle, appreciated unreservedly by all, even by those who do not recognise anything else in his work.

A woman's tenderness and kindness, and the all-absorbing love of a man for a woman... Vysotsky was one of the most striking and fervent singers of that eternal human theme. In a six-volume collection of his songs compiled by selfless collectors and students of his work, this theme takes up a whole volume entitled simply *On Love*. The range of nuances in the emotional and artistic treatment of this subject in that volume is incredible.

I'll make lovers' beds of fields and groves,
Let them sing, awake and in their sleep!..
I am breathing, that means I'm in love!
I'm in love, and that means I'm alive!

Here, the assertion of love is raised to the level of a philosophical postulate, like "Cogito ergo sum".

Only "serious" songs are collected in this volume, but goodness, what great numbers of love songs wander, in carnival guise, through the other volumes, including Vysotsky's parodies of underworld lyrics. Then again, songs of love are also to be found in the volume which the compilers entitled *On the Sea*. You take this song about two gloomy ships, corroded by sea salt and generally the worse for wear, disliking each other on sight when they met in a dry dock for repairs; after rest and repairs they gaze at each other and suddenly see how wonderful the other is. Isn't this a song about human love?

We are speaking here of archetypal values, about those eternal problems which have ever concerned, and will always concern, men and women on all continents. Man's eternal drive towards overcoming difficulties and learning the previously unknown is a value whose significance remains intransient and even continually grows. Vysotsky's long poem *My Hamlet* (about 100 lines) proclaims a constant pursuit of the truth, a pursuit which will never cease, for there are no absolute solutions, for time itself is in motion, incessantly complicating the tasks facing mankind.

There is yet another and probably the most important feature of Vysotsky's talent. It has to be said that Vysotsky kept his quiet smile even in the most dramatic circumstances — a reflection of the national character. Here, I would like to note that his smile was evidence of his true and noble humanity, for no one is truly human unless he or she can see the funnier aspects of the world and of oneself. Vysotsky was human in the full sense of that word; even when he talked of categories that he respected most, like the human thought and its incessant drive towards higher and nobler things, he could grin openly and mischievously; recall his song of Fedya the archeologist, for example.

25

He dug for ancient monuments
Like mad, and often yelled he meant
To find the land in which, he knew,
There were still secret, hidden paths
Where roamed the Pithecanthropus —
And on his chest he beat a wild tattoo.

We have already spoken of the great democratic spirit of his work. In the present context, though, this powerful and archetypal aesthetic value is seen in a special light. Despite the unending efforts of the powers that be to reduce the working masses to the role of serfs or hirelings, these masses have, from olden times, aspired towards elimination of slavery and equality of all men, towards "a free association of producers", in the words of Karl Marx. If all the democratic characters from the Vysotsky theatre were to be gathered in one place, what an extraordinary multitude of individualities they would be! Here, an alcoholic is capable of reasoning in categories of state significance; an ordinary oil-industry worker from Siberia, of displaying great moral staunchness in achieving the national goals, while Vysotsky's lyrical hero, emerging in dozens of guises, splits the most difficult and fundamental questions of life and death like atomic nuclei, releasing colossal energy heretofore peacefully slumbering in verbal depths.

I have here before me an alphabetic index of Vladimir Vysotsky's works. Dozens of songs begin with the word "I", but it would be a grave error to assume, without deeply studying the texts of the songs, that they were written by a self-centred individual. Absolutely not! He simply speaks on behalf of those whom he is capable of personifying, as well as on his own behalf, for he lives and perceives life as those around him do, and his spiritual world is their world.

Vysotsky sang on behalf of many people — and the public took him for those people! He explained this in absolutely clear terms: "I write songs on behalf of different people; I believe I did that because I am an actor. When I write these songs, I act them out. I write on behalf of a person as if he were my old acquaintance, whatever he might be — sailor, pilot, collective farmer, student, industrial worker..." Just hear how convincing and witty his argument sounds: "In *Alice in Wonderland*, n LP for children, I recorded more than twenty musical numbers including the song of a parrot. I sing for that parrot, too. This example explains whether I was that person or persons in whose name I often sing my monologue songs. Here is my answer: I have never been a parrot, in any sense." *

To avoid a systematic listing of all the principal archetypal values, which the people of the earth find in Vladimir Vysotsky's songs, we should conclude our discussion with a reference to a value which will undoubtedly be top on the list in any hierarchical system of values.

In the people's notions, the first and the most important value is life itself. The approach to this issue in folk art is profoundly optimistic. In fairytales, good triumphs over evil, the eternal power of being prevails over the forces of destruction. As for professional writing, the happy end is by no means obligatory, but the feelings and thoughts of the creator of a genuine work of art must necessarilly be those of a person who actively and selflessly loves life, and fervently hates everything that lies in the way of its normal development or even threatens its very existence. In this respect, Vysotsky's work was always beyond reproach! His songs are optimistic in their very essence; assertion of good and overthrow of evil is the message of all his works, from first to last. Beginning with one of his earliest efforts, *The Song of Discontent* ("The dolphin's belly's ripped up by a screw..."), and ending with the last poem, in which he states with quiet pride and dignity that he has his songs "to sing to the Almighty", Vladimir Vysotsky fiercely fought for life, against carrion in all its guises. That is why war veterans come to his grave bringing flowers to express their gratitude to the man whose songs continued their sacred cause. That is why workers from Sverdlovsk are ready to contribute a day's wages to the founding of a Vysotsky Museum. That is why very young girls, having heard so many legends about him, begin to study seriously his real life.

I have said nothing here of Vysotsky the actor. Not because I believe this to be something secondary (Vysotsky the poet and Vysotsky the actor are inseparable!) — the

---

* *Literaturnaya Rossiya,* August 8, 1986, p. 10.

reason is quite different. One can reflect on Vysotsky's poems, the ideas and feelings expressed in them, right before the reader's eyes, while the fascination of his acting and singing, the emotional impact which literally turns one's soul inside out, demands visual support. To some extent these striking sensations will perhaps be conveyed by the reminiscences of those who knew the Artist well, and who were able to capture and retain in words his inimitable image, of something that was neither acting nor singing but Life itself — on the stage, on the screen, in songs, and in the uttered word. You will find some of these reminiscences in the volume offered here. A good read to you, dear reader!

Yuri Andreyev

SELECTED POEMS AND SONGS
(50 OUT OF THE TOTAL 700)

БРАТСКИЕ МОГИЛЫ

На братских могилах не ставят крестов,
И вдовы на них не рыдают —
К ним кто-то приносит букеты цветов,
И Вечный огонь зажигают.

Здесь раньше вставала земля на дыбы,
А нынче — гранитные плиты.
Здесь нет ни одной персональной судьбы —
Все судьбы в единую слиты.

А в Вечном огне — видишь вспыхнувший танк,
Горящие русские хаты,
Горящий Смоленск и горящий рейхстаг,
Горящее сердце солдата.

У братских могил нет заплаканных вдов —
Сюда ходят люди покрепче,
На братских могилах не ставят крестов...
Но разве от этого легче?!

1964

ОН НЕ ВЕРНУЛСЯ ИЗ БОЯ

Почему всё не так? Вроде — всё как всегда:
То же небо — опять голубое,
Тот же лес, тот же воздух и та же вода...
Только — он не вернулся из боя.

Мне теперь не понять, кто же прав был из нас
В наших спорах без сна и покоя.
Мне не стало хватать его только сейчас —
Когда он не вернулся из боя.

COMMON GRAVES *

No crosses stand over these war graves of ours,
No widows come sobbing to mourn here.
But people bring garlands and bouquets of flowers,
And a small flame perpetually burns here.

This place was once bare, the earth ravaged and torn,
Today it has slabs for a cover.
Today in the graves are these dead all made one —
Their separate lives now are over.

But deep in the flame you see gutted tanks smoke,
And razed Russian villages smoulder;
Blazing Smolensk, and the blazing Reichstag,
The fierce blazing heart of the soldier.

No sorrowing wives wet these graves with their tears.
The people who come here are stronger.
No crosses stand over these war graves of ours —
But is there, for all that, less to mourn for?

1964

HE WAS SHOT DOWN
IN YESTERDAY'S FIGHTING

All's gone wrong, although nothing has changed here of late.
Air and water, the sky and the lighting —
They are all just like always, except for my mate:
He was shot down in yesterday's fighting.

I will now never know who was wrong, who was right
In our arguments that went on nightly.
Sad but true: I first missed him like hell this past night,
After he was shot down in the fighting.

---

* © *Sputnik*, Digest of Soviet Press, 1987, No. 11.
Translated by Kathryn Hamilton.

Он молчал невпопад и не в такт подпевал,
Он всегда говорил про другое,
Он мне спать не давал, он с восходом вставал,—
А вчера не вернулся из боя.

То, что пусто теперь,— не про то разговор:
Вдруг заметил я — нас было двое...
Для меня — будто ветром задуло костер,
Когда он не вернулся из боя.

Нынче вырвалась, словно из плена, весна.
По ошибке окликнул его я:
«Друг, оставь покурить!» — а в ответ — тишина...
Он вчера не вернулся из боя.

Наши мертвые нас не оставят в беде,
Наши павшие — как часовые...
Отражается небо в лесу, как в воде,—
И деревья стоят голубые.

Нам и места в землянке хватало вполне,
Нам и время текло — для обоих...
Всё теперь — одному,— только кажется мне —
Это я не вернулся из боя.

1969

МЫ ВРАЩАЕМ ЗЕМЛЮ

От границы мы Землю вертели назад —
Было дело сначала,—
Но обратно ее закрутил наш комбат,
Оттолкнувшись ногой от Урала.

Наконец-то нам дали приказ наступать,
Отбирать наши пяди и крохи,—
Но мы помним, как солнце отправилось вспять
И едва не зашло на востоке.

Мы не меряем Землю шагами,
Понапрасну цветы теребя,—
Мы толкаем ее сапогами —
От себя, от себя!

He could never talk sense, never sang the right song,
He just smiled when I said something biting.
He would not let me sleep, he got up with the sun —
And was shot down in yesterday's fighting.

I felt empty. It struck me: we'd both knocked about
In all kinds of times — dull and exciting.
It felt much like a fire had been blown out
When they downed him in yesterday's fighting.

Spring is here, at long last, royal blue is the sky.
I called out, without thinking, most likely:
"Buddy, leave me the butt!" There's no sound in reply.
He was shot down in yesterday's fighting.

In an hour of trial, our dead will stand by us —
Our dead, they'll be ever our sentries.
In the woods, as in water, are mirrored the skies,
All around, tinted blue, quietly stand trees.

There was plenty of room for us in the dugout,
Even time flew for both of us lightly...
I'm alone now, and I am beginning to doubt:
Wasn't I downed in yesterday's fighting?

1969

WE TURN THE WORLD *

From the frontier we made the earth turn in reverse
(That was at the beginning)
But our squadron commander corrected its course
As his boot sent the Urals spinning.

At last we were given the word to attack,
To retake every inch that we prized so —
But we never forgot how the sun, turning back,
Almost sank on the Eastern horizon.

> With our feet our advance we don't measure,
> Nor vainly the flowers do we crush.
> With our boots we apply all our pressure,
> And we push! And we push!

---

* © *Soviet Literature,* 1988, No. 10.
Translated by Kathryn Hamilton.

33

И от ветра с востока пригнулись стога,
Жмется к скалам отара.
Ось земную мы сдвинули без рычага,
Изменив направленье удара.

Не пугайтесь, когда не на месте закат,
Судный день — это сказки для старших,—
Просто Землю вращают куда захотят
Наши сменные роты на марше.

    Мы ползем, бугорки обнимаем,
    Кочки тискаем — зло, не любя,
    И коленями Землю толкаем —
    От себя, от себя!

Здесь никто б не нашел, даже если б хотел,
Руки кверху поднявших.
Всем живым ощутимая польза от тел:
Как прикрытье используем павших.

Этот глупый свинец всех ли сразу найдет,
Где настигнет — в упор или с тыла?
Кто-то там впереди навалился на дот —
И Земля на мгновенье застыла.

    Я ступни свои сзади оставил,
    Мимоходом по мертвым скорбя,—
    Шар земной я вращаю локтями —
    От себя, от себя!

Кто-то встал в полный рост и, отвесив поклон,
Принял пулю на вдохе,—
Но на запад, на запад ползет батальон,
Чтобы солнце взошло на востоке.

Животом — по грязи, дышим смрадом болот,
Но глаза закрываем на запах.
Нынче по́ небу солнце нормально идет,
Потому что мы рвемся на запад.

    Руки, ноги — на месте ли, нет ли,—
    Как на свадьбе росу пригубя,
    Землю тянем зубами за стебли —
    На себя! От себя!

1972

In the wind from the east the stacked hay is laid low
And the sheep huddle up to the rocks as,
Without using a fulcrum, directing the blow,
We turn the earth round on its axis.

Have no fear when the sun fails to set in the West,
For Doomsday's a tale for the old ones.
The earth's just rotated wherever is best
At the will of our marching battalions.

> We cling to the low hills for protection —
> Hating this evil so much.
> We press down on the earth, our knees flexing,
> And we push! And we push!

In this place shall you find not one soldier alive,
Ready to hand himself over.
But the corpses are useful to those who survive.
To the living the dead offer cover.

Will this stupid lead finish us all off at once,
From the rear, or point-blank find its bullet?
Ahead someone's stormed an emplacement for guns,
And the earth has stood still for a minute.

> My footsteps I've left with my fellows —
> I mourn for each poor fallen soul.
> I turn the earth's sphere with my elbows —
> And I pull! And I pull!

A soldier stands up, and then instantly falls,
Got by a slug in the gizzard.
But westward, still westward our company crawls
To make sure that the sun rises eastward.

We crawl through the mud ignoring the stench
With which the dank marsh is infested.
The sun from its usual path does not flinch,
For we've burst through the battle-lines westward.

> Like wedding guests, fresh dews we sample
> Careless whether our limbs are still whole.
> Our teeth take the earth by the stubble,
> And we push! And we pull!

1972

3*

* * *

Корабли постоят — и ложатся на курс, —
Но они возвращаются сквозь непогоды...
Не пройдет и полгода — и я появлюсь, —
Чтобы снова уйти,
Чтобы снова уйти на полгода.

Возвращаются все — кроме лучших друзей,
Кроме самых любимых и преданных женщин.
Возвращаются все — кроме тех, кто нужней, —
Я не верю судьбе,
Я не верю судьбе, а себе — еще меньше.

Но мне хочется верить, что это не так,
Что сжигать корабли скоро выйдет из моды.
Я, конечно, вернусь — весь в друзьях и в делах, —
Я, конечно, спою,
Я, конечно, спою — не пройдет и полгода.

Я, конечно, вернусь — весь в друзьях и в мечтах, —
Я, конечно, спою,
Я, конечно, спою — не пройдет и полгода.

1967

*   *   *

Anchored ships lie in port
And then put out to sea
But they always return again,
Braving foul   weather.
In six months I'll return
But my journey will be
Ended only to start
            on another.

Everyone returns
But the friends you most trust,
And the dearest of women,
The truest and best.
Everyone returns
Except those you need most.
I have no faith in fate,
          in myself
          even less.

But how good to imagine
Things aren't as they seem,
That to burn all your boats
Will soon pass out of fashion.
I'll be sure to return
Both in friends and in dreams...
Before six months are out
          I'll sing again
          with new passion.

I'll be sure to return
Both in friends and in dreams...
Before six months are out
          I'll sing again
          with new passion.

1967

БЕЛОЕ БЕЗМОЛВИЕ

Все года, и века, и эпохи подряд —
Всё стремится к теплу от морозов и вьюг.
Почему ж эти птицы на север летят —
Если птицам положено только на юг?!

    Слава им не нужна — и величие,
    Вот под крыльями кончится лед —
    И найдут они счастие птичее,
    Как награду за дерзкий полет.

Что же нам не жилось, что же нам не спалось?
Что нас выгнало в путь по высокой волне?
Нам сиянье пока наблюдать не пришлось, —
Это редко бывает — сиянья в цене!

    Тишина. Только чайки — как молнии...
    Пустотой мы их кормим из рук.
    Но наградою нам за безмолвие
    Обязательно будет звук.

Как давно снятся нам только белые сны —
Все иные оттенки снега занесли, —
Мы ослепли давно от такой белизны —
Но прозреем от черной полоски земли.

    Наше горло отпустит молчание,
    Наша слабость растает, как тень, —
    И наградой за ночи отчаянья
    Будет вечный полярный день.

Север, воля, надежда — страна без границ,
Снег без грязи, как долгая жизнь без вранья.
Воронье нам не выклюет глаз из глазниц —
Потому что не водится здесь воронья.

    Кто не верил в дурные пророчества,
    В снег не лег ни на миг отдохнуть —
    Тем наградою за одиночество
    Должен встретиться кто-нибудь!

1972

THE WHITE SILENCE

It has ever and ever been thus on this earth —
Life fears snowstorms and frost. It has ever been so.
Why are birds flying north, why are birds flying north,
When it's natural they should fly south?

> Glory, glamour or fame — they want none of this.
> Where there's no ice below, they'll alight.
> They will find their short-lived, birdlike happiness
> As reward for their daring flight.

So why couldn't we sleep in our warm beds at night?
What high wave drove us forward, what fury and rage?
We have not seen the famous, divine northern lights:
They're rare around here — quite expensive to stage!

> Silence. Seagulls like lightnings through emptiness,
> Pecking hungrily, flash all around.
> Our reward for the silence and frostiness
> Will be surely the long-dreamed-of sound.

Even dreams in the north are in pale, bloodless white,
All the colours are hidden deep under the snow;
With this whiteness around, we have long lost our sight.
With the first strip of black we'll recover it, though.

> Then the silence of night will release our throat,
> And our weakness will melt in the light,
> And the long northern daylight will be our reward
> For the desperate hours of the night.

Hope, and freedom, and limitless space, and the snow —
Clean white snow without mud, like a life without lies...
From the sockets, our eyes won't be pecked by the crows,
For there aren't any crows here to peck out our eyes.

> Those who did not believe in ill prophecies,
> Did not drop in the snow on the way —
> As reward for the long, utter loneliness,
> They are sure to meet someone — some day!

1972

* * *

Штормит весь вечер, и пока
Заплаты пенные латают
Разорванные швы песка —
Я наблюдаю свысока,
Как волны головы ломают.

И я сочувствую слегка
Погибшим — но издалека.

Я слышу хрип, и смертный стон,
И ярость, что не уцелели,—
Еще бы — взять такой разгон,
Набраться сил, пробить заслон —
И голову сломать у цели...

И я сочувствую слегка
Погибшим — но издалека.

А ветер снова в гребни бьёт
И гривы пенные ерошит.
Волна барьера не возьмёт,—
Ей кто-то ноги подсечёт —
И рухнет взмыленная лошадь.

И посочувствуют слегка
Погибшей ей,— издалека.

Придёт и мой черёд вослед:
Мне дуют в спину, гонят к краю.
В душе — предчувствие, как бред,—
Что надломлю себе хребет —
И тоже голову сломаю.

Мне посочувствуют слегка —
Погибшему — издалека.

Так многие сидят в веках
На берегах — и наблюдают
Внимательно и зорко, как
Другие рядом на камнях
Хребты и головы ломают.

Они сочувствуют слегка
Погибшим — но издалека.

1973

* * *

The storm is raging all the night,
I'm listening to the white surf rumble,
And, while the beach is patched with white
Unkempt foam, I watch from a height
Great combers break their necks and crumble.

I'm sorry for the dead, at heart,
But take good care to keep apart.

A rattle of death, a groan, a roar —
I hear mad fury in them all.
No wonder: they rushed for the shore,
They gathered strength, they crossed the bar —
And broke their necks so near their goal.

I'm sorry for the dead, at heart,
But take good care to keep apart.

The wind again will rip and tear
The manes of foam in senseless fury.
This fence the waves will never clear —
A foot will slip, the horse will rear
And crash full length, in white foam buried.

And some will mourn for him, at heart,
But take good care to keep apart.

My turn will come one day, I know,
I'm being pushed towards the border,
Forebodings rip apart my soul —
I'll break my neck, shan't reach my goal;
There's some that will not stop at murder.

And some will mourn for me, at heart,
But take good care to keep apart.

So many folks for ages stay
Put on the beach — and just grow older
Intently studying the way
The others in the white surf play
And break their backs and necks on boulders.

They're sorry for the dead, at heart,
But take good care to keep apart.

1973

БАЛЛАДА О БРОШЕННОМ КОРАБЛЕ

Капитана в тот день называли на «ты»,
Шкипер с юнгой сравнялись в талантах;
Распрямляя хребты и срывая бинты,
Бесновались матросы на вантах.

Двери наших мозгов
Посрывало с петель
В миражи берегов,
В покрывала земель,

Этих обетованных, желанных —
И колумбовых, и магелланных.

Только мне берегов
Не видать и земель —
С хода в девять узлов
Сел по горло на мель,—
А у всех молодцов —
Благородная цель...
И в конце-то концов —
Я ведь сам сел на мель.

И ушли корабли — мои братья, мой флот,
Кто чувствительней — брызги сглотнули.
Без меня продолжался великий поход,
На меня ж парусами махнули.

И погоду и случай
Безбожно кляня,
Мои пасынки кучей
Бросали меня.

Вот со шлюпок два залпа — и ладно! —
От Колумба и от Магеллана.

Я пью пену — волна
Не доходит до рта,
И от палуб до дна
Обнажились борта,
А бока мои грязны —
Таи не таи,—
Так любуйтесь на язвы
И раны мои!

Вот дыра у ребра — это след от ядра,
Вот рубцы от тарана, и даже

THE BALLAD OF AN ABANDONED SHIP

On that day, all derided the Captain, all scoffed;
Ship's boy, skipper — all swore fast and loud.
Proudly rearing and tearing their bandages off,
Sailors bellowed and raged in the shrouds.

> Then the doors of our brains
> Off the hinges were torn
> And were carried away
> To a mirage-like shore,

> In the faraway Promised Lands landing,
> Lands Columbian and Magellanian.

> But it seems I will not
> See those lands newly found:
> Doing eight or nine knots
> I ran firmly aground.
> Ours were dangerous goals,
> But the brave lads were game.
> Someone steered for the shoals.
> I'm the one more to blame.

Then my brothers sailed on — I was left all alone.
The more sensitive ones swallowed spray,
And without me the great daring voyage went on —
They just wrote me off, and sailed away.

> Roundly cursing the weather,
> Fate and pitiless chance,
> They sailed off, all together,
> My unfortunate sons.

> First, two salvoes, and then they would sail on:
> Hail, Columbus! And then, hail, Magellan!

> I drink foam as the waves
> Slap my sides — I don't care.
> Decks to bottom the staves
> Have been crushed and laid bare.
> Slime and seaweed and gore
> Thickly cover my sides.
> You can look at my sores —
> I have nothing to hide.

Here's a cannonball furrow, quite close to the frame;
Here are scars left by ramming and fire;

Видно шрамы от крючьев — какой-то пират
Мне хребет перебил в абордаже.

Киль — как старый неровный
Гитаровый гриф:
Это брюхо вспорол мне
Коралловый риф.

Задыхаюсь, гнию — так бывает:
И просоленное загнивает.

Ветры кровь мою пьют
И сквозь щели снуют
Прямо с бака на ют, —
Меня ветры добьют.
Я под ними стою
От утра до утра, —
Гвозди в душу мою
Забивают ветра.

И гулякой шальным всё швыряют вверх дном
Эти ветры — незваные гости.
Захлебнуться бы им в моих трюмах вином
Или — с мели сорвать меня в злости!

Я уверовал в это,
Как загнанный зверь,
Но не злобные ветры
Нужны мне теперь.

Мои мачты — как дряблые руки,
Паруса — словно груди старухи.

Будет чудо восьмое —
И добрый прибой
Мое тело омоет
Живою водой,
Моря божья роса
С меня снимет табу —
Вздует мне паруса,
Будто жилы на лбу.

Догоню я своих, догоню и прощу
Позабывшую помнить армаду.
И команду свою я обратно пущу:
Я ведь зла не держу на команду.

Только, кажется, нет
Больше места в строю.

You can see where I was many years ago maimed
By a pirate's well-honed grappling irons.

Look, my keel is uneven,
As if gnawed by huge teeth —
My lean belly was riven
Long ago by a reef.

I am rotting and panting and wheezing
Though I've been on the high seas well seasoned.

Winds are sucking my blood
Creeping for'ard by stealth,
Whipping starboard to port...
Winds, they will be my death.
They lambaste me and wail
From first light to first light,
They are driving long nails
In my soul day and night.

Like unbidden guests out on a rampage, the swine,
Winds kick everything here upside down.
How I wish that they choked in my dark holds on wine,
Or in fury pulled me off the ground.

They're stronger, that's sure —
I'm a wild beast at bay.
But it's not the winds' fury
That'll help me today.

Like thin arms are my masts, thin and frail.
Like an old woman's breasts are my sails.

This will be the eighth wonder —
A generous swell
Will sweep over and under
My mouldy old shell.
I will shake off the spell,
I will rise on a crest,
And my white sails will swell
Like a young maiden's breast.

I'll catch up with the fleet, I will show no disdain
For my kin who chose not to remember.
I will let my old crew come on board once again,
I will not rake old memories' embers.

But there's no room for me
In the fleet line today.

Плохо шутишь, корвет,
Потеснись,— раскрою!

Как же так — я ваш брат,
Я ушел от беды...
Полевее, фрегат,
Всем нам хватит воды!

До чего ж вы дошли:
Значит, что — мне уйти?!
Если был на мели —
Дальше нету пути?!
Разомкните ряды,
Всё же мы — корабли,—
Всем нам хватит воды,
Всем нам хватит земли,

Этой обетованной, желанной —
И колумбовой, и магелланной.

1971

You play dangerously,
Cruiser — out of my way!

Are we brothers or not?
I got out of a hole...
Frigate, bear hard a-port,
There's enough sea for all...

That it should come to this —
You reject me, by God!
Once one's stuck on the reefs,
Is one wiped out for good?
Open ranks, heed my call,
We're all ships in the end,
There's enough sea for all
And there is enough land,

So look forward, men, to happy landings
In Columbian lands and Magellanian.

1971

ПЕСНЯ ЗАВИСТНИКА

Мой сосед объездил весь Союз —
Что-то ищет, а чего — не видно,—
Я в дела чужие не суюсь,
Но мне очень больно и обидно.

У него на окнах — плюш и шелк,
Баба его шастает в халате,—
Я б в Москве с киркой уран нашел
При такой повышенной зарплате!

И, сдается мне, что люди врут,—
Он нарочно ничего не ищет:
А для чего? Ведь денежки идут —
Ох, какие крупные деньжищи!

А вчера на кухне ихний сын
Головой упал у нашей двери —
И разбил — нарочно — мой графин,—
А я мамаше — счет в тройном размере.

Ему платят рупь, а мне — пятак?!
Пусть теперь дает мне неустойку!
Я ведь не из зависти, я так,—
Ради справедливости, и только.

...Ничего, я им создам уют —
Живо он квартиру обменяет,—
У них денег — куры не клюют,
А у нас — на водку нехватает!

1965

48

SONG OF A BEGRUDGER *

My next-door neighbour's travelled everywhere,
Away prospecting for some sort of mineral.
Other folk's concerns aren't my affair
But somehow he gets up my nose in general.

  They've had their windows done in silk and plush.
  His lady wife goes round in robe and towel.
  If I'd a wage like his, or half as much,
  I'd find ore in Moscow with a trowel!

It's my belief that all his cronies lie.
He finds nowt on purpose — that's his racket.
But all the same, his salary's sky-high —
Make no mistake, he's worth a bleeding packet!

  At our place yesterday this neighbour's lad
  Fell against our door and knocked his forehead,
  And smashed up my decanter. Well, his dad
  Can pay me back the price with interest on it.

A quid to him is like a bob to me.
So he can pay me three times what the cost is!
It isn't out of spite — that's not my way.
The only thing that interests me is justice.

  I'll give him so much gip that he'll soon move.
  He'll be off, and what's more, pretty briskly.
  He's stiff with loot — his income's through the roof,
  But I can barely keep myself in whiskey!

1965

---

*© *Sputnik,* Digest of Soviet Press, 1987, No. 11.
Translated by Kathryn Hamilton.

49

СМОТРИНЫ

В. Золотухину и Б. Можаеву

Там у соседа — пир горой,
И гость — солидный, налитой,
Ну а хозяйка — хвост трубой —
    Идет к подвалам,—
В замок врезаются ключи,
И вынимаются харчи,
И с тягой ладится в печи,
    И с поддувалом.

А у меня — сплошные передряги:
То в огороде недород, то скот падёт,
То печь чадит от нехорошей тяги,
А то щеку́ на сторону ведёт.

    Там у соседа мясо в щах —
    На всю деревню хруст в хрящах,
    И дочь — невеста, вся в прыщах,—
        Дозрела, значит.
    Смотрины, стало быть, у них —
    На сто рублей гостей одних,
    И даже тощенький жених
        Поет и скачет.

А у меня цепные псы взбесились —
Средь ночи с лая перешли на вой,
Да на ногах моих мозоли прохудились
От топотни по комнате пустой.

    Ох, у соседа быстро пьют!
    А что не пить, когда дают?
    А что не петь, когда уют
        И не накладно?
    А тут, вон, баба на снося́х,
    Гусей некормленных косяк...
    Да дело даже не в гусях,
        А всё неладно.

Тут у меня постены появились,
Я их гоню и так и сяк — они опять,
Да в неудобном месте чирей вылез —
Пора пахать, а тут — ни сесть, ни встать.

    Сосед маленочка прислал —
    Он от щедрот меня позвал,—

A BRIDE-SHOW

To Valery Zolotukhin and Boris Mozhayev

My precious neighbour gives a feast
For his respectable fat guests,
His missus looks uncommon pleased —
    Heads for the cellar.
The keys go smoothly into locks,
There is enough provision stocked
To feed an army round the clock —
    He's rich, that feller.

And I am always in some scrape or other,
My crops all fail; on top of that, my cow drops dead;
The chimney will not draw, so we all smother,
Or else my teeth ache, and I go out of my head.

My neighbour's guests are chewing meat,
And all the village hears them eat,
The daughter rubs her pimply tit —
    She's ripe, that's clear.
Looks like a bride-show, that whole mess,
A hundred roubles' worth, I guess,
The thin bridegroom sings to the guests —
    They only leer.

And in my yard the dogs have gone quite crazy —
They have stopped barking and begun to howl.
My corns are worn by pacing in a frenzy,
As in my empty house all night I prowl.

Boy, aren't the bastards drinking fast!
But then, why shouldn't they, I ask —
It's not as if it was the last
    Of hooch out there.
And here the wife is big with child,
The hungry geese cackle like wild —
It's not the geese that have me riled,
    It's just not fair.

The place is crawling with all kinds of vermin,
I fight them tooth and nail, but there they are again.
A boil on my you know what has me squirming —
It's time to plough, and I can't move with pain.

The neighbour sent his kid for me
In all his generosity;

51

4*

Ну я, понятно, отказал,
   А он — сначала.
Должно, литровую огрел —
Ну и, конечно, подобрел...
И я пошел — попил, поел,—
   Не полегчало.

И посредине этого разгула
Я пошептал на ухо жениху —
И жениха как будто ветром сдуло,—
Невеста, вон, рыдает наверху.

   Сосед орёт, что он — народ,
   Что основной закон блюдёт:
   Что — кто не ест, тот и не пьет,—
      И выпил, кстати.
   Все сразу повскакали с мест,
   Но тут малец с поправкой влез:
   «Кто не работает — не ест,—
      Ты спутал, батя!»

А я сидел с засаленною трёшкой,
Чтоб завтра гнать похмелие моё,
В обнимочку с обшарпанной гармошкой —
Меня и пригласили за неё.

   Сосед другую литру съел —
   И осовел, и опсовёл,
   Он захотел, чтоб я попел,—
      Зря, что ль, поили?!
   Меня схватили за бока
   Два здоровенных мужика:
   «Играй, паскуда, пой, пока
      Не удавили!»

Уже дошло веселие до точки,
Уже невесту тискали тайком —
И я запел про светлые денёчки,
«Когда служил на почте ямщиком».

   Потом у них была уха,
   И заливные потроха,
   Потом поймали жениха
      И долго били,
   Потом пошли плясать в избе,
   Потом дрались не по злобе —
   И всё хорошее в себе
      Доистребили.

Of course I wouldn't go, but he
Said not to blather.
A fifth he must have put away,
No wonder he felt kind today...
I went and drank and ate; can't say
I felt much better.

And in the midst of all this razzle-dazzle
I whispered softly in the bridegroom's ear:
It wasn't nice to sit around and guzzle —
The bride was drowning in her room in tears.

The neighbour then kicked up a stink:
"I'm people — who are you, d'you think?
Who eats not, neither shall he drink!"
    He yelled and slobbered.
The company leaped from their seats,
But here spoke up his little kid:
"Who works not, neither shall he eat —
    That is the law, Dad!"

I sat there, my last greasy rouble hoarding
(I'd need a shot or two the following day),
Embracing my decrepit old accordion:
That's what I was invited for — to play.

The neighbour guzzled one more fifth
And bawled and banged and spouted filth,
And yelled I must sing for his kith —
    "Whose booze you're suckin'?"
Before I could my noodle nod,
They started roughing me, the sods —
"Get on, you shithead, or by God
    We'll bash your mug in!"

The feast was in full swing, the guests went batty,
Some merry souls were feeling up the bride,
And I began to sing that ancient ditty —
"When I was young, I loved like mad to ride."

And after that they drank again
And had fat tripe and fish, and then
They caught the puny bridegroom, and
    They slapped him silly.
And then they danced till they would fall,
And then there was a free-for-all;
There might be good in them — that brawl
    Was sure to kill it.

А я стонал в углу болотной выпью,
Набычась, а потом и подбочась,—
И думал я: а с кем я завтра выпью
Из тех, с которыми я пью сейчас?!

Наутро там всегда покой,
И хлебный мякиш за щекой,
И без похмелья перепой,
    Еды навалом,
Никто не лается в сердцах,
Собачка мается в сенцах,
И печка — в синих изразцах
    И с поддувалом.

А у меня — и в ясную погоду
Хмарь на душе, которая горит,—
Хлебаю я колодезную воду,
Чиню гармошку, и жена корит.

                                    1973

МАСКИ

Смеюсь навзрыд — как у кривых зеркал,—
Меня, должно быть, ловко разыграли:
Крючки носов и до ушей оскал —
Как на венецианском карнавале!

Вокруг меня смыкается кольцо —
Меня хватают, вовлекают в пляску,—
Так-так, мое нормальное лицо
Все, вероятно, приняли за маску.

Петарды, конфетти... Но все не так,—
И маски на меня глядят с укором,—
Они кричат, что я опять — не в такт,
Что наступаю на ноги партнерам.

Что делать мне — бежать да поскорей?
А может, вместе с ними веселиться?..
Надеюсь я — под масками зверей
Бывают человеческие лица.

I whimpered in a corner in black sorrow,
Bemoaning like a bittern my sad plight:
And will I want, I thought, to drink tomorrow
With any jerks that I drink with tonight?

Come morning, everything is quiet,
And for a while all's peace and light,
There's booze enough to set things right,
    And food a-plenty.
There's no one there to swear and rail,
The puppy even wags its tail,
The stove is covered with blue tile
    And looks so dainty.

And not a thing works with me as it ought to.
My soul is cloudy — now and all my life.
I'm drinking by the pint ice-cold well-water,
Fix my accordion — and listen to the wife.

1973

MASKS *

I laugh, but with wild laughter nearer tears.
As if seen in distorting mirrors, all
Have crooked noses and grin from ear to ear
Like grotesques at a Venetian carnival.

The circle closes in and rings me round.
They seize me, forcing me to take my place
And join the dance. My features they confound
And see a mask where there is but my face.

Confetti fills the hall and fireworks flare!
The masks scowl balefully and look askance:
I'm out of step, they cry, and take no care —
I tread upon the others in the dance.

. . . .

What shall I do? Shall I take flight, I ask,
Or shall I stay and frolic with these creatures?
Can I not hope, behind an animal mask,
To find a face endowed with human features?

---

* © *Sputnik,* Digest of Soviet Press, 1987, No. 11.
   Translated by Kathryn Hamilton.

Все в масках, в париках — все как один,—
Кто — сказочен, а кто — литературен...
Сосед мой слева — грустный арлекин,
Другой — палач, а каждый третий — дурень.

Один — себя старался обелить,
Другой — лицо скрывает от огласки,
А кто — уже не в силах отличить
Свое лицо от непременной маски.

Я в хоровод вступаю, хохоча,—
И все-таки мне неспокойно с ними:
А вдруг кому-то маска палача
Понравится — и он ее не снимет?!

Вдруг арлекин навеки загрустит,
Любуясь сам своим лицом печальным;
Что, если дурень свой дурацкий вид
Так и забудет на лице нормальном?!

Как доброго лица не прозевать,
Как честных отличить наверняка мне? —
Все научились маски надевать,
Чтоб не разбить свое лицо о камни.

Я в тайну масок все-таки проник,—
Уверен я, что мой анализ точен:
Что маски равнодушья у иных —
Защита от плевков и от пощечин.

1971

ТОВАРИЩИ УЧЕНЫЕ

Товарищи учёные, доценты с кандидатами!
Замучились вы с иксами, запутались в нулях,
Сидите, разлагаете молекулы на атомы,
Забыв, что разлагается картофель на полях.

Из гнили да из плесени бальзам извлечь пытаетесь
И корни извлекаете по десять раз на дню,—

For each of them is wearing mask and wig,
Some from literature, some from old romances.
The one beside me sports a harlequin's rig,
The next a hangman's and a third a dunce's.

. . . .

With loud guffaws I join the merry round,
But still I feel uneasy, though I laugh.
Supposing one — a hangman — grows too fond
Of his grim mask and will not take it off?

What if a harlequin should learn to love
His mournful face, and so be sad forever?
Or if a fool should like his mask enough
To forget his wits and lose them altogether?!

But how can I spot goodness? Recognise
The rogues and tell them from the honest ones?
Each dons his mask and put on his disguise
So as not to dash his face against the stones.

And yet, I've plumbed their secret. If correct —
And I've no serious grounds for doubting it —
I know the indifferent mask is to protect
The real face from blows and gobs of spit.

1971

COMRADE SCIENTISTS! *

Comrade scientists, academicians, candidates and such!
You're nuts on x's, y's and z's — watch out, they'll be your
death!
In labs and stuffy libraries for days on end you mope
and slouch,
Without a thought for tons of taters rotting in the earth.

You want to turn mould into balm, you put all trash to use,
And every blessed day you try to find the cubic root,

---

* Every autumn, Soviet intellectuals are sent, along with the
rest of the urban population, to harvest crops on collective and
state farms. Vysotsky's is one of a great many satirical sketches
on the subject.— *Tr.*

57

Ох, вы там добалуетесь, ох, вы доизвлекаетесь,
Пока сгниёт, заплесневеет картофель на корню!

Автобусом до Сходни доезжаем,
А там — рысцой, и не стонать!
Небось картошку все мы уважаем,—
Когда с сольцой ее намять.

Вы можете прославиться почти на всю Европу, коль
С лопатами проявите здесь свой патриотизм,—
А то вы всем кагалом там набросились на опухоль,
Собак ножами режете, а это — бандитизм!

Товарищи учёные, кончайте поножовщину,
Бросайте ваши опыты, гидрид и ангидрид:
Садитеся в полуторки, валяйте к нам в Тамбовщину,—
А гамма-излучение денёк повременит.

Полуторкой к Тамбову подъезжаем,
А там — рысцой, и не стонать!
Небось картошку все мы уважаем,—
Когда с сольцой ее намять.

К нам можно даже с семьями, с друзьями и знакомыми —
Мы славно тут разместимся, и скажете потом,
Что бог, мол, с ними, с генами, бог с ними, с хромосомами,
Мы славно поработали и славно отдохнем!

Товарищи учёные, Эйнштейны драгоценные,
Ньютоны ненаглядные, любимые до слёз!
Ведь лягут в землю общую остатки наши бренные,—
Земле — ей всё едино: апатиты и навоз.

Так приезжайте, милые,— рядами и колоннами!
Хотя вы все там химики, и нет на вас креста,
Но вы ж ведь там задохнетесь за синхрофазотронами,—
А тут места отличные — воздушные места!

But while you're playing all them tricks, which really amuse
Good folks, potatoes in the fields just lie about and rot.

We ride as far as buses' wheels can get us,
And then, look smart, folks! At a trot!
No whimpering! We all of us like taters,
I guess — when mushed with eggs and salt.

Come on, you can set records here, you can gain European
fame,
And digging spuds, you can display your patriotism, too,
Instead of ganging up on dogs — we know the way you maim
Them curs, and carve them up with knives — a nasty thing
to do!

Dear comrade scientists, stop all this carving critters
with your blades,
Knock off all those experiments on mammals and reptiles,
Pile into lorries, come out here, it's time for you to swing
a spade,
And gamma radiations, they can surely wait awhile.

We ride as far as buses' wheels can get us,
And then, look smart, folks! At a trot!
No whimpering! We all of us like taters,
I guess — when mushed with eggs and salt.

Come over with your families and friends — it'll be your home
from home.
There will be room for everyone, and when the job is done,
To hell with molecules, you'll say, and blast the genes
and chromosomes,
We've done a job of work — it's time we had a little fun.

Dear scientists, our precious Ensteins and our clever — clever
Bohrs,
Beloved Newtons, there's one thing that I would like to ask:
D'you know where all our mortal remains go? Just think on it,
because
It's all the same to Mother Earth — dung, phosphorites, or us.

So come in ranks and columns, dears! Remember you're
welcome, straight!
Of course you are smart Alecs all, and atheists to boot,
But with those cyclotrons around you'll like as not soon
suffocate,
And here we have fresh air for free — and what a beauty
spot!

Товарищи учёные, не сумлевайтесь, милые:
Коль что у вас не ладится,— ну, там, не тот аффект,—
Мы мигом к вам заявимся с лопатами и с вилами,
Денёчек покумекаем — и выправим дефект!

1972

Dear scientists, you can rely on us — we're with you all
the way:
If things do not run smooth with you — you get the wrong
effect —
We'll get our spades, we'll get our forks, and hurry to
your aid,
We'll use our noodles — in one day we'll clear any defect!

1972

ПЕСНЯ О ДРУГЕ

Если друг
    оказался вдруг
И не друг, и не враг,
    а — так...
Если сразу не разберёшь,
Плох он или хорош,—
Парня в горы тяни —
    рискни! —
Не бросай одного
    его:
Пусть он в связке в одной
    с тобой —
Там поймешь, кто такой.

Если парень в горах —
    не ах,
Если сразу раскис —
    и вниз,
Шаг ступил на ледник —
    и сник,
Оступился — и в крик,—
Значит, рядом с тобой —
    чужой.
Ты его не брани —
    гони:
Вверх таких не берут,
    и тут —
Про таких не поют.

Если ж он не скулил,
    не ныл,

FRIENDSHIP *

If a chum
    begins acting rum,
Not a friend, not a foe,
    but so...
And if suddenly you can't tell
If he means ill or well,
Take him off mountaineering —
    dare!
But don't let him stray
    away!
When he's roped on one rope
    with you
You'll find out if he's true.

If, as the chap scales,
    he quails,
If his nerve starts to go,
    and so —
He steps backwards, appalled,
    and falls
On a glacier, and bawls —
Then you'll know in a trice —
    no dice.
Chase him off — there's no use
    in abuse:
You'll do better — no doubt —
    without him,
And don't sing about him.

If the chap doesn't moan,
    or groan,

---

* © *Soviet Literature*, 1988, No. 10.
Translated by Kathryn Hamilton.

Пусть он хмур был и зол,
        но шёл,
А когда ты упал
        со скал,
Он стонал,
        но держал;
Если шёл он с тобой
        как в бой,
На вершине стоял — хмельной,—
Значит, как на себя самого
Положись на него.

1966

If, though angry or glum,
    he'll come,
And when you miss your step
    and tumble,
He'll hang on,
    though he'll grumble;
If he'll stay with you
    all the way
To the top, as though into the fray —
Then you'll know that the man is a friend
You can trust to the end.

1966

ПРО ДИКОГО ВЕПРЯ

В королевстве, где все тихо и складно,
Где ни войн, ни катаклизмов, ни бурь,
Появился дикий вепрь огромадный —
То ли буйвол, то ли бык, то ли тур.

Сам король страдал желудком и астмой,
Только кашлем сильный страх наводил,—
А тем временем зверюга ужасный
Коих ел, а коих в лес волочил.

И король тотчас издал три декрета:
«Зверя надо одолеть наконец!
Вот кто отчается на это, на это,
Тот принцессу поведет под венец».

А в отчаявшемся том государстве —
Как войдешь, так прямо наискосок —
В бесшабашной жил тоске и гусарстве
Бывший лучший, но опальный стрелок.

На полу лежали люди и шкуры,
Пели песни, пили мёды — и тут
Протрубили во дворе трубадуры,
Хвать стрелка — и во дворец волокут.

И король ему прокашлял: «Не буду
Я читать тебе морали, юнец,—
Но если завтра победишь чуду-юду,
То принцессу поведёшь под венец».

А стрелок: «Да это что за награда?!
Мне бы — выкатить портвейну бадью!»
Мол, принцессу мне и даром не надо —
Чуду-юду я и так победю!

А король: «Возьмёшь принцессу — и точка!
А не то тебя раз-два — и в тюрьму!

A SONG ABOUT A WILD BOAR

In a kingdom where it's all peace and quiet,
And there are no storms, no cataclysms nor war,
There appeared a beast, a wild monstrous giant —
Could be aurochs, could be bison, could be boar.

Now, the king of that land suffered from colic,
All he did was pester folks and talk posh.
In the meantime, that wild beast romped and frolicked,
Eating men and dragging maids in the bush.

And the king then promptly passed a decision:
"That foul monster must be shot — that's my behest!
He who carries out this dangerous mission —
He will marry our sweet child the Princess."

In that kingdom, which was close to distraction,
As you enter, just a short walk sideways,
Lived a fellow in debauch and inaction —
Once the king's best shooter, now in disgrace.

On the floor lay skins, old buddies and strumpets,
Singing songs and drinking mead, and what not.
There was suddenly a flourish of trumpets,
And the shooter was dragged straight to the court.

Here the king coughed to the shooter, "Look,
                                       youngster,
We all know you are a fine shot — the best.
If you kill in single combat the monster,
You will marry our sweet child, the Princess."

"Do you call that a reward?" cried the shooter.
"I will do it for a bucket of port!
And the Princess you can have, or I'll boot her;
I will shoot the beast — you keep the reward!"

In a fury bawled the king at the shooter:
"You mill marry her, or end up in gaol!

Ведь это все же королевская дочка!..»
А стрелок: «Ну хоть убей — не возьму!»

И пока король с им так препирался,
Съел уже почти всех женщин и кур
И возле са́мого дворца ошивался
Этот самый то ли бык, то ли тур.

Делать нечего — портвейн он отспорил,—
Чуду-юду уложил — и убег...
Вот так принцессу с королём опозорил
Бывший лучший, но опальный стрелок.

1966

After all, she is my own royal daughter!"
And the shooter yelled, "You keep that female!"

And while these two went on swearing and screaming,
That wild monster — could be bison or boar —
Put away almost all chickens and women,
And was skulking by the palace's door.

What a stew! The shooter got what he ought to,
Shot the monster and skipped off to his place.
Thus he put to shame the king and his daughter —
Once the king's best shooter, now in disgrace.

1966

О ФАТАЛЬНЫХ ДАТАХ И ЦИФРАХ

Моим друзьям — поэтам

Кто кончил жизнь трагически, тот — истинный поэт,
А если в точный срок, так — в полной мере:
На цифре 26 один шагнул под пистолет,
Другой же — в петлю слазил в «Англетере».

А в 33 Христу — он был поэт, он говорил:
«Да не убий!» Убьёшь — везде найду, мол.
Но — гвозди ему в руки, чтоб чего не сотворил,
Чтоб не писал, и чтобы меньше думал.

С меня при цифре 37 в момент слетает хмель,—
Вот и сейчас — как холодом подуло:
Под эту цифру Пушкин подгадал себе дуэль
И Маяковский лег виском на дуло.

Задержимся на цифре 37! Коварен Бог —
Ребром вопрос поставил: или — или!
На этом рубеже легли и Байрон, и Рембо,—
А нынешние — как-то проскочили.

Дуэль не состоялась, или — перенесена,
А в 33 распяли, но не сильно,
А в 37 — не кровь, да что там кровь! — и седина
Испачкала виски не так обильно.

«Слабо́ стреляться?! В пятки, мол, давно ушла душа!» —
Терпенье, психопаты и кликуши!

ON FATAL DATES AND FIGURES

To my friends the poets

They are true poets, those who end their days in tragedy,
Especially when they choose well when and where.
At twenty-six, one went and stopped a bullet one fine day,
Another, hanged himself in the Angleterre*.

Or you take Christ — at 33, He was a poet; He said,
"Thou shalt not kill," and generally disabused the rabble.
They nailed Him to the cross — He would be safer dead,
He would not teach or preach or stir up trouble.

Now, 37... What a gloomy date, and what a cruel
Sign — leaves me sober as a judge, that figure.
At 37, Pushkin went to fight a hopeless duel,
And Mayakovsky pulled the pistol trigger.

Let's dwell on this grim figure 37. Yes or no —
Good God would ask point-blank, and few would tarry.
Along this line some good men fell, like Byron or
Rimbaud!
Today, most bards slip neatly past this barrier.

The duel is delayed awhile, and sometimes never fought.
At thirty-three, one's crucified, but slightly.
At thirty-seven, tears are sometimes shed, but blood is not,
One's hair turns grey, perhaps — but only lightly.

"Poets chicken out these days — their hearts are in their
lyric boots!"
But patience, psychopaths and sullen ghouls!

---

* Mikhail Lermontov (1814-1841) was killed in a duel ; Sergei
Yesenin (1895-1925) slashed his veins, wrote his last poem in blood
and hanged himself in the Angleterre in Leningrad.— *Tr.*

71

Поэты ходят пятками по лезвию ножа —
И режут в кровь свои босые души!

На слово «длинношеее» в конце пришлось три «е»,—
Укоротить поэта! — вывод ясен,—
И нож в него! — но счастлив он висеть на острие,
Зарезанный за то, что был опасен!

Жалею вас, приверженцы фатальных дат и цифр,—
Томитесь, как наложницы в гареме!
Срок жизни увеличился — и, может быть, концы
Поэтов отодвинулись на время!

1971

НАТЯНУТЫЙ КАНАТ

Он не вышел ни званьем, ни ростом,
Не за славу, не за плату —
На свой, необычный манер.
Он по жизни шагал над помостом —
По канату, по канату,
Натянутому, как нерв.

    Посмотрите — вот он
       без страховки идёт.
    Чуть правее наклон —
       упадёт, пропадёт!
    Чуть левее наклон —
       всё равно не спасти...
    Но, должно быть, ему очень нужно пройти
    четыре четверти пути.

И лучи его с шага сбивали,
И кололи, словно лавры.
Труба надрывалась — как две.
Крики «Браво!» его оглушали,
А литавры, а литавры —
Как обухом по голове!

    Посмотрите — вот он
       без страховки идет.
    Чуть правее наклон —
       упадёт, пропадёт!
    Чуть левее наклон —

In these days, too, the poets walk on razors barefoot,
And slash to ribbons naked hearts and souls!

A poet will stick out his neck, he will torment his heart.
Slash at his neck, this self-appointed angel!
They stick a knife in him, but he is happy to shed blood —
This man ripped up for being such a danger.

I'm sorry for you all, you hostages of fatal dates.
You are like concubines in harems longing.
Our life expectancy has grown considerably of late —
Perhaps now poets also will last longer.

1971

THE TIGHTROPE

He was neither imposing nor sprightly,
Not a hero out of a fable —
In his own curious way, with some verve
He was walking through life, stepping lightly
High above our heads on a cable
Stretched taut as a nerve.

> Look, he's walking without
>   Any belt, any net.
> If he leans too far out —
>   He's a goner, he's dead!
> He is dead, anyway,
>   If he slips, if he sways...
> He is crazy, that fellow
>   If he wants to play
>   With death all four fourths of the way.

Spotlights blinded him, searing as lava,
Lights like pinpricks — Steady! Slowly...
The trumpet mourned as for the dead.
He was deafened by shrill cries of Bravo!
And the kettledrums kept rolling —
As if pounding him on the head!

> Look, he's walking without
>   Any belt, any net.
> If he leans too far out —
>   He's a goner, he's dead!
> He is dead, anyway,

всё равно не спасти...
Но теперь ему меньше осталось пройти —
уже три четверти пути.

«Ах как жутко, как смело, как мило!
Бой со смертью — три минуты!» —
Раскрыв в ожидании рты,
Из партера глядели уныло —
Лилипуты, лилипуты —
Казалось ему с высоты.

Посмотрите — вот он
   без страховки идёт.
Чуть правее наклон —
   упадёт, пропадёт!
Чуть левее наклон —
   всё равно не спасти...
Но спокойно,— ему остается пройти
   всего две четверти пути!

Он смеялся над славою бренной,
Но хотел быть только первым —
Такого попробуй угробь!
Не по проволоке над ареной,—
Он по нервам — нам по нервам —
Шёл под барабанную дробь!

Посмотрите — вот он
   без страховки идёт.
Чуть правее наклон —
   упадёт, пропадёт!
Чуть левее наклон —
   всё равно не спасти...
Но замрите,— ему остается пройти
   не больше четверти пути!

Закричал дрессировщик — и звери
Клали лапы на носилки...
Но прост приговор и суров:
Был растерян он или уверен —
Но в опилки, но в опилки
Он пролил досаду и кровь!

И сегодня другой
   без страховки идёт.
Тонкий шнур под ногой —
   упадёт, пропадёт!

If ne slips, if he sways...
But he's inching ahead, he has less time to play
With death — some three fourths of the way.

"Oh, how awful, how daring, how lovely!
Fighting death — must be all an illusion!"
The slack silly mouths gaping wide,
From the stalls they looked up at him glumly —
Liliputians, Liliputians
They all seemed to him from the height.

Look, he's walking without
Any belt, any net.
If he leans too far out —
He's a goner, he's dead!
He is dead, anyway,
If he slips, if he sways...
Silence, everyone! All this man now has to play
With death is two fourths of the way.

He would mock at all fame and renown,
But he would be the first ever —
And anything less could be damned!
Not a tightrope he danced on now,
It was our nerves — in a fever —
To the rolling of the drum!

Look, he's walking without
Any belt, any net.
If he leans too far out —
He's a goner, he's dead!
He is dead, anyway,
If he slips, if he sways...
But — be quiet! He has but a short time to play
With death — just a fourth of the way.

The trainer cried out, and the horses
Stood quite still — they understood us.
And the sentence was simple and crude:
Lost his nerve — that's the worst of all losses.
In the sawdust, in the sawdust
He spilled his resentment and blood.

Now another walks without
Any belt, any net.
If he leans too far out —
He's a goner, he's dead!

Вправо, влево наклон —
　　и его не спасти...
Но зачем-то ему тоже нужно пройти
　　четыре четверти пути.

1972

I. ПЕВЕЦ У МИКРОФОНА

Я весь в свету, доступен всем глазам,—
Я приступил к привычной процедуре:
Я к микрофону встал, как к образам...
Нет-нет, сегодня точно — к амбразуре.

И микрофону я не по нутру —
Да, голос мой любому опостылет.
Уверен, если где-то я совру —
Он ложь мою безжалостно усилит.

　　　Бьют лучи от рампы мне под рёбра,
　　　Светят фонари в лицо недобро,
　　　И слепят с боков прожектора,
　　　И — жара!.. Жара!.. Жара!..

Сегодня я особенно хриплю,
Но изменить тональность не рискую,—
Ведь если я душою покривлю —
Он ни за что не выпрямит кривую.

Он, бестия, потоньше острия —
Слух безотказен, слышит фальшь до йоты.
Ему плевать, что не в ударе я,—
Но пусть я верно выпеваю ноты!

　　　Бьют лучи от рампы мне под ребра,
　　　Светят фонари в лицо недобро,
　　　И слепят с боков прожектора,
　　　И — жара!.. Жара!.. Жара!..

На шее гибкой этот микрофон
Своей змеиной головою вертит:
Лишь только замолчу — ужалит он,—
Я должен петь — до одури, до смерти.

Не шевелись, не двигайся, не смей!
Я видел жало — ты змея, я знаю!

He is dead, anyway,
   If he slips, if he sways...
But there's also something that drives him to play
   With death all four fourths of the way.

1972

I. A SINGER AT THE MICROPHONE

I'm bathed in light, before the crowd, alone;
I'm here to give my darling public pleasure.
It's like an icon-stand, this microphone...
But — no! Tonight, it's more like an embrasure.

This microphone seems to dislike my voice —
Indeed, there's quite a few who find it trying.
I'm sure if I make one, just one false noise —
It'll mercilessly amplify my lying.

     Footlights beat me fiercely from below,
     In the darkness, evil lanterns glow,
     Spotlights blind me — I am in a spot —
     And it's hot! It's hot! It's hot! It's hot!

Tonight my voice sounds more than ever hoarse,
But I can't change the key — I do not dare,
I know that if I slip, if I sound false,
The mike will not put right my slightest error.

The beast is like a well-honed razor sharp.
Pitch absolute — it hears the least false quarter.
I'm not in voice — it does not give a crap:
I am onstage, I must sing as I ought to!

     Footlights beat me fiercely from below,
     In the darkness, evil lanterns glow,
     Spotlights blind me — I am in a spot —
     And it's hot! It's hot! It's hot! It's hot!

The snakehead writhes, keeping time with my song,
It's rearing like a cobra before stinging.
The moment I fall silent, I am gone —
Till I drop dead, I'll have to go on singing.

Don't stir, don't move, you snake, do not you dare!
I've seen your tongue — you are a deadly viper!

И я — как будто заклинатель змей,
Я не пою — я кобру заклинаю!

   Бьют лучи от рампы мне под ребра,
   Светят фонари в лицо недобро,
   И слепя́т с боков прожектора,
   И — жара!.. Жара!.. Жара!..

Прожорлив он, и с жадностью птенца
Он изо рта выхватывает звуки.
Он в лоб мне влепит девять грамм свинца,
Рук не поднять — гитара вяжет руки!

Опять!.. Не будет этому конца!
Что есть мой микрофон — кто мне ответит?
Теперь он — как лампада у лица,
Но я не свят, и микрофон не светит.

Мелодии мои попроще гамм,
Но лишь сбиваюсь с искреннего тона —
Мне сразу больно хлещет по щекам
Недвижимая тень от микрофона.

   Бьют лучи от рампы мне под ребра,
   Светят фонари в лицо недобро,
   И слепя́т с боков прожектора,
   И — жара!.. Жара!..

                                          1971

II. ПЕСНЯ МИКРОФОНА

Я оглох от удара ладоней,
Я ослеп от улыбок певиц —
Сколько лет я страдал от симфоний,
Потакал подражателям птиц!

Сквозь меня многократно просеясь,
Чистый звук в ваши души летел.
Стоп! Вот — тот, на кого я надеюсь,
Для кого я все муки стерпел.

   Сколько раз в меня шептали про луну,
   Кто-то весело орал про тишину,

Me, I'm a charmer, I do not sing airs,
I'm charming snakes — a latterday Pied Piper!

Footlights beat me fiercely from below,
In the darkness, evil lanterns glow,
Spotlights blind me — I am in a spot —
And it's hot! It's hot! It's hot! It's hot!

It's greedy like a nestling, it will strain
To snatch voraciously at every sound.
It's sure to put a bullet through my brain:
My hands hold the guitar, my hands are bound!

Again!.. There is no end to this disgrace!
To what can I the microphone liken?
It's like an icon-lamp now near my face,
But I am not a saint — and it's no icon!

My melodies are simpler than the scales,
But if I wander from the truthful tone,
I get a stinging smart slap in the face
From that slick shadow of the microphone!

Footlights beat me fiercely from below,
In the darkness, evil lanterns glow,
Spotlights blind me — I am in a spot —
And it's hot! It's hot!

1971

II. SONG OF A MICROPHONE

I am deafened by clapping and cheers,
I am blinded by singers' wide grins,
I have suffered for so many years,
From the high C's and pop idols' din.

Sounds were sifted through me, and went flying
Off the stage, through the air, to your soul.
There's the man on whom all hope I'm laying —
It's for him that I've suffered it all.

I heard sighs enough about the silver moon,
Beaming stars of blissful nights would bawl or croon,

79

На пиле один играл — шею спиливал,—
А я усиливал,
        усиливал,
                усиливал...

На «низах» его голос утробен,
На «верхах» он подобен ножу,—
Он покажет, на что он способен,—
Но и я кое-что покажу!

Он поёт задыхаясь, с натугой —
Он устал, как солдат на плацу,—
Я тянусь своей шеей упругой
К золотому от пота лицу.

    Сколько лет в меня шептали про луну,
    Кто-то весело орал про тишину,
    На пиле один играл — шею спиливал,—
    А я усиливал,
            усиливал,
                    усиливал...

Только вдруг: «Человече, опомнись,—
Что поёшь?! Отдохни — ты устал.
Это — патока, сладкая помесь!
Зал, скажи, чтобы он перестал!..»

Всё напрасно — чудес не бывает,—
Я качаюсь, я еле стою,—
Он бальзамом мне горечь вливает
В микрофонную глотку мою.

    Сколько лет в меня шептали про луну,
    Кто-то весело орал про тишину,
    На пиле один играл — шею спиливал,—
    А я усиливал,
            усиливал,
                    усиливал...

В чем угодно меня обвините—
Только против себя не пойдёшь:
По профессии я — усилитель,—
Я страдал — но усиливал ложь.

Застонал я — динамики взвыли,—
Он сдавил мое горло рукой...
Отвернули меня, умертвили —
Заменили меня на другой.

There was one played on a saw — I nearly died,
But I magnified,
              and magnified,
                          and magnified...

His voice booms in the lower keys,
In the upper, it's sharp as a blade.
He will show what a great star he is.
In my way, though, I may be as great!

He is breathing so hard, he is straining
Every sinew — I fear he'll drop dead.
My long, flexible neck I'm craning
Towards his face that seems golden with sweat.

I heard sighs enough about the silver moon,
Beaming stars of blissful nights would bawl or croon,
There was one played on a saw — I nearly died,
But I magnified,
              and magnified,
                          and magnified...

Suddenly I blow up: "Can't you hear it —
This is bilge, what you sing, cut the crap!
It's like treacle it's saccharine syrop.
People, tell him that he should shut up!"

Voice in wilderness! In vain, my call,
I am wobbling, all things seem afloat.
He is pouring, like balm, bitter gall
In my long and long-suffering throat.

I heard sighs enough about the silver moon,
Beaming stars of blissful nights would bawl or croon,
There was one played on a saw — I nearly died,
But I magnified,
              and magnified,
                          and magnified...

I have always disliked lies and liars.
What of that? I had really no choice.
It's my job, I am an amplifier,
So I suffered, yet amplified lies.

Then I groaned, and the loudspeakers hollered,
But he twisted my neck, and I quaked.
They unscrewed me — I was deftly murdered
And replaced by some lousy old fake.

Тот, другой,— он все стерпит и примет,—
Он навинчен на шею мою.
Часто нас заменяют другими,
Чтобы мы не мешали вранью.

...Мы в чехле очень тесно лежали —
Я, штатив и другой микрофон,—
И они мне, смеясь, рассказали,
Как *он* рад был, что я заменен.

1971

ЧУЖАЯ КОЛЕЯ

Сам виноват — и слёзы лью,
                    и охаю:
Попал в чужую колею
                глубокую.
Я цели намечал свои
                  на выбор сам —
А вот теперь из колеи
                не выбраться.

Крутые скользкие края
Имеет эта колея.

Я кляну проложивших её —
Скоро лопнет терпенье моё —
И склоняю, как школьник плохой:
Колею, в колее, с колеёй...

Но почему неймётся мне —
                   нахальный я,—
Условья, в общем, в колее
                нормальные:
Никто не стукнет, не притрёт —
                 не жалуйся!
Желаешь двигаться вперед —
                пожалуйста!

Отказа нет в еде-питье
В уютной этой колее —

И я живо себя убедил:
Не один я в неё угодил,
Так держать — колесо в колесе! —
И доеду туда, куда все.

It will meekly accept all they say —
That is why on my neck it's now screwed:
We are often replaced — that they may
Go on mouthing their lies undeterred.

...We were lying, a few hours after,
Tightly packed in a hot, dusty case,
And the other mike told me, with laughter,
"*He* was so glad that you'd been replaced."

1971

SOMEONE ELSE'S RUT

No one to blame now for my lot —
                      I groan and weep:
In someone else's rut I got,
              it's very deep.
I used to pick and choose my goals,
                I felt so proud,
And in this rut, it's just no go —
                 no getting out.

     It has such slippery and steep
     Rough edges, and it is so deep.

     I am cursing those who made this rut,
     I'm afraid I shall soon burst a gut,
     I'm declining the noun, like a nut:
     "Of the rut, to the rut, by the rut..."

I wonder why I can't stay put —
                 such cockiness.
Conditions in the rut are good —
                 well, more or less.
No one will slap you down, no fear —
                   no fear at all!
And if you want a nice career —
                get on the ball!

     The folks are always nice and fat,
     Quite comfortable in the rut,

     And I quickly convinced myself that
     We are all in the same cosy rut.
     Steady, mate, as you go: wheel to wheel —
     You'll end up where everyone will.

Вот кто-то крикнул сам не свой:
                              «А ну, пусти!» —
И начал спорить с колеёй
                    по глупости.
Он в споре сжёг запас до дна
                        тепла души —
И полетели клапана и вкладыши.

      Но покорежил он края —
      И шире стала колея.

      Вдруг его обрывается след...
      Чудака оттащили в кювет,
      Чтоб не мог он нам, задним, мешать
      По чужой колее проезжать.

Вот и ко мне пришла беда —
                      стартёр заел,—
Теперь уж это не езда,
                  а ёрзанье.
И надо б выйти, подтолкнуть —
                          но прыти нет,—
Авось подъедет кто-нибудь
                      и вытянет.

      Напрасно жду подмоги я —
      Чужая это колея.

      Расплеваться бы глиной и ржой
      С колеей этой самой — чужой,—
      Тем, что я ее сам углубил,
      Я у задних надежду убил.

Прошиб меня холодный пот
                        до косточки,
И я прошелся чуть вперед
                        по досточке,—
Гляжу — размыли край ручьи
                        весенние,
Там выезд есть из колеи —
                        спасение!

      Я грязью из-под шин плюю
      В чужую эту колею.

Then someone shouted boiling mad,
                              "Make way, you there!"
And he began to fight the rut,
                    the crazy bear.
He burnt in argument his whole
                    tank of goodwill,
Phut went the inserts of his soul —
                              snap went the wheel!

   And still, the silly ass fought hard,
   It's wider now, the bloody rut.

   Soon we see that his track is cut short —
   Someone's booted the crank off the road.
   And indeed, who was he to obstruct
   Heavy traffic in that good old rut?

My turn to fret, the cooler's dead,
                              it will not cool.
No driving, this — it's blood and sweat,
                              it's push and pull.
I mean, I should get out and push —
                    I really ought,
But other stragglers in the slush
                    may pull me out.

   I wait and wait for help in vain,
   "This rut's all wrong," I think again.

   How I'd like to spit slush, slime and muck
   In this alien rut's stupid mug —
   I dug deeper, and got firmly stuck,
   And killed all hope for those at the back.

I felt myself break out in sweat,
                    now cold, now hot,
And I went gingerly ahead
                    along a board.
Just look, the rut's been washed away
                              by springtime floods,
We're saved at last — there is a way
                              out of this rut!

      My wheels kept spitting viscous mud —
      To hell with this ungodly rut!

Эй вы, задние, делай как я!
Это значит — не надо за мной,
Колея эта — только моя,
Выбирайтесь своей колеёй!

1973

БЕГ ИНОХОДЦА

Я скачу, но я скачу иначе —
По камням, по лужам, по росе.
Бег мог назван иноходью — значит:
По-другому, то есть — не как все.

        Мне набили раны на спине,
        Я дрожу боками у воды.
        Я согласен бегать в табуне —
        Но не под седлом и без узды!

Мне сегодня предстоит бороться,—
Скачки! — я сегодня фаворит.
Знаю, ставят все на иноходца,—
Но не я — жокей на мне хрипит!

        Он вонзает шпоры в рёбра мне,
        Зубоскалят первые ряды...
        Я согласен бегать в табуне —
        Но не под седлом и без узды!

Нет, не будут золотыми горы —
Я последним цель пересеку:
Я ему припомню эти шпоры —
Засбою, отстану на скаку!..

        Колокол! Жокей мой на коне —
        Он смеётся в предвкушенье мзды.
        Ох, как я бы бегал в табуне,—
        Но не под седлом и без узды!

Что со мной, что делаю, как смею —
Потакаю своему врагу!
Я собою просто не владею —
Я прийти не первым не могу!

        Что же делать остаётся мне?
        Вышвырнуть жокея моего —

Listen you, stragglers, do as I do!
Do not trail me, I'll go it alone.
This is my rut, it isn't for you —
So get out by a rut of your own!

1973

THE PACER'S RACE

On the stones and sands and dewey grasses
I am racing at my curious pace,
For my gait's unlike all other horses':
I am not like everybody else.

> On my back the sores are oozing blood,
> And my sides are trembling with the pain.
> I would race, and gladly, with the herd —
> But without the saddle and the rein!

I shall run today with other racers.
Racing time! I'm favourite today.
Everyone lays money on the pacers —
That's the way the jockey's money lay.

> And he urges me with whip and spur,
> Crowds are cheering, jeering like insane...
> I would race, and gladly, with the herd —
> But without the saddle and the rein!

No, today the jockey will not force me,
I will be the last one past the post;
I will teach the swine to use the horsewhip —
I will rear and kick, and come in last!

> There's the bell! My master pulls ahead.
> He is grinning: victory spells gain.
> Ah, how I would gallop with the herd —
> But without the saddle and the rein!

What is this? What is it I am doing?
Aiding him, my enemy — the worst!
I'm beside myself, I'm spurting, flying —
It's beyond me, not to be the first!

> Ah, what can I do but spurt ahead!
> Only first, I'll throw him on his can —

И бежать, как будто в табуне, —
Под седлом, в узде, но — без него!

Я пришел, а он в хвосте плетётся —
По камням, по лужам, по росе...
Я впервые не был иноходцем —
Я стремился выиграть, как все!

1970

Я ИЗ ДЕЛА УШЕЛ

Я из дела ушел, из такого хорошего дела!
Ничего не унёс — отвалился в чем мать родила, —
Не затем, что приспичило мне, — просто время приспело,
Из-за синей горы понагнало другие дела.

Мы многое из книжек узнаём,
А истины передают изустно:
«Пророков нет в отечестве своём», —
Но и в других отечествах — не густо.

Растащили меня, но я счастлив, что львиную долю
Получили лишь те, кому я б ее отдал и так.
Я по скользкому полу иду, каблуки канифолю,
Подымаюсь по лестнице и прохожу на чердак.

Пророков нет — не сыщешь днем с огнем, —
Ушли и Магомет, и Заратустра.
Пророков нет в отечестве своем, —
Но и в других отечествах — не густо.

А внизу говорят — от добра ли, от зла ли — не знаю:
«Хорошо, что ушел — без него стало дело верней!»
Паутину в углу с образов я ногтями сдираю,
Тороплюсь — потому что за домом седлают коней.

Открылся лик — я встал к нему лицом,
И он поведал мне светло и грустно:
«Пророков нет в отечестве своём, —
Но и в других отечествах — не густо».

Then I will race on, as with my herd,
With a saddle, but without the man!

I came first — and he can count his losses —
Only this time, pace or no pace,
I was just like all the other horses —
Out to win, like everybody else!

1970

I HAVE QUIT MY OLD JOB

I have quit my old job, such a fine one, things really were
                                                    humming;
I did not gain a lot: I was poor, now I'm poorer still.
It was not just a whim — I had seen it for quite a while
                                                    coming,
Other jobs, other griefs rolling on from behind the blue hill.

    Some things are pretty hard to understand,
    By word of mouth passed from one to another:
    "There are no prophets in a prophet's land,
    In other lands there aren't too many, either."

I have been pulled apart, but I'm glad that the full lion's share
Was received by the folks who'd have got it from me anyway.
I am shuffling along, up the slippery, steep, rotten stairs,
To a tiny old garret where few people, if ever, stray.

    No prophets now — perhaps there's no demand
    For Zoroasters, Mahomets, Isaiahs.
    There are no prophets in a prophet's land,
    In other lands there aren't too many, either.

People talking below — I don't know if in kindness or malice:
"Just as well that he left — if he hadn't things would have
                                                    been worse."
I am tearing away cobwebs off ancient icons with my nails,
I must hurry because in the backyard they're saddling
                                                    my horse.

    The image radiantly shone under my hand,
    And sadly said to me the blessed Father:
    "There are no prophets in a prophet's land,
    In other lands there aren't too many either."

Я влетаю в седло, я врастаю в коня — тело в тело,—
Конь падёт подо мной — я уже закусил удила!
Я из дела ушёл, из такого хорошего дела:
Из-за синей горы понагнало другие дела.

Скачу — хрустят колосья под конём,
Но ясно различаю из-за хруста:
«Пророков нет в отечестве своём,—
Но и в других отечествах — не густо»,

1973

МОЙ ГАМЛЕТ

Я только малость объясню в стихе —
На всё я не имею полномочий...
Я был зачат, как нужно, во грехе —
В поту и в нервах первой брачной ночи.

Я знал, что, отрываясь от земли, —
Чем выше мы, тем жестче и суровей;
Я шел спокойно прямо в короли
И вёл себя наследным принцем крови.

Я знал — все будет так, как я хочу,
Я не бывал внакладе и в уроне,
Мои друзья по школе и мечу
Служили мне, как их отцы — короне.

Не думал я над тем, что говорю,
И с лёгкостью слова бросал на ветер, —
Мне верили и так, как главарю,
Все высокопоставленные дети.

Пугались нас ночные сторожа,
Как оспою, болело время нами.
Я спал на кожах, мясо ел с ножа
И злую лошадь мучил стременами.

Я знал — мне будет сказано: «Царуй!» —
Клеймо на лбу мне рок с рожденья выжег.
И я пьянел среди чеканных сбруй,
Был терпелив к насилью слов и книжек.

Я улыбаться мог одним лишь ртом,
А тайный взгляд, когда он зол и горек,

I leap into the saddle, I'm one with my steed, and he's
                                                        spuming,
He is rearing to go, and I give him his head with a will.
I have quit my old job, such a fine one — but I saw it coming:
Other jobs, other griefs rolling on from behind the blue hill.

> I'm galloping along an empty strand —
> The wind seems to be singing to the rider:
> "There are no prophets in a prophet's land,
> In other lands there aren't too many, either."

1973

MY HAMLET

Let me explain a few things in my verse —
To speak of all of them I have no right.
I was conceived in sin, like all of us, —
The sweat and jitters of the wedding night.

I knew that as we rise above the earth
We learn the harshness that's in power inherent.
I neared the throne with dignity and worth,
With all the hubris of an heir apparent.

I knew I'd have my way no matter what,
I never suffered loss or was let down,
Companions of the schooldesk and the sword
All served me as their fathers served the crown.

I never bothered to select my words,
What came into my head, I simply tossed
To highborn youths, and was believed: I was
By right of birth their undisputed boss.

Night watchmen feared us, feared for their life.
We were the time's disease, the time's murrain.
I slept on skins, I ate meat off a knife,
I always gave my vicious horse free rein.

I knew I would be told one day, "Be king!"
Since birth, I felt a mark on my brow burning.
The sounds of tourneys were like heady drink,
But I was patient, too, with books and learning.

I smiled — the smile, though, at the eyes would stop.
When life seemed vulgar, empty, vicious, boring,

Умел скрывать, воспитанный шутом, —
Шут мертв теперь: «Аминь!» Бедняга Йорик!..

Но отказался я от дележа
Наград, добычи, славы, привилегий:
Вдруг стало жаль мне мертвого пажа,
Я объезжал зеленые побеги...

Я позабыл охотничий азарт,
Возненавидел и борзых и гончих,
Я от подранка гнал коня назад
И плетью бил загонщиков и ловчих.

Я видел — наши игры с каждым днем
Всё больше походили на бесчинства, —
В проточных водах по ночам, тайком
Я отмывался от дневного свинства.

Я прозревал, глупея с каждым днем,
Я прозевал домашние интриги.
Не нравился мне век, и люди в нем
Не нравились, — и я зарылся в книги.

Мой мозг, до знаний жадный, как паук,
Всё постигал: недвижность и движенье, —
Но толку нет от мыслей и наук,
Когда повсюду — им опроверженье.

С друзьями детства перетёрлась нить,
Нить Ариадны оказалась схемой.
Я бился над словами "быть, не быть",
Как над неразрешимою дилеммой.

Но вечно, вечно плещет море бед, —
В него мы стрелы мечем — в сито просо,
Отсеивая призрачный ответ
От вычурного этого вопроса.

Зов предков слыша сквозь затихший гул,
Пошел на зов, — сомненья крались с тылу,
Груз тяжких дум наверх меня тянул,
А крылья плоти вниз влекли, в могилу.

В непрочный сплав меня спаяли дни —
Едва застыв, он начал расползаться.
Я пролил кровь, как все, — и, как они,
Я не сумел от мести отказаться.

My bitter anguish I concealed, brought up
By Jester, now long dead. Amen, poor Yorick!

But I refused to enter in the fight
For privileges, glory, spoils and booty.
All of sudden, for a page who died,
For all young, fragile life I felt such pity...

I soon forgot my passion for the chase,
I hated now my greyhounds and my beagles;
Away from wounded quarry I would race,
And I would lash at huntsmen and at beaters.

I now could see our games with every day
Become more crude, outrageous, pitiless.
At night, in secret I would wash away
The filth and scum of daytime swinishness.

My eyes were opened, but my plight grew worse.
Intrigues and schemes at court I overlooked.
I scorned the age, its men — and I immersed
Myself in ancient manuscripts and books.

All knowledge, like a sponge, absorbed my brain,
I studied rest and motion in elation,
But sciences and Muses are in vain
When everywhere you see their refutation.

What tied me to my mates I could not see,
And Ariadne's thread proved a false schema.
I racked my brains — to be or not to be —
As if it really were a great dilemma.

Our arrows fall on this eternal sea
Of troubles, wretchedness and slavery.
Like millet in a sieve, we try to sift
A ghostly answer from this mannered query.

Through rumbles, I could hear my father's cry.
I answered it, though doubts rose like a wave.
My thoughts — my burden — pulled me to the sky,
The wings of flesh drove me towards the grave.

I was an alloy smelted by my days,
So fragile it broke up before it set.
Like all the world, I shed blood, and, as they,
Could not resist revenge — it was too sweet.

А мой подъём пред смертью — есть провал.
Офелия! Я тленья не приемлю.
Но я себя убийством уравнял
С тем, с кем я лег в одну и ту же землю.

Я Гамлет, я насилье презирал,
Я наплевал на датскую корону, —
Но в их глазах — за трон я глотку рвал
И убивал соперника по трону.

Но гениальный всплеск похож на бред,
В рожденье смерть проглядывает косо.
А мы всё ставим каверзный ответ
И не находим нужного вопроса.

1972

My rise before my death was a descent.
Ophelia, I reject filth and decay,
But through a murder I debased myself —
No better than the man I had to slay.

I'm Hamlet, I abhorred all violence,
I did not care much for the Danish crown,
But in their eyes I was a cut-throat prince
Who killed a rival for his father's throne.

A genius bursts like a delirious cry.
At birth, death shows his visage, grim and leery.
We pose again the tricky old reply
And cannot find the necessary query.

1972

БАЛЛАДА О ДЕТСТВЕ

Час зачатья я помню неточно, —
Значит, память моя — однобока, —
Но зачат я был ночью, порочно
И явился на свет не до срока.

Я рождался не в муках, не в злобе, —
Девять месяцев — это не лет!
Первый срок отбывал я в утробе, —
Ничего там хорошего нет.

    Спасибо вам, святители,
    Что плюнули да дунули,
    Что вдруг мои родители
    Зачать меня задумали —

    В те времена укромные,
    Теперь — почти былинные, —
    Когда срока огромные
    Брели в этапы длинные.

    Их брали в ночь зачатия,
    А многих — даже ранее, —
    А вот живёт же братия —
    Моя честна компания!

Ходу, думушки резвые, ходу!
Слóва, строченьки милые, слóва!..
В первый раз получил я свободу
По указу от тридцать восьмого.

Знать бы мне, кто так долго мурыжил, —
Отыгрался бы на подлеце!
Но родился, и жил я, и выжил, —
Дом на Первой Мещанской — в конце.

THE BALLAD OF CHILDHOOD

I'm afraid I don't know the precise
Hour in which they conceived me, although
They conceived me at night, and in vice,
Not in virtue — that much I do know.

I was not born in pain or in gloom,
Nine months is not nine years, I daresay,
And I did my first term in the womb,
Not in gaol, but it's all much the same.

How can I thank you, angels dear,
You chanted out the magic word —
My parents had the bright idea
To up and bring me in this world,

In those unblest times long ago —
Now something out of folklore tales —
When endless columns used to go
To serve their endless terms in gaols,

Some nabbed right on conception night,
And others, earlier even,
Yet here we are, we are all right,
Me and my gang, thank heaven!

Get away, gloomy thoughts, do not tease me!
My best verse my best words will set free.
For the first time in life, they released me
In 1938, by decree *.

If I knew who kept me in the cooler,
I would pay back the scoundrel, the fiend,
Still, I lived, I lived really and truly —
In an old Moscow street, at the end.

---

* The Decree in question dealt with maternity leaves. Even in these days. "decree" is often used as a euphemism for pregnancy.— *Tr.*

Там за стеной, за стеночкою,
За перегородочкой
Соседушка с соседочкою
Баловались водочкой.

Все жили вровень, скромно так, —
Система коридорная,
На тридцать восемь комнаток —
Всего одна уборная.

Здесь нá зуб зуб не попадал,
Не грела телогреечка,
Здесь я доподлинно узнал,
Почём она — копеечка.

...Не боялась сирены соседка,
И привыкла к ней мать понемногу,
И плевал я — здоровый трехлетка —
На воздушную эту тревогу!

Да не всё то, что сверху, — от бога,
И народ «зажигалки» тушил;
И как малая фронту подмога —
Мой песок и дырявый кувшин.

И било солнце в три луча,
Сквозь дыры крыш просеяно,
На Евдоким Кирилыча
И Гисю Моисеевну.

Она ему: «Как сыновья?»
«Да без вести пропавшие!
Эх, Гиська, мы одна семья, —
Вы тоже пострадавшие!

Вы тоже — пострадавшие,
А значит — обрусевшие:
Мои — без вéсти павшие,
Твои — безвинно севшие».

...Я ушел от пеленок и сосок,
Поживал, не забыт, не заброшен,
И дразнили меня: «Недоносок», —
Хоть и был я нормально доношен.

Маскировку пытался срывать я:
Пленных гонят — чего ж мы дрожим?!
Возвращались отцы наши, братья
По домам — по своим да чужим.

Here, in the next room, there would be
A super row — you couldn't snooze.
The neighbours there, both he and she,
Enjoyed their daily doze of booze.

Here, everyone lived modestly,
In comfort somewhat dubious:
There was just one amenity —
One loo to forty cubicles.

On walls in winter grew hoar-frost,
The kids would be too cold to bawl,
And here I learnt how much it cost
To make two loose ends meet at all.

Air alerts didn't worry the neighbour,
Ma made out like she was unafraid,
I, a brave healthy three-year-old shaver,
Didn't give a good damn for those raids.

Not all things from the sky are divine —
Folks kept fighting incendiary bombs,
So I offered toy buckets of mine
To the soldiers of that Front-at-Home.

Through shattered roofing shone the sun,
The rays kept cutely peering in
At Gisya, an old Jewish crone,
And Russian peasant Yevdokim.

She asks about his sons, "What's new?"
"Both missing, they're telling me.
But you — you carry your cross, too.
Ah Gisya, we're one family.

Yes, we're one family — perhaps
You feel it all, like Russians feel:
Your sons are, guiltless, in the camps,
My sons have fallen in the field."

I was long out of rompers and diapers,
I don't think I was then too much bother.
People teased me, and called whipper-snapper,
Though I was a kid like any other.

Black-out curtains I'd try to tear down:
Germans beaten! Now all fears were gone.
Dads and brothers were now back in town,
Coming home — sometimes not to their own.

У тети Зины кофточка
С драконами да змеями, —
То у Попова Вовчика
Отец пришел с трофеями.

Трофейная Япония,
Трофейная Германия...
Пришла страна Лимония,
Сплошная Чемодания!

Взял у отца на станции
Погоны, словно цацки, я, —
А из эвакуации
Толпой валили штатские.

Осмотрелись они, оклемались,
Похмелились — потом протрезвели.
И отплакали те, кто дождались,
Недождавшиеся — отревели.

Стал метро рыть отец Витькин с Генкой, —
Мы спросили — зачем? — он в ответ:
«Коридоры кончаются стенкой,
А тоннели — выводят на свет!»

Пророчество папашино
Не слушал Витька с корешем —
Из коридора нашего
В тюремный коридор ушёл.

Да он всегда был спорщиком,
Припрут к стене — откажется...
Прошел он коридорчиком —
И кончил «стенкой», кажется.

Но у отцов — свои умы,
А что до нас касательно —
На жизнь засматривались мы
Уже самостоятельно.

Все — от нас до почти годовалых —
«Толковищу» вели до кровянки, —
А в подвалах и полуподвалах
Ребятишкам хотелось под танки.

A nylon blouse with snakes — not bad! —
Our Auntie Zina these days wore.
That was because Volodka's Dad
Returned home with the spoils of war.

The spoils of war from Germany,
The spoils of war from far Japan...
Hail from the Land of Lemony,
The fairy Suitcase Land!

When I met Father, I said, "Please,
Give me those shoulder straps to wear."
And all around, evacuees
Were streaming back home in a tear.

They looked round and then settled back slowly,
Sobered up after vodka and beers.
Those who waited in vain, stopped their howling,
Those who didn't, just ran out of tears.

Vitka's Dad built the new Underground;
When we asked him what for? he replied:
"All our staircases somehow lead down.
And some tunnels can lead towards light."

But Vitka did not care a straw
For his wise Dad's prophetic words,
So he went down our corridor
And ended up as a jailbird.

But he was just that kind of lad,
Bound for a bad end — one could tell.
Like his Dad said, our staircase led
Him straight into a prison cell.

Well, fathers have their fine ideas,
But we were learning to think, too:
Of life, and of life's mysteries,
We took an independent view.

Everywhere, kids were arguing, screaming,
Fights broke out amid bloodthirsty yells.
In their basements, teenagers were dreaming —
Blowing up German tanks, and themselves *.

---

* A recurrent episode in World War II on the Russian front:
in the absence of other defences against tanks, soldiers would tie
several hand grenades round their body and throw themselves under
a tank. The episode figured in several wartime films.— *Tr.*

Не досталось им даже по пуле —
В «ремеслухе» — живи да тужи:
Ни дерзнуть, ни рискнуть, — но рискнули
Из напильников делать ножи.

Они воткнуться в лёгкие,
От никотина чёрные,
По рукоятки лёгкие
Трехцветные наборные...

Вели дела обменные
Сопливые острожники —
На стройке немцы пленные
На хлеб меняли ножики.

Сперва играли в «фантики»,
В «пристенок» с крохоборами, —
И вот ушли романтики
Из подворотен ворами.

...Спекулянтка была номер перший —
Ни соседей, ни бога не труся,
Жизнь закончила миллионершей —
Пересветова тётя Маруся.

У Маруси за стенкой говели, —
И она там втихую пила...
А упала она — возле двери, —
Некрасиво так, зло умерла.

Нажива — как наркотика, —
Не выдержала этого
Богатенькая тётенька
Маруся Пересветова.

Но было все обыденно:
Заглянет кто — расстроится.
Особенно обидело
Богатство — метростроевца.

Он дом сломал, а нам сказал:
«У вас носы не вытерты,
А я, за что я воевал?!» —
И разные эпитеты.

...Было время — и были подвалы,
Было дело — и цены снижали,

Not a bullet for them — they had missed it.
What a life, doing time at trade schools;
Neither courage nor risk — but they risked it,
They made knives out of steel files, the fools.

And later someone would get killed —
A knife would slide into a lung,
All nicotined, up to the hilt —
And yet another would die young.

The times were hard, all things were tight,
The snotty jailbirds did a trade:
The Krauts on construction sites
Exchanged their hand-made knives for bread.

At first they played at petty theft
And fooled at cards, them silly mugs,
And then the young romantics left
Their native gutter to play thugs.

An old woman, our Auntie Maria,
Never feared either God or her neighbours.
When she died, this small-time profiteer,
She'd gained millions through her shameless labours.

Neighbours went without food all about,
And she drank in her room on the sly,
But one day she dropped dead, just fagged out —
Such a lousy and sad way to die.

It looked like money was her dope —
She got an overdose.
Alone with millions, she would mope,
And then she croaked, the louse.

The people came, and peered, and found
An ordinary room, no more.
Our worker from the Underground,
He felt particularly sore.

He pulled the house down, and he swore:
"You're greenhorns, now, but you take me —
What did I fight for, in the war?"
Plus words banned in mixed company.

There were times when we all lived like herrings,
There were times when the prices were lowered,

И текли куда надо каналы,
И в конце куда надо впадали.

Дети бывших старшин да майоров
До ледовых широт поднялись,
Потому что из тех коридоров,
Им казалось, сподручнее — вниз.

1975

БАНЬКА ПО-БЕЛОМУ

Протопи ты мне баньку, хозяюшка,—
Раскалю я себя, распалю.
На полоке, у самого краешка,
Я сомненья в себе истреблю.

Разомлею я до неприличности,
Ковш холодной — и всё позади,—
И наколка времён культа личности
Засинеет на левой груди.

Протопи ты мне баньку по-белому,—
Я от белого свету отвык,—
Угорю я — и мне, угорелому,
Пар горячий развяжет язык.

** A lengthy treatise would be needed to really explain the
role of the bath-hut in the Russian way of life — or what used
to be the way of life in peasant Russia. It was, and in some
areas still is, an institution — much like the ancient Roman baths,
the Turkish baths, the Japanese baths, or the Finnish saunas, the
difference being that Russian bath-huts are family affairs, not public
institutions, each farmstead having a bath-hut (endearingly referred to
as *banka*, not the formal *banya*) of its own. (For a more detailed
description of these see Zolotukhin's contribution to the present collection.) With Russia's severe climate, warming oneself in the steam
of the bath-hut, accompanied by ritual self-flagellation with a birch-
twig besom, rolling naked in the snow or dipping in an ice-hole
in a lake or river to cool off, is a real delight. Steaming oneself
in the bath-hut was also a necessary prelude to a religious or any

Dams were built, and the builders were buried,
Rivers flowed where they ought to have flowed *.

Sergeants' children, the children of majors
Ended up in Siberian camps —
All because in our house the staircases
All led down — there were none leading up.

1975

---

* These are all signs of the times — the late 1940s and early
1950s: prices *were* lowered (after first being raised, but no one seems
to remember that), great canals were built (by prison labour),
and grandiose plans were made for the "transformation of nature",
better known as "ecological disaster" at present.— *Tr.*

BATH-HUT **

Warm the bath-hut, my love, set it steaming,
I will lash myself glowing red,
On a shelf somewhere near the ceiling
I will squash all my doubts — kill them dead.

I'll ease off to the point of brutality,
Then a roll in the snow will feel good,
And the face of that cult personality
Will stand out on my left breast, tattoo'd.

Warm the bath-hut, my love, set it steaming,
I've been out in the cold for so long.
It still seems to me I must be dreaming...
Heady steam, it will loosen my tongue.

---

other kind of feast, a remedy for nearly all types of illnesses, and
sometimes an act of preparation for death.— The hero of this song is
apparently a Siberian peasant branded *kulak* during forced collectivi-
sation who resisted arrest and was deported from his native village.
Peasants from European Russia were taken to Siberia, while those in
Siberia could naturally be taken merely to another part of Siberia
(this explains verse seven). Many peasants had faith in Stalin even in
the camps, they believed he knew nothing of his hirelings' atrocities ;
hence the widespread custom of tattooing his profile on the breast,
described in the song — and the anguished soul-searching on finding
out that Stalin hadn't been all that blameless, after all. Touching as
it does on the raw nerves of society, this is probably the most
important, and characteristic, of all of Vysotsky's poem-songs.—*Tr.*

Сколько веры и лесу повалено,
Сколь изведано горя и трасс!
А на левой груди — профиль Сталина,
А на правой — Маринка анфас.

Эх, за веру мою беззаветную
Сколько лет отдыхал я в раю!
Променял я на жизнь беспросветную
Несусветную глупость мою.

  Протопи ты мне баньку по-белому,—
  Я от белого свету отвык,—
  Угорю я — и мне, угорелому,
  Пар горячий развяжет язык.

Вспоминаю, как утречком раненько
Брату крикнуть успел: «Пособи!» —
И меня два красивых охранника
Повезли из Сибири в Сибирь.

А потом на карьере ли, в топи ли,
Наглотавшись слезы и сырца,
Ближе к сердцу кололи мы профили,
Чтоб *он* слышал, как рвутся сердца.

  Не топи ты мне баньку по-белому,—
  Я от белого свету отвык,—
  Угорю я — и мне, угорелому,
  Пар горячий развяжет язык.

Ох, знобит от рассказа дотошного!
Пар мне мысли прогнал от ума.
Из тумана холодного прошлого
Окунаюсь в горячий туман.

Застучали мне мысли под темечком:
Получилось — я зря *им* клеймен,—
И хлещу я берёзовым веничком
По наследию мрачных времен.

  Протопи ты мне баньку по-белому,—
  Чтоб я к белому свету привык,—
  Угорю я — и мне, угорелому,
  Пар горячий развяжет язык.

Протопи!..
  Не топи!..
    Протопи!..

1968

How much timber and faith have since fallen,
How much grief fell in all of our days!
On my left breast, a profile of Stalin,
On my right one, Marina full face.

For my utter devotion and loyalty
Half my life I spent in paradise...
Yeah, my utter and selfless stupidity
Cost me thousands of hopeless black days.

> Warm the bath-hut, my love, set it steaming,
> I've been out in the cold for so long.
> It still seems to me I must be dreaming...
> Heady steam, it will loosen my tongue.

I remember my yell, I still hear it:
"Brother, help!" Back to back, we fought hard.
Then they marched me across half Siberia
To the other half, those pretty guards.

Later, lost among marshes or snowpiles,
Sucking down rotgut and bitter tears,
We tattoo'd next to our hearts those profiles
That the breaking of hearts *He* might hear.

> Christ, the steam is too hot near the ceiling —
> I've been out in the cold for too long.
> It still seems to me I must be dreaming...
> Heady steam, it will loosen my tongue.

How my story sets my own flesh crawling!
But the steam drives away all my cares —
I fly back from the fog, bleakly rolling ·
From the past, into hot, steamy air.

Seems I branded myself for no reason
With that image — doubts rips up my mind,
And I lash with a thick birch-twig besom
At my heart — and the evil times' sign.

> Warm the bath-hut, my love, set it steaming,
> I've been out in the cold for so long.
> It still seems to me I must be dreaming...
> Icy water will loosen my tongue.

It's so hot!
        Ah my God!
                It's too hot!..

1968

ПЕСНЯ О ВРЕМЕНИ

За́мок временем срыт и укутан, укрыт
В нежный плед из зелёных побегов,
Но... развяжет язык молчаливый гранит —
И холодное прошлое заговорит
О походах, боях и победах.

Время подвиги эти не стёрло:
Оторвать от него верхний пласт
Или взять его крепче за горло —
И оно свои тайны отдаст.

Упадут сто замков, и спадут сто оков,
И сойдут сто потов с целой груды веков,
И польются легенды из сотен стихов —
Про турниры, осады, про вольных стрелков.

Ты к знакомым мелодиям ухо готовь
И гляди понимающим оком,—
Потому что любовь — это вечно любовь,
Даже в будущем вашем далеком.

Звонко лопалась сталь под напором меча,
Тетива от натуги дымилась,
Смерть на копьях сидела, утробно урча,
В грязь валились враги, о пощаде крича,
Победившим сдаваясь на милость.

Но не все, оставаясь живыми,
В доброте сохраняли сердца,
Защитив свое доброе имя
От заведомой лжи подлеца.

Хорошо, если конь закусил удила
И рука на копьё поудобней легла,
Хорошо, если знаешь — откуда стрела,
Хуже, если по-подлому — из-за угла.

Как у вас там с мерзавцами? Бьют? Поделом!
Ведьмы вас не пугают шабашем?
Но... не правда ли, зло называется злом
Даже там — в добром будущем вашем?

И во веки веков, и во все времена
Трус, предатель — всегда презираем,
Враг есть враг, и война всё равно есть война,

A SONG ABOUT TIME

Time has brought down the castle, and covered with grass.
Where the walls stood, grow thistles and nettles.
But the silence of granite will not always last,
And one day these old, cold stones will talk of the past —
Of old triumphs, campaigns and great battles.

It's not all been razed, under the thistle.
If you rip away time's upper crust,
Or if you squeeze time's gullet a little,
It will part with its lore of the past.

Scores of padlocks will fall, scores of chains will be shed,
And a vast heap of ages will break out in sweat,
Scores of legends will pour, in sonorous old verse,—
About tournaments, sieges and brave francs-tireurs.

These old times will to you be familiar enough,
And to you, too, they will seem sublime.
And the reason is, love will forever be love,
Even in your remote future time.

Armour split with a crunching sound, hit by the sword,
And the bowstring smoked, hot with the strain.
Death on halberds sat greedily yelling for blood,
Shrilly begging for mercy, foes dropped in the mud —
Their entreaties, though, would be in vain.

But not all remained human who came
Out on top, or escaped with their lives —
Even if they'd protected their name
From a scoundrel's obvious lies.

It feels fine to be rocked by the horse's smooth gait,
When the hand wields the spear's reassuring weight;
When you know where the arrow comes from — it's all
right.
It's much worse when it pierces your back, in the night.

Do you still slap your scoundrels silly? That's great!
You're no longer afraid of vile witches?
You still call evil evil, isn't that right? —
Even there, in your nice, friendly future?

Ages come, ages go, but at all times deceit,
Treason, cowardice are loathed and despised.
At all times war is war, and defeat is defeat,

И темница тесна, и свобода одна —
И всегда на неё уповаем.

Время эти понятья не стёрло,
Нужно только поднять верхний пласт —
И дымящейся кровью из горла
Чувства вечные хлынут на нас.

Ныне, присно, во веки веков, старина,—
И цена есть цена, и вина есть вина,
И всегда хорошо, если честь спасена,
Если другом надёжно прикрыта спина.

Чистоту, простоту мы у древних берём,
Саги, сказки — из прошлого тащим,
Потому что добро остается добром —
В прошлом, будущем и настоящем!

1975

БАЛЛАДА О БОРЬБЕ

Средь оплывших свечей и вечерних молитв,
Средь военных трофеев и мирных костров
Жили книжные дети, не знавшие битв,
Изнывая от детских своих катастроф.

Детям вечно досаден
    Их возраст и быт —
И дрались мы до ссадин,
    До смертных обид.
Но одежды латали
    Нам матери в срок,
Мы же книги глотали,
    Пьянея от строк.

Липли волосы нам на вспотевшие лбы,
И сосало под ложечкой сладко от фраз,
И кружил наши головы запах борьбы,
Со страниц пожелтевших слетая на нас.

И пытались постичь —
    Мы, не знавшие войн,
За воинственный клич
    Принимавшие вой,—
Тайну слова «приказ»,

Dungeons ever are dark, freedom always is sweet —
It is always above all things prized.

Ages could not have razed these ideas.
If one rips away time's upper crust,
Like hot, pulsing blood or burning tears
Ageless feelings will sweep over us.

Now and always, old-timer, and forevermore —
Guilt is guilt, and the cost is the cost, war is war,
And it always feels fine when your honour is safe
And a friend shields your back from a treacherous knife.

We seek pureness and sweetness in old legends' hoard,
Though they mix up what was with what wasn't.
Good and evil remain, ever, evil and good —
In the future, the past and the present!

1975

A BALLAD ABOUT STRUGGLE

In the candle-light and among prayers at night,
Among trophies of war and serene peaceful fires,
Children lived steeped in books, far from crude, real-life fights,
By their childish mishaps mortified.

Somehow kids always feel
A disgust with their age,
And in fights we would spill
Hidden hurt and dark rage.
But our mothers would mend
Those patched-up rags of ours,
While our hearts would be rent
By the books we devoured.

Then our foreheads would suddenly glisten with sweat,
We would feel as if endlessly falling through space,
As the rumble of battle turned our little heads
And we breathed in the smell of old dust and suspense.

We who'd seen no wars fought,
Either big ones or small
(Someone howled — and we thought,
What a brave, daring call),
We would try to divine

111

        Назначенье границ,
      Смысл атаки и лязг
        Боевых колесниц.

А в кипящих котлах прежних боен и смут
Столько пищи для маленьких наших мозгов!
Мы на роли предателей, трусов, иуд
В детских играх своих — назначали врагов.

      И злодея следам
        Не давали остыть,
      И прекраснейших дам
        Обещали любить;
      И, друзей успокоив
        И ближних любя,
      Мы на роли героев
        Вводили себя.

Только в грёзы нельзя насовсем убежать:
Краткий век у забав — столько боли вокруг!
Попытайся ладони у мертвых разжать
И оружье принять из натруженных рук.

      Испытай, завладев
        Еще теплым мечом
      И доспехи надев,—
        Что почём, что почём!
      Разберись, кто ты — трус
        Иль избранник судьбы,—
      И попробуй на вкус
        Настоящей борьбы.

И когда рядом рухнет израненный друг,
И над первой потерей ты взвоешь, скорбя,
И когда ты без кожи останешься вдруг
Оттого, что убили — его, не тебя,—

      Ты поймешь, что узнал,
        Отличил, отыскал
      По оскалу забрал —
        Это смерти оскал! —
      Ложь и зло,— погляди,
        Как их лица грубы,
      И всегда позади —
        Вороньё и гробы!

Если путь прорубая отцовским мечом
Ты соленые слезы на ус намотал,

The deep meaning of orders,
Of attacks, skirmish lines,
And the purpose of borders.

In the cauldrons of battles fought ages ago
There was much food for thought, for our little live brains.
We appointed our enemies to play the roles
Of cowards, Judases, traitors and such, in our games.

We would always see through
Any villainous ploys,
We would ever stay true
To sweet maids of our choice;
Upright warriors at heart,
We would spoil for the fray —
The heroic parts
Ourselves we would play.

But you can't live forever in this make-believe.
Games are over quite soon — so much grief in the land!
So you have to begin in real earnest to live
And to take up the arms from dead men's tired hands.

Still warm armour put on,
Take your father's old sword —
And you'll very soon learn
Who is who and what's what.
Coward or hero — this
Will be easy to see,
You will know how it feels
In a real fight to be.

When a friend in a battle at your side falls dead,
And your heart is with anguish about your loss filled,
When your whole soul feels raw, as if you had been flayed,
All because it was he, and not you, who got killed,

You will know your twin foes —
They are Evil and Lie,
For wherever they go
People die, people die
So that these two might live,
These assassins depraved.
Where these ghouls go, they leave
Only ravens and graves.

If you hacked your way through with your father's old sword,
For the loss of your comrades-in-arms tears shed,

113

Если в жарком бою испытал что почём,—
Значит, нужные книги ты в детстве читал!

    Если мяса с ножа
        Ты не ел ни куска,
    Если руки сложа
        Наблюдал свысока
    И в борьбу не вступил
        С подлецом, с палачом —
    Значит, в жизни ты был
        Ни при чём, ни при чём!

1975

РАССТРЕЛ ГОРНОГО ЭХА

В тиши перевала, где скалы ветрам не помеха,
                    помеха,
На кручах таких, на какие никто не проник,
Жило-поживало веселое горное,
              горное эхо,—
Оно отзывалось на крик — человеческий крик.

Когда одиночество комом подкатит под горло,
                 под горло
И сдавленный стон еще слышно в обрыв упадет,
Крик этот о помощи эхо подхватит,
               подхватит проворно,
Усилит — и бережно в руки своих донесет.

Должно быть, не люди, напившись дурмана и зелья,
                 и зелья,
Чтоб не был услышан никем громкий топот и храп,
Пришли умертвить, обеззвучить живое,
             живое ущелье,—
И эхо связали, и в рот ему всунули кляп.

Всю ночь продолжалась кровавая злая потеха,
               потеха,—
И эхо топтали — но звука никто не слыхал.
К утру расстреляли притихшее горное,
             горное эхо —
И брызнули слезы, как камни, из раненых скал!
И брызнули слезы, как камни, из раненых скал.
И брызнули камни, как слезы, из раненых скал...

1974

If in fierce bloody battles you learnt what is what —
We can say that in childhood the right books you read.

But if meat off a knife
　　You have not even tried,
If in all of your life
　　You have not taken sides,
Never joined in the strife
　　With the base, the unfair —
Then you've been in this life
　　Neither here, nor there!

1975

THE SHOOTING OF THE MOUNTAIN ECHO *

In hushed mountain passes where the cliffs cannot bar the
　　　　　　　　　　　　　　wind's way, the wind's way,
On sheer soaring ridges that no living soul has come near, has
　　　　　　　　　　　　　　　　　　come near,
There once lived a genial echo, kindly, kindly and gay,
And the sounds that it echoed were cries, cries of human despair.
When solitude surged and then lodged like a lump in the throat,
　　　　　　　　　　　　　　　　　in the throat,
And a choked, barely audible moan down the cliff would
　　　　　　　　　　　　　　　descend, would descend,
Then deftly that faint cry for help by the echo, the echo was
　　　　　　　　　　　　　　　　　　caught,
And, swelling, born tenderly off to the arms of a friend.
There were no tramping feet or coarse shouts, so they cannot
　　　　　　　　　　　　　　　have been, have been.
Simply men in whom sense had been dulled, whether drunken
　　　　　　　　　　　　　　or drugged, drunken or drugged,
But they went out to murder, to silence the living, the living
　　　　　　　　　　　　　　　　　ravine,
And the echo was bound fast and held, and its mouth roughly
　　　　　　　　　　　　　　　　　gagged.
Their vicious and murderous sport lasted all the night long,
　　　　　　　　　　　　　　　　the night long,
And they trampled the echo, killed its voice, until nothing was
　　　　　　　　　　　　　　　left, nothing was left...
Though the echo was silenced, the shooting continued, continued
　　　　　　　　　　　　　　　　　till dawn,
And stones spilled and cascaded like tears, as the wounded
　　　　　　　　　　　　　　　　cliffs wept.

---

* © *Soviet Literature*, 1988, No. 10.
Translated by Kathryn Hamilton.

1974

ДВЕ СУДЬБЫ

Жил я славно в первой трети
Двадцать лет на белом свете —
      по учению,
Жил безбедно и при деле,
Плыл, куда глаза глядели,—
      по течению.

Заскрипит ли в повороте,
Затрещит в водовороте —
      я не слушаю.
То разуюсь, то обуюсь,
На себя в воде любуюсь —
      брагу кушаю.

И пока я наслаждался,
Пал туман и оказался
      в гиблом месте я,—
И огромная старуха
Хохотнула прямо в ухо,
      злая бестия.

Я кричу,— не слышу крика,
Не вяжу от страха лыка,
      вижу плохо я,
На ветру меня качает...
«Кто здесь?» Слышу — отвечает:
      «Я, Нелёгкая!
Брось креститься, причитая,—
Не спасет тебя святая
      Богородица:
Кто рули да весла бросит,
Тех Нелёгкая заносит —
      так уж водится!»

И с одышкой, ожиреньем
Ломит, тварь, по пням, кореньям
      тяжкой поступью.

TWO FATES

Without trouble, without fear
I lived in my younger years —
        like it was a dream.
Life was soft, and thoughts were pleasing,
So I floated, free and easy —
        drifting with the stream.

There'd be scowling and yearning,
Something squeaking at a turning —
        I would pay no heed.
It got cooler, it got hotter,
I just peered into the water
        and kept sipping mead.

While I had it nice and pretty,
Fog descended, and I drifted
        to a wretched place.
There, a huge old woman leered,
She guffawed right in my ear,
        damn her stupid face.

I stood still, I thought I'd never
Put two simple words together,
        I thought: That's the end!
When at last I yelled, "Who's there?"
That old hippo hoarsely blared,
        "It's me, Heavy Hand!

You stop muttering your prayer,
It's no use for you to swear
        by your holy God:
Those who drift and seek no landing
Get some Heavy-Handed handling —
        that's the way things go!"

Wheezing fatly, she went crunching,
Hitting stumps and fallen branches,
        with a heavy tread.

117

Я впотьмах ищу дорогу,
Но уж брагу понемногу —
            только пó сту пью.

Вдруг навстречу мне — живая
Колченогая Кривая —
            морда хитрая:
«Не горюй,— кричит,— болезный,
Горемыка мой нетрезвый,—
            слезы вытру я!»

Взвыл я, ворот разрывая:
«Вывози меня, Кривая,—
            я на привязи!
Мне плевать, что кривобока,
Криворука, кривоока,—
            только вывези!»

Влез на горб к ней с перепугу,—
Но Кривая шла по кругу —
            ноги разные.
Падал я и полз на брюхе —
И хихикали старухи
            безобразные.

Не до жиру — быть бы жúвым,—
Много горя над обрывом,
            а в обрыве — зла.
«Слышь, Кривая, четверть ставлю —
Кривизну твою исправлю,
            раз не вывезла!

Ты, Нелёгкая, маманя!
Хочешь истины в стакане —
            на лечение?
Тяжело же столько весить,
А хлебнешь стаканов десять —
            облегчение!»

И припали две старухи
Ко бутыли медовухи —
            пьянь с ханыгою,—
Я пока за кочки прячусь,
К бережку тихонько пячусь —
            с кручи прыгаю.

Огляделся — лодка рядом,—
А за мною по корягам,
            дико охая,

And I followed, through the nettle,
Taking now and then a little —
      just a sip of mead.

Suddenly an old Clubfooted
Witch ran into me and hooted,
      with a cunning leer:
"Why so glum, you drunken devil?
Why's your pickled heart so heavy?
      I shall wipe your tears!"

And I howled, tearing my hair,
"Clubfoot, get me out of here,
      I am stuck, d'you hear?
I don't care if you're one-eyed and
Bandy-legged, stiff-armed, lopsided —
      get me out of here!"

On her back, scared stiff, I rode —
Clubfoot, though, went round and round,
      hobbling crookedly.
I would fall, and on my belly
Crawl — the ugly crones kept yelling,
      jeering, mocking me.

Things were getting really ugly,
Though I wriggled and kept struggling
      with abysmal woe.
"Look, Clubfoot, I'll stand a round,
Drink may make your clubfoot sound —
      then we'll really go.

Heavy-hand, make with the wine-glass.
Would you like some truth-in-wine, lass?
      Just to put you right!
Must be tough, to weigh so heavy,
Have a few — you'll feel in heaven —
      You'll feel feather-light."

The two witches by the river
Drank — it seemed as if they'd never
      ever have enough.
In the meantime I backed slowly
And toward the bank kept crawling —
      then went off the bluff.

I looked round — the boat was near,
But I could already hear
      how they cursed and cried.

Припустились, подвывая,
Две судьбы мои — Кривая
               да Нелёгкая.

Грёб до умопомраченья,
Правил против ли теченья,
               на стремнину ли,—
А Нелёгкая с Кривою
От досады, с перепою
               там и сгинули!

1976

* * *

Мне судьба — до последней черты, до креста
Спорить до хрипоты (а за ней — немота),
Убеждать и доказывать с пеной у рта,
Что — не то это вовсе, не тот и не та!

Что — лабазники врут про ошибки Христа,
Что — пока ещё в грунт не влежалась плита,—
Триста лет под татарами — жизнь ещё та:
Маета трехсотлетняя и нищета.

Но под властью татар жил Иван Калита,
И уж был не один, кто один против ста.
Пот намерений добрых и бунтов тщета,
Пугачёвщина, кровь и опять — нищета...

Пусть не враз, пусть сперва не поймут ни черта,—
Повторю даже в образе злого шута,—
Но не стоит предмет, да и тема не та,—
Суета всех сует — всё равно суета.

Только чашу испить — не успеть на бегу,
Даже если разлить — все равно не смогу,—

My two fates towards me trotted —
Heavy-handed and Clubfooted —
         out to get my hide.

Then I pulled away like crazy —
Heading upstream, in a frenzy —
         how I held my breath!
Gone with drink and malice dotty,
Heavy-handed and Clubfooted
         drank themselves to death.

1976

*   *   *

It's my fate, to fight on to the end, to the cross,
It's my lot, to keep wrangling and shout myself hoarse,
And to argue and fight, till I froth at the mouth,
That it's all of it wrong — silly words, crooked path;

That the hucksters are lying about Christ's mistakes,
That the wailing still echoes at countless wakes,
That we still bear the scars of the cursed Tartar yoke,
Of the three hundred years that all went up in smoke.

Yoke or not, Kalita * strengthened Muscovy's throne,
Those who fought one to ten felt no longer alone.
Then — more proof that goodwill and revolt are in vain:
Pugachov **, blood and misery, and blood again.

I'll repeat it, though people won't get it, at first.
I will say it in earnest, in malice and jest,
Though I sometimes believe that the point has been lost:
It's all vanity, and of all vain things, the worst.

But I can't drain the cup, not as long as I run.
Even if I spill half, I do not think I can.

---

    * Ivan Kalita (?—1340) — Prince of Muscovy, Grand Duke
of Vladimir. Under Kalita, the resurgence of Russian national consciousness and power began.— *Tr.*
    ** Yemelyan Pugachov (1740-1775) — leader of a peasant upri-
sing under Catherine the Great. Sergei Yesenin wrote *Pugachov*,
a drama in verse. In its Taganka production, Vysotsky played
Khlopusha, one of Pugachov's closest associates. The part is remembered
as an embodiment of the spirit of revolt.— *Tr.*

Или выплеснуть в наглую рожу врагу —
Не ломаюсь, не лгу — все равно не могу!

На вертящемся гладком и скользком кругу
Равновесье держу, изгибаюсь в дугу!
Что же с чашею делать?! Разбить — не могу!
Потерплю — и достойного подстерегу.

Передам — и не надо держаться в кругу
И в кромешную тьму и в неясную згу —
Другу передоверивши чашу, сбегу!
Смог ли он ее выпить — узнать не смогу.

Я с сошедшими с круга пасусь на лугу,
Я о чаше невыпитой здесь ни гугу —
Никому не скажу, при себе сберегу,—
А сказать — и затопчут меня на лугу.

Я до рвоты, ребята, за вас хлопочу!
Может, кто-то когда-то поставит свечу
Мне за голый мой нерв, на котором кричу,
За веселый манер, на котором шучу...

Даже если сулят золотую парчу
Или порчу грозят напустить — не хочу,—
На ослабленном нерве я не зазвучу —
Я уж свой подтяну, подновлю, подвинчу!

Лучше я загуляю, запью, заторчу,
Всё, что ночью кропаю,— в чаду растопчу,
Лучше голову песне своей откручу,—
Но не буду скользить, словно пыль по лучу!

... Если всё-таки чашу испить мне судьба,
Если музыка с песней не слишком груба,
Если вдруг докажу, даже с пеной у рта,—
Я уйду и скажу, что не всё суета!

1978

And I can't throw the cup in an enemy's face —
I'm not lying or bragging, I simply confess.

On a slippery disk, swiftly turning, I reel.
I keep losing my balance, I writhe like an eel.
Shall I smash into pieces my cup? But I can't!
For a worthier man I shall patiently hunt.

I'd hand over the cup, and I'd slide off the disk.
I'd be free from the worry, I would be released.
I would hide in the darkness, the sleet and the snow.
He might finish the cup — only I'd never know.

Now I graze in a meadow, with other old bums.
Not a hint at the cup left undrained — I keep mum.
Not a murmur — I guess I had best save my breath.
If I don't, I'm afraid I'll be trampled to death.

I am breaking my back, boys, I do what I can,
And some day one of you may for me light a candle —
For the naked nerves' sting as I sing and I choke,
For the tough jolly manner in which I make jokes.

Even if I am threatened with all kinds of woe,
Even if I am promised rewards, I say no!
I will not sound too good if my nerves dangle loose —
I best take up the slack and then tighten the screws.

I would rather carouse, romp, raise all hell and fight,
I would rather tear up what I wrote in the night,
I would rather knock down and kick senseless my song
Than dance happily like butterflies in the sun.

If I do drain the cup — after all, it's my fate —
If my songs aren't too crude, and the tunes do not grate,
I shall froth at the mouth, but I shall not complain;
I shall go — but I'll prove that not all is in vain!

1978

ОХОТА НА ВОЛКОВ

Рвусь из сил — и из всех сухожилий,
Но сегодня — опять как вчера:
Обложили меня, обложили —
Гонят весело на номера!

Из-за елей хлопочут двустволки —
Там охотники прячутся в тень,—
На снегу кувыркаются волки,
Превратившись в живую мишень.

    Идёт охота на волков, идёт охота —
    На серых хищников, матёрых и щенков!
    Кричат загонщики, и лают псы до рвоты,
    Кровь на снегу — и пятна красные флажков.

Не на равных играют с волками
Егеря — но не дрогнет рука,—
Оградив нам свободу флажками,
Бьют уверенно, наверняка.

Волк не может нарушить традиций,—
Видно, в детстве — слепые щенки —
Мы, волчата, сосали волчицу
И всосали: нельзя за флажки!

    И вот — охота на волков, идёт охота —
    На серых хищников, матёрых и щенков!
    Кричат загонщики, и лают псы до рвоты,
    Кровь на снегу — и пятна красные флажков.

Наши ноги и челюсти быстры,—
Почему же, вожак,— дай ответ —
Мы затравленно мчимся на выстрел
И не пробуем — через запрет?!

Волк не может, не должен иначе.
Вот кончается время моё:
Тот, которому я предназначен,
Улыбнулся — и поднял ружьё.

    Идёт охота на волков, идёт охота —
    На серых хищников, матёрых и щенков!

WOLF HUNT *

In my flight, sinews bursting, I hurtle,
But as yesterday — so now today,
They've cornered me! Driven me, encircled,
Towards the huntsmen that wait for their prey!

From the fir-trees the rifle-shots quicken —
In the shadows the huntsmen lie low.
As they fire, the wolves somersault, stricken,
Living targets brought down on the snow.

>They're hunting wolves! The hunt is on, pursuing
>The wily predators, the she-wolf and her brood.
>The beaters shout, the dogs bay, almost spewing.
>The flags on the snow are red, as red as the blood.

In the fight heavy odds have opposed us,
But the merciless huntsmen keep ranks.
With the flags on their ropes they've enclosed us.
They take aim and they fire at point blank.

For a wolf cannot break with tradition.
With milk sucked from the she-wolf's dugs
The blind cubs learn the stern prohibition
Never, never to cross the red flags!

>They're hunting wolves! The hunt is on, pursuing
>The wily predators, the she-wolf and her brood.
>The beaters shout, the dogs bay, almost spewing.
>The flags on the snow are red, as red as the blood.

We are swift and our jaws are rapacious.
Why then, chief, like a tribe that's oppressed,
Must we rush towards the weapons that face us
And that precept be never transgressed?

For a wolf cannot change the old story.
The end looms and my time's almost done.
Now the huntsman who's made me his quarry
Gives a smile as he raises his gun.

>They're hunting wolves! The hunt is on, pursuing
>The wily predators, the she-wolf and her brood.

© *Sputnik,* Digest of Soviet Press, 1987, No. 11.
Translated by Kathryn Hamilton.

Кричат загонщики, и лают псы до рвоты,
Кровь на снегу — и пятна красные флажков.

Я из повиновения вышел —
За флажки — жажда жизни сильней!
Только сзади я радостно слышал
Удивленные крики людей.

Рвусь из сил — и из всех сухожилий,
Но сегодня не так, как вчера:
Обложили меня, обложили —
Но остались ни с чем егеря!

Идёт охота на волков, идёт охота —
На серых хищников, матёрых и щенков!
Кричат загонщики, и лают псы до рвоты,
Кровь на снегу — и пятна красные флажков.

1968

ПЕСНЯ О СУДЬБЕ

Куда ни втисну душу я, куда себя ни дену,
За мною пес — Судьба моя, беспомощна, больна,—
Я гнал ее каменьями, но жмётся пёс к колену —
Глядит, глаза навыкате, и с языка — слюна.

Морока мне с нею —
Я оком грустнею,
Я ликом тускнею
И чревом урчу,
Нутром коченею,
А горлом немею,—
И жить не умею,
И петь не хочу!

Должно быть, старею,—
Пойти к палачу...
Пусть вздёрнет на рею,
А я заплачу.

Я зарекался столько раз, что на Судьбу я плюну,
Но жаль ее, голодную — ласкается, дрожит,—

126

The beaters shout, the dogs bay, almost spewing.
The flags on the snow are red, as red as the blood.

But revolt and the life-force are stronger
Than the fear that the red flags instil.
From behind come dismayed cries of anger
As I cheat them, with joy, of their kill.

In my flight, sinews bursting, I hurtle,
But the outcome is different today!
I was cornered! They trapped me, encircled!
But the huntsmen were foiled of their prey!

They're hunting wolves! The hunt is on, pursuing
The wily predators, the she-wolf and her brood.
The beaters shout, the dogs bay, almost spewing.
The flags on the snow are red, as red as the blood.

1968

A SONG ABOUT MY FATE

Wherever I may drag my soul, adrift or gone to ground,
My helpless fate — a mangy dog — trots everywhere along.
I tried to pelt the cur with stones — but she still stuck around;
With bulging eyes she gazed at me, spit dribbling from
                                        her tongue.

My fate's such a bother,
I'm lost in a pother,
My eyes become duller,
My heart feels a sting.
My guts begin freezing,
I can't go on breathing,
I'm not good at living,
I don't want to sing.

But these aren't sorrows
A hangman can't cure.
I'll swing from the gallows —
And pay him his due.

I often swore I'd boot my fate to hell, and stop this nonsense,
But she would whine and tremble so — I pitied the damn
                                        clod.

Я стал тогда из жалости подкармливать Фортуну —
Она, когда насытится, всегда подолгу спит.

      Тогда я гуляю,
      Петляю, вихляю,
      Я ваньку валяю
      И небо копчу.
      Но пса охраняю,
      Сам вою, сам лаю —
      О чем пожелаю,
      Когда захочу.

      Нет, не постарею —
      Пойду к палачу,—
      Пусть вздёрнет скорее,
      А я приплачу́

Бывают дни, я голову в такое пекло всуну,
Что и Судьба попятится, испуганна, бледна,—
Я как-то влил стакан вина для храбрости в Фортуну —
С тех пор ни дня без стака́на, еще ворчит она:

      Закуски — ни корки!
      Мол, я бы в Нью-Йорке
      Ходила бы в норке,
      Носила б парчу!..
      Я ноги — в опорки,
      Судьбу — на закорки,—
      И в гору и с горки
      Пьянчугу влачу.

      Когда постарею,
      Пойду к палачу,—
      Пусть вздёрнет на рею,
      А я заплачу́.

Однажды пере-перелил Судьбе я ненароком —
Пошла, родимая, вразнос и изменила лик,—
Хамила, безобразила и обернулась Роком,—
И, сзади прыгнув на меня, схватила за кадык.

Then out of pity I began to feed her juicy morsels —
When she has eaten all she wants, she always sleeps a lot.

> Then I will go whooping
> It up — I'll go ripping —
> How I will go nipping
> All over the place!
> But I guard the puppy,
> And I do the yapping —
> Whenever I'm happy,
> Whenever I please!

> I'd rather die young, man,
> I should be strung up.
> A job for the hangman —
> I'll pay for the job.

I sometimes get into such scrapes, such free-for-alls and
                                        carnage,
That even fate in fear recoils, and cowers, pale, a-tremble.
One day I poured the fink a drink, to give it liquid
                                        courage.
Since then, the cur has turned a booze-hound, and — she'll
                                        even grumble:

> What swill we're drinking!
> You know, I keep thinking
> You'd be less a stinker
> In New York — by far!..
> Then I in a hurry
> Fate on my back carry —
> I know I can't tarry —
> We must find a bar!

> It seems I grow callous,
> I'm getting fed up.
> I'd swing from the gallows —
> And pay for the job.

One day my fate went over the eight — I poured and erred
                                        a little.
She went completely off the rails and off her chump,
                                        the sot.
She bawled and swore and snarled and kicked, my ugly fate
                                        turned fatal,
And, jumping on me from behind, she caught me by
                                        the throat.

129

Мне тяжко под нею,
Гляди — я синею,
Уже сатанею,
Кричу на бегу:
«Не надо за шею!
Не надо за шею!
Не надо за шею, —
Я петь не смогу!»

Судьбу, коль сумею,
Снесу к палачу —
Пусть вздёрнет на рею,
А я заплачу́!

⟨1976⟩

* * *

Дурацкий сон, как кистенём,
Избил нещадно:
Невнятно выглядел я в нём
И неприглядно.

Во сне — и лгал, и предавал,
И льстил легко я...
А я и не подозревал
В себе такое!

...Еще — сжимал я кулаки
И бил с натугой, —
Но мягкой кистию руки,
А не упругой...

Тускнело сновиденье, но
Опять являлось:
Смыкал я веки — и оно
Возобновлялось!

...Я не шагал, а семенил
На ровном брусе, —
Ни разу ногу не сменил —
Труси́л и тру́сил.

Я перед сильным — лебезил,
Пред злобным — гнулся...
И сам себе я мерзок был —
Но не проснулся.

Unbearable, really,
I choke — it's too silly,
I plead willy-nilly —
Half-strangled, I wheeze:
Let go, you damn bully!
Let go, you damn bully!
Let go, you damn bully!
I can't sing like this!

I'm telling you fellows,
If someone strings up
My fate from the gallows —
I'll pay for the job!

⟨ *1976* ⟩

* * *

A stupid dream lambasted me —
And maybe rightly:
I seemed in it quite vague to be,
And quite unsightly.

I was a traitor, and I lied,
I scraped and bowed...
I'd never even thought that I
Could fall so low!

And then, I'd hit out with a fist
With full force, madly,
But at the last second, my wrist
Would go all flabby.

The vision would grow pale and dim,
And sort of sear,
But once I closed my eyes, the dream
Would reappear!

I never strode, I only minced,
Not always forward.
When threatened, I would flinch and wince,
I cowered, a coward.

I'd fawn and grovel like a serf
On power and evil,
I was disgusting to myself —
But waked not, even.

Да это бред — я свой же стон
Слыхал сквозь дрёму!
Но — это мне приснился он,
А не другому.

Очнулся я — и разобрал
Обрывок стона,
И с болью веки разодрал —
Но облегчённо.

И сон повис на потолке —
И распластался...
Сон — в руку ли? И вот в руке
Вопрос остался.

Я вымыл руки — он в спине
Холодной дрожью!
...Что было правдою во сне,
Что было ложью?

Коль этот сон — виденье мне,—
Ещё везенье!
Но — если было мне во сне
Ясновиденье?!

Сон — отраженье мыслей дня?
Нет, быть не может!
Но вспомню — и всего меня
Перекорёжит.

А после скажут: «Он вполне
Всё знал и ведал!...» —
Мне будет мерзко, как во сне,
В котором предал.

Или — в костер! Вдруг нет во мне
Шагнуть к костру сил,—
Мне будет стыдно, как во сне,
В котором струсил.

Но скажуте мне: «Пой в унисон —
Жми что есть духу!..» —
И я пойму: вот это сон,
Который в руку!

⟨*До 1978*⟩

It's mad! I slept, but I could hear
My own groans, smothered.
And yet — that dream had come to me,
And not another.

I still could hear, when I awaked,
A groan drift faintly:
The pain of coming-to was great,
Relief was greater.

The dream dissolved — and yet it seemed
To be still goading.
And what if it was not a dream
But a foreboding?

I quake, I do not see a gleam
Of hope — but why?
What was the truth in this odd dream?
What was a lie?

I'm lucky if it was a sign,
If I was warned.
But what if in this dream of mine
I was clairvoyant?

A mirror of my real soul?
No, not a mirror!
But then — when I my dream recall,
I writhe in horror.

"He knew he'd be a rat," they'll claim.
"He's ever at it."
I'd feel disgust, as in the dream
In which I ratted.

Suppose I cannot fill the breach —
Beyond my power?
The nightmare would be back in which
I was a coward.

But if I'm told, "Man, join the crowd —
Make your career!"
I'll realise I'm down and out:
I was a seer.

⟨*Before 1978*⟩

Я НЕ ЛЮБЛЮ

Я не люблю фатального исхода,
От жизни никогда не устаю.
Я не люблю любое время года,
Когда весёлых песен не пою.

Я не люблю холодного цинизма,
В восторженность не верю, и еще —
Когда чужой мои читает письма,
Заглядывая мне через плечо.

Я не люблю, когда — наполовину
Или когда прервали разговор.
Я не люблю, когда стреляют в спину,
Я также против выстрелов в упор.

Я ненавижу сплетни в виде версий,
Червей сомненья, почестей иглу,
Или — когда все время против шерсти,
Или — когда железом по стеклу.

Я не люблю уверенности сытой,—
Уж лучше пусть откажут тормоза.
Досадно мне, что слово «честь» забыто
И что в чести наветы за глаза.

Когда я вижу сломанные крылья —
Нет жалости во мне, и неспроста:
Я не люблю насилье и бессилье —
Вот только жаль распятого Христа.

HOW I DETEST... *

How I detest the fatal final curtain!
I never find life dull or wearying.
I've got no time for any time or season
When I don't have a cheerful song to sing.

I've got no time for cynicism cold, nor
Can I be fooled by hankerings for the Grail.
I hate when people peer over my shoulder
And crane their necks to try to read my mail.

I cant't stant those whose actions are half-hearted.
Or who interrupt a cordial exchange;
Or shoot you in the back, an easy target,
Or pull a gun on you at point-blank range.

I can't stand idle talk in any vein,
The worms of doubt, the needles of false praise,
Or things that are meant to go against the grain
And grate your nerves like metal scraped on glass.

I don't like self-assured complacency.
You're better off being hanged and letting rip.
I don't like those who forget all decency
And give an eager ear to slanderous gossip.

I don't feel sympathy for damaged limbs
Or broken wings — lame ducks I can't abide.
I don't like bullies or acquiescent victims —
Yet pity moves me for Christ crucified.

---

* © *Sputnik*, Digest of Soviet Press, 1987, No. 11.
Translated by Kathryn Hamilton.

Я не люблю себя, когда я трушу,
Досадно мне, когда невинных бьют.
Я не люблю, когда мне лезут в душу,
Тем более — когда в неё плюют.

Я не люблю манежи и арены:
На них мильон меняют по рублю.
Пусть впереди большие перемены —
Я это никогда не полюблю!

1969

ОЧИ ЧЁРНЫЕ

I. *Погоня*

Во хмелю слегка
Лесом правил я.
Не устал пока, —
Пел за здравие.
А умел я петь
Песни вздорные:
«Как любил я вас,
Очи чёрные...»

То плелись, то неслись, то трусили рысцой,
И болотную слизь конь швырял мне в лицо.
Только я проглочу вместе с грязью слюну,
Штофу горло скручу — и опять затяну:

«Очи чёрные!
Как любил я вас...»
Но — прикончил я
То, что впрок припас.
Головой тряхнул,
Чтоб слетела блажь,
И вокруг взглянул —
И присвистнул аж:

Лес стеной впереди — не пускает стена, —
Кони прядут ушами, назад подают.
Где просвет, где прогал — не видать ни рожна!
Колют иглы меня, до костей достают.

Коренной ты мой,
Выручай же, брат!

I hate it when I've played the coward's part.
I hate to see the guiltless victimised.
I hate when people pry into my heart,
The more so when it's spat on and despised.

I can't abide the stadium or ring
Where all is vilely cheapened and defiled.
Whatever alterations time may bring
To these I know I won't be reconciled.

1969

THOSE BIG DARK EYES

I. *The Chase*

> Driving through the woods,
> I was slightly gone.
> A felt fine and strong
> As I sang a song.
> And the song I sang
> Wasn't deep or wise —
> Of how fond I was
> Of those big dark eyes...

And my horses would trot, then start off on a race;
Hoofs kicked up the slime, and it hit my face.
I would swallow the slime and the droplets of rain,
Break a fresh bottle's neck, and start singing again:

> "Ah, those big dark eyes,
> How I loved those eyes..."
> But I finished soon
> All of my supplies.
> Then I shook my head
> To drive off the cloud,
> And I looked around —
> And I whistled loud:

For the forest ahead was a blank solid wall.
My wild horses kept shying, and trying to turn.
There was no glade or road, not a damn thing at all,
Needles pricking my skin, right through to the bone.

> Giddup, thill-horse, brother,
> Let's get out of here!

Ты куда, родной,—
Почему назад?!
Дождь — как яд с ветвей —
Недобром пропах.
Пристяжной моей
Волк нырнул под пах.

Вот же пьяный дурак, вот же на́лил глаза!
Ведь погибель пришла, а бежать — не суметь,—
Из колоды моей утащили туза,
Да такого туза, без которого — смерть!

Я ору волкам:
«Побери вас прах!..» —
А коней пока
Подгоняет страх.
Шевелю кнутом —
Бью кручёные
И ору притом:
«Очи чёрные!..»

Храп, да топот, да лязг, да лихой перепляс —
Бубенцы плясовую играют с дуги.
Ах вы кони мои, погублю же я вас,—
Выносите, друзья, выносите, враги!

...От погони той
Даже хмель иссяк.
Мы на кряж крутой —
На одних осях,—
В хлопьях пены мы —
Струи в кряж лились,—
Отдышались, отхрипели
Да откашлялись.

Я лошадкам забитым, что не подвели,
Поклонился в копыта, до самой земли,
Сбросил с воза манатки, повел в поводу...
Спаси бог вас, лошадки, что целым иду!

What on earth, bay — why
Are you backing, dear?
Drops of rain off trees
Of some poison reeked.
My outrunner! Wolves
By its belly streaked.

Oh you drunken old fool, damn your stinking red eyes!
You will not get away, not this time — understand?
They have stolen an ace from my deck — such an ace
That I now can do nothing but wait for the end.

So I cursed the wolves:
"Blast your rotten hides!"
And the horses flew
Like the wind, in fright.
I lashed with the whip
At the horses' sides,
And yelled all the time,
"Oh, those big dark eyes!"

Thudding hoofs, heavy snorts, and the dance of the bells —
Harness bells singing tunes of the nearing end.
Hey, my horses, I'll kill you — but save me from hell!
Save me, enemies, dear! And save yourselves, friends!

I was stone-cold sober
After that mad chase.
Nearly dead, my horses
Up a steep hill raced.
Froth and lather fell,
But we knew we'd live,
As we stood there, reeling,
Breathing heavily.

"You have not let me down, my true horses," I said,
And I bowed to the hoofs of my horses half-dead.
Then I pushed off the load, led the team by the rein...
Bless you, horses, God bless you! I will live again.

II. *Старый дом*

Что за дом притих,
Погружен во мрак,
На семи лихих
Продувных ветрах,
Всеми окнами
Обратясь в овраг,
А воротами —
На проезжий тракт?

Ох устал я, устал,— а лошадок распряг.
Эй, живой кто-нибудь, выходи, помоги!
Никого,— только тень промелькнула в сенях
Да стервятник спустился и сузил круги.

В дом заходишь как
Все равно в кабак,
А народишко —
Кажный третий — враг.
Своротят скулу,
Гость непрошеный.
Образа в углу —
И те перекошены.

И затеялся смутный, чудной разговор,
Кто-то песню стонал и гитару терзал,
И припадочный малый — придурок и вор —
Мне тайком из-под скатерти нож показал.

«Кто ответит мне —
Что за дом такой,
Почему — во тьме,
Как барак чумной?
Свет лампад погас,
Воздух вылился...
Али жить у вас
Разучилися?

Двери настежь у вас, а душа взаперти.
Кто хозяином здесь? — напоил бы вином».
А в ответ мне: «Видать, был ты долго в пути —
И людей позабыл,— мы всегда так живем!

Тра́ву кушаем,
Век — на щавеле,
Скисли душами,
Опрыщавели,

II. *The Old House*

What's this house, so still,
Sunk so low in gloom?
Swept by evil winds,
It but vaguely looms.
All its windows look
On a deep ravine,
And the broken gates
Towards the highway lean.

Ah, how fagged I was! I unharnessed the team.
Hey, folks, lend us a hand — are you all of you dead?
Not a soul, just a shadow moved near, quick and dim,
And a buzzard in circles flew low overhead.

Like a dirty dive,
This house surely is,
And the people here
Look like enemies.
For unbidden guests,
A fist in the eye.
Even icons hang
Anyhow, awry.

I sat down, and a meaningless, strange talk began.
Someone beat a guitar, someone crooned pitiously,
And a slobbering fellow, a mad hooligan,
Pulled a razor-sharp blade, and he wagged it at me.

"Look, what house is this —
Who the deuce can tell?
Was it hit by plague?
Or — by what the hell?
Why no candles burn.
And the air's so foul?
There's no life, no song —
It's all death and howl?

All the doors here are open but all souls are barred.
Who's the host in this house? Can't you give me a shot?"
And they told me, "You really have come from afar.
We have long lived like this — or have you forgot?

Now we feed on grass,
We have gone to pot,
And our soured souls
Stink of muck and rot.

Да ещё вином
Много тешились,—
Разоряли дом,
Дрались, вешались».

«Я коней заморил,— от волков ускакал.
Укажите мне край, где светло от лампад,
Укажите мне место, какое искал,—
Где поют, а не стонут, где пол не покат».

«О таких домах
Не слыхали мы,
Долго жить впотьмах
Привыкали мы.
Испокону мы —
В зле да шёпоте,
Под иконами
В чёрной копоти».

И из смрада, где косо висят образа,
Я башку очертя гнал, забросивши кнут,
Куда кони несли да глядели глаза,
И где люди живут, и — как люди живут.

...Сколько кануло, сколько схлынуло!
Жизнь кидала меня — не докинула.
Может, спел про вас неумело я,
Очи чёрные, скатерть белая?!

1974

МОЯ ЦЫГАНСКАЯ

В сон мне — жёлтые огни,
И хриплю во сне я:
«Повремени, повремени —
Утро мудренее!»
Но и утром всё не так,
Нет того веселья:
Или куришь натощак,
Или пьёшь с похмелья.

В кабаках — зелёный штоф,
Белые салфетки,—
Рай для нищих и шутов,
Мне ж — как птице в клетке.

Most amuse themselves
Swilling rotgut wine,
Fight and hang themselves,
Ruin the house, the swine."

"Wolves have chased me, I've driven my horses to death.
Tell me where is the land lit with icon-lamp light.
Tell me where is that place, where's that spot on the earth,
Where they sing and not howl, and where wrong is not right?"

"We have never heard
Of a place like that,
And we've always lived
In the dark, like rats.
We have always known
That the good's no good,
All our icons are
Black with greasy soot."

Then away from the stench, icons hanging awry,
I went tearing along, off the highway again,
Dropped the whip and the reins, let the team bolt away
For the land where lived men, and where men lived like men.

How much water's flowed off the good old earth!
I've been smashed by life — thank God, not to death.
Maybe this my song wasn't deep or wise —
I had better sing of those dark big eyes.

1974

MY GYPSY SONG

In my dream burn yellow lights,
And I spill my sorrow:
"Do not go — please, stay the night!
Wait! Fresh for the morrow!"
But the morning seems all wrong,
No joy — more's the pity —
Ugh — the hair of the dog,
Of the dog that bit you!

In the bars, red, bloodshot eyes,
All that sparkling poison —
Clowns' and beggars' paradise
And my gilded prison.

143

В церкви — смрад и полумрак,
Дьяки курят ладан...
Нет, и в церкви всё не так,
Всё не так, как надо!

Я — на гору впопыхах,
Чтоб чего не вышло,—
На горе стоит ольха,
Под горою — вишня.
Хоть бы склон увить плющом —
Мне б и то отрада,
Хоть бы что-нибудь еще...
Всё не так, как надо!

Я — по полю вдоль реки:
Света — тьма, нет бога!
В чистом поле — васильки,
Дальняя дорога.
Вдоль дороги — лес густой
С бабами-ягами,
А в конце дороги той —
Плаха с топорами.

Где-то кони пляшут в такт,
Нехотя и плавно,
Вдоль дороги всё не так,
А в конце — подавно.
И ни церковь, ни кабак —
Ничего не свято!
Нет, ребята, всё не так,
Всё не так, ребята...

Зима 1967/68

In the church, stench, Evensong,
Even gold looks shabby...
No, the church, it feels all wrong,
Not the way it should be!

In a hurry, I climb up,
Why? I do not know.
There's an alder-tree on top,
A cherry-tree below.
Wish there was plush on the slope —
It would look less scrubby.
There is not a bloody hope,
Nothing's as it should be.

I keep searching high and low:
Oh my God, where are you?
By the roadside, bluebells grow,
And the road climbs higher.
All along the road, a wood
Full of witches, fellows.
At the end of that long road
Nothing but the gallows.

Horses dancing all along,
Smoothly dance the horses.
On the road it seems all wrong,
At the end, much worser.
Nothing's holy anymore,
Neither drink nor prayer.
It's all wrong, boys, by the Lord,
No, boys, it's not fair...

Winter 1967/1968

145

КУПОЛА

Как засмотрится мне нынче, как задышится?!
Воздух крут перед грозой, крут да вязок.
Что споётся мне сегодня, что услышится?
Птицы вещие поют — да все из сказок.

Птица Сирин мне радостно скалится —
Веселит, зазывает из гнёзд,
А напротив — тоскует-печалится,
Травит душу чудной Алконост.

Словно семь заветных струн
Зазвенели в свой черёд —
Это птица Гамаюн
Надежду подаёт!

В синем небе, колокольнями проколотом,—
Медный колокол, медный колокол —
То ль возрадовался, то ли осерчал...
Купола в России кроют чистым золотом,—
Чтобы чаще Господь замечал.

Я стою, как перед вечною загадкою,
Пред великою да сказочной страною —
Перед солоно- да горько-кисло-сладкою,
Голубою, родниковою, ржаною.

Грязью чавкая жирной да ржавою,
Вязнут лошади по стремена,
Но влекут меня сонной державою,
Что раскисла, опухла от сна.

Словно семь богатых лун
На пути моём встаёт —
То мне птица Гамаюн
Надежду подаёт!

THE DOMES

Wonder what I'll see today, how I will breathe today.
Soon there'll be a thunderstorm — the air is tingling.
Wonder what I'll sing today, what songs I'll hear, pray?
Seems like birds from fairytales are sweetly singing.

    Sirin's * flapping its wings, laughing joyously,
    Calling gaily to me from the nest;
    And the sad bird is crying most grievously —
    My heart's riven by weird Alkonost.

        Seven magical strings rang
        Wondrously, melodiously —
        That is holy Hamayun
        Giving hope to me.

Over countless domes of churches blue skies hover.
Copper bells are pealing, over, over and over...
Hard to say if it's in anger or in joy.
Here in Russia, domes with purest gold are covered —
That they oftener may catch the Lord's eye.

Here I stand before a hoary ancient mystery,
Here I stand before a fairytale vast land —
Salty, bitter, sour, sweet and slightly gingery —
Land of blue skies, rye and clear springs, here I stand.

    Horses sink in the mud to the stirrups,
    In the rusty mud, glossy and deep,
    But they drag me across this unstirring
    Drowsy land, limp and swollen with sleep.

        It's as if seven rich moons
        Lit my pathway suddenly:
        That is holy Hamayun
        Giving hope to me!

---

* Sirin — in Russian folklore, a mythological bird with a woman's face and breast (cf. "siren"). Alkonost is the Alcyone or Halcyone of Greek mythology, daughter of Aeolus, turned into a diver by the gods for her impertinence. Hamayun is a fabulous clairvoyant bird with a human face. One may assume that the three birds did not fly into Vysotsky's song straight from folklore but via two of Blok's poems: "Hamayun, the Prophetic Bird" and "Sirin and Alkonost. The Birds of Joy and Sadness".— *Tr.*

Душу, сбитую утратами да тратами,
Душу, стёртую перекатами,—
Если до́ крови лоскут истончал,—
Залатаю золотыми я заплатами,—
Чтобы чаще Господь замечал!

1975

РАЗБОЙНИЧЬЯ

Как во смутной волости
Лютой, злой губернии
Выпадали молодцу
Всё шипы да тернии.

Он обиды зачерпнул, зачерпнул
Полные пригоршни,
Ну а горе, что хлебнул,—
Не бывает горше.

    Пей отраву, хочь залейся!
    Благо, денег не берут.
    Сколь верёвочка ни вейся —
    Всё равно совьёшься в кнут!

Гонит неудачников
По́ миру с котомкою,
Жизнь течёт меж пальчиков
Паутинкой тонкою.

А которых повело, повлекло
По лихой дороге —
Тех ветрами сволокло
Прямиком в остроги.

    Тут на милость не надейся —
    Стиснуть зубы да терпеть!
    Сколь верёвочка ни вейся —
    Всё равно совьёшься в плеть!

Ах, лихая сторона,
Сколь в тебе ни рыскаю,—
Лобным местом ты красна
Да верёвкой склизкою!

А повешенным сам дьявол-сатана
Голы пятки лижет.

Now, my soul's been worn by losses and by loneliness,
Torn by eddies, rapids, and by my unrest;
Now that my blood oozes slowly, and goes dry
I will patch it up with golden brocade — with the best —
That it oftener might catch the Lord's eye!

1975

HIGHWAYMAN'S SONG

In the darkest corner of
Evil lands, out in the sticks,
Once a fine brave fellow roved,
Getting all the thorns and kicks.

In offence he walked knee-deep, yeah, knee-deep,
Hurt by handfuls swallowed,
And his endless, cruel grief
Tasted worse than wormwood.

> Drink the poison, if you're thirsty.
> In the end, it'll cost you cheap.
> It's no use, turning and twisting —
> It will all end with the whip.

Through the wide world grim fate drives
Hapless ones to beg their bread.
Life slips between fingers — life,
Like a gossamer thin thread.

And the other ones who went — those who went —
Hunting luck on highways,
They were driven by ill winds
Straight into the dark gaols.

> Here, there is no hope of mercy —
> Bear it all, though your teeth gnash!
> It's no use, turning and twisting —
> It will all end with the lash.

No, you evil, evil land,
You leave folks no hope,
You are best at scaffolds, and
Long and well-soaped ropes.

And the hanged men's heels, their bare heels in his hole
Stupid Satan's licking.

Смех, досада, мать честна! —
Ни пожить, ни выжить!

Ты не вой, не плачь, а смейся —
Слёз-то нынче не простят.
Сколь верёвочка ни вейся —
Всё равно укоротят!

Ночью думы муторней.
Плотники не мешкают —
Не успеть к заутрене:
Больно рано вешают.

Ты об этом не жалей, не жалей,—
Что тебе отсрочка?!
На верёвочке твоей
Нет ни узелочка!

Лучше ляг да обогрейся —
Я, мол, казни не просплю.
Сколь верёвочка ни вейся —
А совьёшься ты в петлю!

1975

ПРЕРВАННЫЙ ПОЛЁТ

Кто-то высмотрел плод, что неспел,—
Потрусили за ствол — он упал...
Вот вам песня о том, кто не спел,
И что голос имел — не узнал.

Может, были с судьбой нелады
И со случаем плохи дела,
А тугая струна на лады
С незаметным изъяном легла.

Он начал робко с ноты до,
Но не допел ее, не до...

Не дозвучал его аккорд
И никого не вдохновил.
Собака лаяла, а кот —
Мышей ловил.

Смешно, не правда ли, смешно!
А он шутил — недошутил,

Ah, how funny — bless my soul!
People call this living!

> Laugh! It is no use, this whining —
> They will not forgive the tears.
> It's no use twisting and turning —
> Fate is ready with the shears.

In the night, the thoughts are dreary,
And the carpenters look sour:
No time for their morning prayer —
Hangmen keep such early hours.

Don't be angry about this, about that:
Why wait, if you're ready?
There is not a single knot
On your long rope, laddie.

> Better lie awhile — get rested
> For the hanging, take a snooze.
> Any way the rope is twisted,
> It will coil into a noose.

1975

STOPPED MID FLIGHT

Someone saw that the fruit wasn't ripe,
And he shook the branch, and it dropped.
Hear the tale of a voice never tried,
For the voice was too soon rudely stopped.

Fate was harder on him than he'd thought,
And the chances were somehow all wrong,
And the strings may have been much too taut,
And off key was the tune of the song.

> He started timidly with *do*,
> But was cut short at once, and so —

> And so the chord, cut short, fell flat.
> Who was inspired by his voice?
> The dog barked fiercely, and the cat —
> It hunted mice.

> It is so funny, is it not?
> He laughed — but never learnt to jest.

Недораспробовал вино,
И даже недопригубил.

Он пока лишь затеивал спор,
Неуверенно и неспеша,—
Словно капельки пота из пор,
Из-под кожи сочилась душа.

Только начал дуэль на ковре —
Еле-еле, едва приступил,
Лишь чуть-чуть осмотрелся в игре,
И судья еще счёт не открыл.

Он знать хотел всё от и до,
Но не добрался он, не до...

Ни до догадки, ни до дна,
Не докопался до глубин
И ту, которая одна,—
Недолюбил.

Смешно, не правда ли, смешно!
А он спешил — недоспешил,—
Осталось недорешено
Все то, что он недорешил.

Ни единою буквой не лгу —
Он был чистого слога слуга,
И писал ей стихи на снегу...
К сожалению, тают снега!

Но тогда ещё был снегопад,
И свобода писать на снегу,—
И большие снежинки и град
Он губами хватал на бегу.

Но к ней в серебряном ландо
Он не добрался и не до...

Не добежал бегун, беглец,
Не долетел, не доскакал,
А звёздный знак его — Телец —
Холодный Млечный Путь лакал.

Смешно, не правда ли, смешно,
Когда секунд недостаёт,—
Недостающее звено,
И недолёт, и недолёт!

He'd taste the finest wines, he thought,—
He did not live to know the taste.

He was itching to join in the sport,
Too unsure of himself to begin,
And, like droplets of sweat from the pores,
His young soul oozed from under the skin.

He was trying to learn all the ropes,
He was getting the feel of the court,
He flew high on his first timid hopes
Though they hadn't yet started the score.

    He thought one day he'd know it all,
    How could he know he'd trip and fall

    Before he sensed the coming dawn,
    Before he mused and mulled his fill,
    Before he loved the only one
    Up to the hilt.

    It is so funny, is it not?
    He hurried only to get stalled.
    It's all remained unsolved, all what
    He never had time to resolve.

Not a shadow of lie in my song, I vow —
Faithful knight of the purest style,
He would write her long poems on the snow...
Pity all snow melts after a while!

But that was in the great snowfall
And the freedom to write on the snow —
Snow came endlessly, squall after squall,
And he seemed with the whirlwind to float.

    He ran, but he ran much too slow
    To catch up with the white landau...

    He knew that he would never win,
    That runner — or the runaway.
    The Taurus sign, his Zodiac twin,
    Meanwhile lapped at the Milky Way.

It's all so funny, is it not,
When misses are as good as miles,
And when all shells keep falling short,
When fate guffaws but never smiles.

Смешно, не правда ли? Ну вот,—
И вам смешно, и даже мне —
Конь на скаку и птица влёт,—
По чьей вине?..

1973

ПЕСНЯ КОНЧЕНОГО ЧЕЛОВЕКА

Истома ящерицей ползает в костях,
И сердце с трезвой головой не на ножах,
И не захватывает дух на скоростях,
Не холодеет кровь на виражах.

И не прихватывает горло от любви,
И нервы больше не внатяжку,— хочешь — рви,—
Провисли нервы, как верёвки от белья,
И не волнует, кто кого,— он или я.

На коне,—
            толкани —
                        я с коня.
    Только *не*,
            только *ни*
                        у меня.

Не пью воды — чтоб стыли зубы — питьевой
И ни событий, ни людей не тороплю.
Мой лук валяется со сгнившей тетивой,
Все стрелы сломаны — я ими печь топлю.

Не напрягаюсь, не стремлюсь, а как-то так...
Не вдохновляет даже самый факт атак.
Сорви-голов не принимаю и корю,
Про тех, кто в омут с головой,— не говорю.

На коне,—
            толкани —
                        я с коня.
    Только *не*,
            только *ни*
                        у меня.

И не хочу ни выяснять, ни изменять,
И ни вязать и ни развязывать узлы.
Углы тупые можно и не огибать,
Ведь после острых — это не углы.

So funny, is it not? So there!
You laugh — I grin — all in the game.
Horse at full tilt, bird on the air —
And who's to blame?

1973

THE SONG OF A GONER

Dull languor's crawling like a lizard through my bones,
My heart and sober head are not at daggers drawn.
The world is hurtling by, but I'm as cool as stone.
Blood does not freeze when I pull into a blind turn.

And love is different — there's no lump in my throat,
It's easy now to rend my nerves, no longer taut —
They sag now like a line of washing in the wind.
I do not care much whether I win or he wins.

    I'm in the saddle —
                just a jolt —
                            and I will fall.
  It may be sad —
             but *no* and *not* —
                        that is my all.

I drink no longer icy water from a spring,
I do not hurry either people or events.
My bow lies somewhere, with a rotten bow-string,
I throw my arrows in the fire, and sit content.

I do not strain now, or aspire — sort of relax.
I'm not inspired even by unfair attacks.
I don't like madcaps, and for daring hold no brief,
I never talk of guys who have jumped off a cliff.

    I'm in the saddle —
                just a jolt —
                            and I will fall.
  It may be sad —
             but *no* and *not* —
                        that is my all.

I do not want to alter things, or put to use,
To pull more strings, or undo knots,— I'm in no mood.
You can ignore the angles, if they are obtuse —
They seem no angles after handling the acute.

Свободный ли, тугой ли пояс — мне-то что!
Я пули в лоб не удостоюсь — не за что.
Я весь прозрачный, как раскрытое окно,
И неприметный, как льняное полотно.

        На коне, —
                толкани —
                        я с коня.
        Только *не*,
                только *ни*
                        у меня.

Не ноют раны, да и шрамы не болят —
На них наложены стерильные бинты.
И не волнуют, не свербят, не теребят
Ни мысли, ни вопросы, ни мечты.

Любая нежность душу не разбередит,
И не внушит никто, и не разубедит.
А так как чужды всякой всячины мозги,
То ни предчувствия не жмут, ни сапоги.

        На коне, —
                толкани —
                        я с коня.
        Только *не*,
                только *ни*
                        у меня.

Ни философский камень больше не ищу,
Ни корень жизни, — ведь уже нашли женьшень.
Не вдохновляюсь, не стремлюсь, не трепещу
И не надеюсь поразить мишень.

Устал бороться с притяжением земли —
Лежу, — так больше расстоянье до петли.
И сердце дёргается словно не во мне, —
Пора туда, где только *ни* и только *не*.

        На коне, —
                толкани —
                        я с коня.
        Только *не*,
                только *ни*
                        у меня.

1971

My belt is tight, my belt is loose — who gives a hoot?
I shan't be shot — there's no one kind enough to shoot.
I am transparent like a window open wide,
And inconspicuous as white is white on white.

    I'm in the saddle —
                  just a jolt —
                                and I will fall.
    It may be sad —
                  but *no* and *not* —
                              that is my all.

My wounds no longer ache, and scars give me no pain —
They were well-cauterised, I guess I'm in good shape.
I'm not excited, or concerned, I can't complain
That I am worried by a dream or idle hope.

There is no tenderness that could my soul pervade,
No one can make me think, and no one can dissuade.
And since my mind is alien to that kind of rot,
My shoes may hurt me, but presentiments do not.

    I'm in the saddle —
                  just a jolt —
                                and I will fall.
    It may be sad —
                  but *no* and *not* —
                              that is my all.

I look no longer for the philosophic stone,
Nor for the root of life — for ginseng has been found.
I do not tremble or aspire, I'm not highflown,
I do not hope to hit the target first time 'round.

I'm tired fighting gravitation — can't break loose.
I'm lying down to keep me further from the noose.
My heart's not mine — it is a distant frozen clot —
It's time I went where all there is, is *no* and *not*.

    I'm in the saddle —
                  just a jolt —
                                and I will fall.
    It may be sad —
                  but *no* and *not* —
                              that is my all.

1971

Мы все живем как будто, но
Не будоражат нас давно
Ни паровозные свистки,
Ни пароходные гудки.
Иные,— те, кому дано,—
Стремятся вглубь — и видят дно,—
Но — как навозные жуки
И мелководные мальки...

А рядом случаи летают, словно пули,—
Шальные, запоздалые, слепые на излёте,—
Одни под них подставиться рискнули —
И сразу: кто — в могиле, кто — в почёте.

А мы — так не заметили
И просто увернулись,—
Нарочно, по примете ли —
На правую споткнулись.

Средь суеты и кутерьмы
Ах, как давно мы не прямы! —
То гнёмся бить поклоны впрок,
А то — завязывать шнурок...
Стремимся вдаль проникнуть мы,—
Но даже светлые умы
Всё размещают между строк —
У них расчёт на долгий срок...

Стремимся мы подняться ввысь —
Ведь думы наши поднялись,—
И там царят они, легки,
Свободны, вечны, высоки.
И так нам захотелось ввысь,
Что мы вчера перепились —
И горьким думам вопреки
Мы ели сладкие куски...

Открытым взломом, без ключа,
Навзрыд об ужасах крича,
Мы вскрыть хотим подвал чумной —
Рискуя даже головой.
И трезво, а не сгоряча
Мы рубим прошлое с плеча,—
Но бьем расслабленной рукой,
Холодной, дряблой — никакой.

* * *

We all seem to be living, but
It's been a long time since our heart
Was stirred by distant hoot or wail
Of ship or train speeding away.
Some people get out of the rut,
And they go deep but deep, man, but
All this is no more than child's play —
So let the fry play while they may.

And all around, our chances fly nearby, like bullets —
Stray, spent, belated, blind, some real stunners;
Some took the risk, jumped at a chance — and duly
Reaped the reward: some, coffins, others, honours.

And we just looked aside
And nimbly past them ambled,
And, mindful of the signs,
Took good care not to stumble.

In this fuss and hullabaloo
We've long grown used to bending low:
Our torso's constantly inclined —
To take a bow, to tow the line.
We love to know what's false, what's true,
We know, though, what the bright ones do:
They squeeze all meanings between lines
For future use by better minds.

How we would like to rise sky high —
Our thoughts soar high up in the sky —
Eternally up there they reign,
Without a blemish or restraint.
And we, too, longed so much to fly
That yesterday we got quite high:
To ease the bitterness and strain,
We drank again — and drank again...

By horrors shaken to the core
We'd like to batter down the door
Of basements filled with our past's dead —
Though we may put at risk our head.
And soberly, without furor,
We hit the past all stained with gore —
Our arms, though, are inert as lead,
And weak with unforgotten dread.

Приятно сбросить гору с плеч —
И всё на божий суд извлечь,
И руку выпростать, дрожа,
И показать — в ней нет ножа, —
Не опасаясь, что картечь
И безоружных будет сечь.
Но нас, железных, точит ржа —
И психология ужа...

А рядом случаи летают, словно пули, —
Шальные, запоздалые, слепые на излёте, —
Одни под них подставиться рискнули —
И сразу: кто — в могиле, кто — в почёте.

А мы — так не заметили
И просто увернулись, —
Нарочно, по примете ли —
На правую споткнулись.

1974

ПРИТЧА О ПРАВДЕ И ЛЖИ

Булату Окуджаве

Нежная Правда в красивых одеждах ходила,
Принарядившись для сирых, блаженных, калек, —
Грубая Ложь эту Правду к себе заманила:
Мол, оставайся-ка ты у меня на ночлег.

И легковерная Правда спокойно уснула,
Слюни пустила и разулыбалась во сне, —
Грубая Ложь на себя одеяло стянула,
В Правду впилась — и осталась довольна вполне.

И поднялась, и скроила ей рожу бульдожью:
Баба как баба, и что её ради радеть?! —
Разницы нет никакой между Правдой и Ложью, —
Если, конечно, и ту и другую раздеть.

Выплела ловко из кос золотистые ленты
И прихватила одежды, примерив на глаз;
Деньги взяла, и часы, и еще документы, —
Сплюнула, грязно ругнулась — и вон подалась.

A load off our minds feels so nice.
Nice, to bare all before God's eyes,
To show your empty hand, so they
Can see we aren't armed for a fray, —
Though, armed or not, one simply dies
When shrapnel flesh at random slice.
But our ironsides decay,
To rust and wormlike spirit prey.

And all around, our chances fly nearby, like bullets —
Stray, spent, belated, blind, some real stunners;
Some took the risk, jumped at a chance — and duly
Reaped the reward: some, coffins, others, honours.

And we just looked aside
And nimbly past them ambled,
And, mindful of the signs,
Took good care not to stumble.

1974

A PARABLE OF TRUTH AND LIE

To Bulat Okudzhava

Truth walked the earth once in fine clothes — which she used
to wear
Only to please all the poor and the cripples in their plight.
Crude Lie decoyed tender Truth one night into her lair,
Telling her, Why don't you stay at my place overnight?

Gullible Truth went to bed and slept quietly and soundly,
Dribbling saliva, and smiling a radiant smile.
Crude Lie first hogged all the blankets and then started
sucking
At Truth's lifeblood, feeling as pleased as Punch all the while.

Then she rose swiftly and made a crude face at the other:
Ha! Just a dame! What's so special about this damn bitch?
Truth or Lie, there is no difference at all, whatever —
If you undress them, of course — you can't tell which
is which.

Then golden ribbons she nimbly pulled out of the tresses,
Put on the dress and the shoes that the other one wore,
Picked up the money, the watch and the papers, with curses
Spat on the floor, coarsely swore, and skipped out of the door.

161

Только к утру обнаружила Правда пропажу —
И подивилась, себя оглядев делово:
Кто-то уже, раздобыв где-то чёрную сажу,
Вымазал чистую Правду, а так — ничего.

Правда смеялась, когда в неё камни бросали:
«Ложь это все, и на Лжи одеянье моё...»
Двое блаженных калек протокол составляли
И обзывали дурными словами её.

Стервой ругали её, и похуже чем стервой,
Мазали глиной, спустили дворового пса...
«Духу чтоб не было, — на километр сто первый
Выселить, выслать за двадцать четыре часа!»

Тот протокол заключался обидной тирадой
(Кстати, навесили Правде чужие дела):
Дескать, какая-то мразь называется Правдой,
Ну а сама — пропилась, проспалась догола.

Чистая Правда божилась, клялась и рыдала,
Долго скиталась, болела, нуждалась в деньгах, —
Грязная Ложь чистокровную лошадь украла —
И ускакала на длинных и тонких ногах.

Некий чудак и поныне за Правду воюет, —
Правда, в речах его правды — на ломаный грош:
«Чистая Правда со временем восторжествует, —
Если проделает то же, что явная Ложь!»

Часто, разлив по сто семьдесят граммов на брата,
Даже не знаешь, куда на ночлег попадёшь.

Truth in the morning woke up, and her losses discovered,
And felt amused as she looked at herself in the light:
Somebody'd got hold of soot and her body had covered
In dirty streaks, but the rest — more or less — looked all right.

Truth merely laughed when they stoned her, and told those dense
people:
"These are all lies, and the fine clothes Lie's wearing
are mine."
But a report was made out by a couple of cripples
Who called her all the bad names they could think of,
the swine.

They called her bitch, and much worse; and with jeers
and with howls
She was all tarred, and then baited with dogs by the hoods.
"Get lost, and stay lost!" They gave her just twenty-
four hours
In which to pack and get out of the city for good.

That report ended in brazen-faced, impudent slander
(Jobs done by others were pinned on the poor Truth,
to boot):
This bum who called herself Truth, they wrote, went
on a bender,
Hocked all her clothes to get booze, and was found
in the nude.

How pure Truth pleaded, sobbed and swore by all that
is holy!
Knocking all over the world, she was broke and in pain.
One dark night, Dirty Lie stole a fast, thoroughbred filly
And rode away with a whoop of delight and disdain.

A certain crank tried to vindicate Truth — he's still trying.
True, there's no truth in his speeches — they're cunning
and sly:
"Time will come, brothers, when Truth will be certain
to triumph —
Always provided it acts in the same way as Lie."

Often, when you split a bottle of booze with two others *,
You don't know where you will spend the night, with whom
or why.

---

* Vysotsky refers here to the accepted way of dealing with
vodka: a bottle (half a litre) is poured into three glasses which
are downed at a draught. In the drinking circles, the system is known
as "for three" (*na troikh*).— *Tr.*

163

Могут раздеть, — это чистая правда, ребята, —
Глядь — а штаны твои носит коварная Ложь.
Глядь — на часы твои смотрит коварная Ложь.
Глядь — а конём твоим правит коварная Ложь!

1977

* * *

Я бодрствую, но вещий сон мне снится.
Пилюли пью — надеюсь, что усну.
Не привыкать глотать мне горькую слюну:
Организации, инстанции и лица
Мне объявили явную войну
За то, что я нарушил тишину,
За то, что я хриплю на всю страну,
Чтоб доказать — я в колесе не спица,
За то, что мне неймётся и не спится,
За то, что в передачах заграница
Передаёт мою блатную старину,
Считая своим долгом извиниться:
«Мы сами, без согласья...» — ну и ну!
За что ещё, — быть может, за жену,
Что, мол, не мог на нашей подданной жениться;
Что, мол, упрямо лезу в капстрану
И очень не хочу идти ко дну;
Что песню написал — и не одну —
Про то, как мы когда-то били фрица,
Про рядового, что на дзот валится,
А сам — ни сном ни духом про войну.
Кричат, что я у них украл луну
И что-нибудь ещё украсть не премину,
И небылицу догоняет небылица.
Не спится мне. Ну как же мне не спиться?!
Нет, не сопьюсь, я руку протяну
И завещание крестом перечеркну,
И сам я не забуду осениться,
И песню напишу — и не одну, —
И в песне той кого-то прокляну,
Но в пояс не забуду поклониться
Всем тем, кто написал, чтоб я не смел ложиться.
Пусть чаша горькая — я их не обману.

⟨*До 1978*⟩

You can be picked clean — I swear it's the purest truth,
brothers —
Look — those are your trousers, stolen by insidious Lie.
Look — that is your watch, now worn by insidious Lie.
Look — that is your horse that carries insidious Lie!

1977

* * *

I am awake, yet dream prophetic verses.
I want to sleep, and swallow pills galore.
No matter — I have taken bitter pills before:
Organisations, institutions, persons —
They've all declared on me a total war
For my disturbing peace and quiet, and
For my hoarse singing filling this whole land,
For my disrepute and for my renown;
For being impotent to keep me down;
For my old ballads that come flitting
On short-wave radio from abroad,
With notices attached — I think, quite fitting —
"Unauthorised by author..." Oh, my God!
What else? It may well be my foreign wife.
I should have married Soviet — done my duty.
How dare I choose a foreign way of life?
And, above all, how dare I to survive?
They hate me for my songs about the years
When we beat bloody hell out of the Fritzes,
For writing songs of dogfights and of blitzes,
Not having fought, or been anywhere near.
They yell that I have pinched the moon, and will
Find something else again, as valuable, to steal.
So dirty lies keep chasing one another.
With all these blots, I'll soon be blotto, brother!
No, I won't drink myself to death — I will
Tear up or just cross off my testament and will,
And cross myself — God, bear with this offender! —
And go on writing songs, with all my heart and skill, —
And there'll be those whom in my songs I'll damn
But also those to whom I'll homage render,
All those who wrote to me that I dare not surrender.
And though my cup be bitter, I'll be true to them.

⟨*Before 1978*⟩

ПАМЯТИ ВАСИЛИЯ ШУКШИНА

Еще — ни холодов, ни льдин,
Земля тепла, красна калина, —
А в землю лёг ещё один
На Новодевичьем мужчина.

Должно быть, он примет не знал, —
Народец праздный суесловит, —
Смерть тех из нас всех прежде ловит,
Кто понарошку умирал.

Коль так, Макарыч, — не спеши,
Спусти колки, ослабь зажимы,
Пересними, перепиши,
Переиграй, — останься живым!

Но, в слёзы мужиков вгоняя,
Он пулю в животе понёс,
Припал к земле, как верный пёс...
А рядом куст калины рос —
Калина красная такая.

Смерть самых лучших намечает —
И дергает по одному.
Такой наш брат ушёл во тьму! —
Не поздоровилось ему, —
Не буйствует и не скучает.

А был бы «Разин» в этот год...
Натура где? Онега? Нарочь?

IN MEMORY OF VASILY SHUKSHIN *

The earth was warm, no frost, no ice,
Bright-red were guelder-rose's berries **.
It seemed all wrong, when one of us
in Novodevichye *** was buried.

He did not know the signs, they say,
But simple people know the menace:
"Death goes for those of us in earnest
Who play at death, and die in play."

If that is true — relax, Vasily,
The real game is to survive.
Film it again, and don't be silly —
Rewrite it all, and stay alive!

But, driving grown-up men to tears,
He hugged the dear earth as he bled,
And looked up, fainting, nearly dead,
Towards a guelder-rose bright-red —
It was all red, it was so near...

Death marks out but the best and pluckiest
And plucks them out, one by one.
Ah, what a man this time is gone
In outer darkness, having run
Clean out of luck in the earthly ruckus.

This year, your *Razin* would be shot —
You chose locations near Lake Naroch.

---

* Vasily Shukshin — Vysotsky's friend, film actor, director, and a superb realistic writer.— *Tr.*

** *Red Guelder-rose* (lit. *Guelder-rose Red*) was the title of one of Shukshin's films. The poem is full of allusions to it.— *Tr.*

*** Novodevicheye — a cemetery on the grounds of the Novodevichy Monastery in Moscow.— *Tr.*

Всё — печки-лавочки, Макарыч, —
Такой твой парень не живёт!

Вот после временной заминки
Рок процедил через губу:
«Снять со скуластого табу —
За то, что он видал в гробу
Все панихиды и поминки.

Того, с большой душою в теле
И с тяжким грузом на горбу, —
Чтоб не испытывал судьбу, —
Взять утром тёпленьким с постели!»

И после непременной бани,
Чист перед богом и трезв,
Вдруг взял да умер он всерьёз —
Решительней, чем на экране.

1974

What was that other film, Makarych *?
There Lives a Lad — but he does not.

After a second's hesitation
Fate angrily let loose a yell:
"Come on, let's close in for the kill —
The fellow said he'd see in hell
All requiems and lamentations.

Him with the soul so great and warming,
And on his back a load so great,
That he might no more tempt his fate —
Drag from the warm bed in the morning!"

After a steam-bath, like all honest **
Folks, clean and sober before God,
He up and died, like someone shot,
Not on the screen this time — in earnest.

1974

---

* Makarych — Shukshin's patronymic (Vasily Makarych). This
is a curious Russian form of address combining respect and familiarity.—*Tr.*
** See comment on Vysotsky's song *Bath-hut.*— *Tr.*

КОНИ ПРИВЕРЕДЛИВЫЕ

Вдоль обрыва, по-над пропастью, по самому по краю
Я коней своих нагайкою стегаю, погоняю...
Что-то воздуху мне мало — ветер пью, туман глотаю, —
Чую с гибельным восторгом: пропадаю, пропадаю!

    Чуть помедленнее, кони, чуть помедленнее!
    Вы тугую не слушайте плеть!
    Но что-то кони мне попались привередливые —
    И дожить не успел, мне допеть не успеть.

    Я коней напою,
            я куплет допою —
    Хоть мгновенье ещё постою
                на краю...

Сгину я — меня пушинкой ураган сметёт с ладони,
И в санях меня галопом повлекут по снегу утром, —
Вы на шаг неторопливый перейдите, мои кони,
Хоть немного, но продлите путь к последнему приюту!

    Чуть помедленнее, кони, чуть помедленнее!
    Не указчики вам кнут и плеть.
    Но что-то кони мне попались привередливые —
    И дожить не успел, мне допеть не успеть.

    Я коней напою,
            я куплет допою —
    Хоть мгновенье ещё постою
                на краю...

Мы успели: в гости к Богу не бывает опозданий, —
Что ж там ангелы поют такими злыми голосами?!

UNRULY HORSES *

Along the chasm's edge, upon the precipice's brink
I urge my horses onward, I coerce them, whiplash flying.
I'm somehow short of breath, I gulp the air, the wind I
                                                    drink...
I'm gripped with mortal ecstasy: I'm dying, oh, I'm dying!

    Slower, slower, oh my horses, slowly run, slowly run!
    Pay no heed to the lash's taut thong.
    The horses that fell to my lot are unruly ones...
    I've not lived out my life, I can't finish my song.

    I'll water my horses,
                I'll sing some more verses —
    Yet a moment I'll stand on the brink
                   ere I sink.

I'll perish: from its outstretched hand the frenzied
                                        wind will blow me,
At a gallop through the morning snow my sleigh's drawn
                                            helter-skelter.
Be patient, patient, wayward horses, make the journey slowly,
And delay if but a while before we reach the final shelter.

    Slower, slower, oh my horses, slowly run, slowly run!
    You don't serve the whip or the thong.
    The horses that fell to my lot are unruly ones...
    I've not lived out my life, I can't finish my song.

    I'll water my horses,
                I'll sing some more verses —
    Yet a moment I'll stand on the brink
                   ere I sink.

It's all over: guests to God cannot delay until the morrow.
But why then should the angels' voices sound so harsh
                                            and hoarse?

---

* © *Soviet Leterature,* 1988, No. 10.
Translated by Kathryn Hamilton.

Или это колокольчик весь зашёлся от рыданий,
Или я кричу коням, чтоб не несли так быстро сани?!

Чуть помедленнее, кони, чуть помедленнее!
Умоляю вас вскачь не лететь!
Но что-то кони мне попались привередливые...
Коль дожить не успел, так хотя бы — допеть!

Я коней напою,
         я куплет допою —
Хоть мгновенье ещё постою
                 на краю...

1972

ПАМЯТНИК

Я при жизни был рослым и стройным,
Не боялся ни слова, ни пули
И в привычные рамки не лез, —
Но с тех пор, как считаюсь покойным,
Охромили меня и согнули,
К пьедесталу прибив ахиллес.

Не стряхнуть мне гранитного мяса
И не вытащить из постамента
Ахиллесову эту пяту,
И железные рёбра каркаса
Мёртво схвачены слоем цемента, —
Только судороги по хребту.

Я хвалился косою саженью —
     Нате смерьте! —
Я не знал, что подвергнусь суженью
     После смерти, —
Но в привычные рамки я всажен —
     На́ спор вбили,
А косую неровную сажень
     Распрямили.

И с меня, когда взял я да умер,
Живо маску посмертную сняли
Расторопные члены семьи, —

Is it but the harness bell that jangles wildly out of sorrow,
Or do I harangue the horses to slow down their hectic
                                                    course?

Slower, slower, oh my horses, slowly run, slowly run!
I implore you, don't gallop headlong!
The horses that fell to my lot are unruly ones...
I've not lived out my life, yet I'd finish my song.

I'll water my horses,
                        I'll sing some more verses —
Yet a moment I'll stand on the brink
                                        ere I sink.

1972

THE MEMORIAL *

When I lived I was straight and stout-hearted,
I feared neither the word nor the bullet,
And I scorned all the usual ways.
But now that this life I've departed
They've made me all crippled and crooked,
With "Achilles" inscribed on the base.

I can't shake off this granite flesh from me,
From the monument's plinth even more so
I can't wrench this Achillean heel.
A layer of cement presses numbly
The iron ribcage supporting my torso —
Spinal spasms are all that I feel.

I boasted fine shoulders, none broader.
    Gauge their breadth!
I'd no inkling I'd face the recorder
    After death.
But I've been forced back into line.
    Straight they set
Those uneven broad shoulders of mine
    For a bet.

I had no sooner died than my kindred,
The most efficient and quick ones,
Came and moulded a mask of my face.

_____

* © *Soviet Literature*, 1988, No. 10.
Translated by Kathryn Hamilton.

173

И не знаю, кто их надоумил, —
Только с гипса вчистую стесали
Азиатские скулы мои.

Мне такое не мнилось, не снилось,
И считал я, что мне не грозило
Оказаться всех мертвых мертвей, —
Но поверхность на слепке лоснилась,
И могильною скукой сквозило
Из беззубой улыбки моей.

    Я при жизни не клал тем, кто хищный,
        В пасти палец,
    Подходившие с меркой обычной —
        Отступались, —
    Но по снятии маски посмертной —
        Тут же в ванной —
    Гробовщик подошел ко мне с меркой
        Деревянной.

А потом, по прошествии года —
Как венец моего исправленья —
Крепко сбитый литой монумент
При огромном скопленьи народа
Открывали под бодрое пенье, —
Под моё — с намагниченных лент.

Тишина надо мной раскололась —
Из динамиков хлынули звуки,
С крыш ударил направленный свет, —
Мой отчаяньем сорванный голос
Современные средства науки
Превратили в приятный фальцет.

    Я немел, в покрывало упрятан, —
        Все там будем! —
    Я орал в то же время кастратом
        В уши людям.
    Саван сдернули — как я обужен, —
        Нате, смерьте! —
    Неужели *такой* я вам нужен
        После смерти?!

Командора шаги злы и гулки.
Я решил: как во времени оном —
Не пройтись ли, по плитам звеня? —
И шарахнулись толпы в проулки,

And I've no idea who recommended
That they take off my high Asian cheekbones,
But they scraped them away without trace.

I never remotely suspected
Or entertained even a thought of
My ending up deader than dead.
But they smoothed down the mask to correct it
And death's tedious blandness smiled out of
The toothless grin in my head.

> When I lived I would not put my hand out
>   To the sharks.
> They were scared to apply common standards
>   To my work.
> But, to measure my corpse for the coffin,
>   As his tool
> The mortician used only a rough one,
>   A wood rule.

And now, a year after my burial,
As the crown of their work to adjust me,
They've gathered a huge crowd to gape,
And unveiled their fine solid memorial
To the sound of loud singing and lusty —
My singing, recorded on tape.

The loudspeakers blare out the music,
Their din bursting in on my stillness;
From the rooftops the spotlight beams glare.
The marvels of modern acoustics
Have reduced to a saccharine shrillness
My voice that was hoarse with despair.

> I lie speechless, for so we're all fated,
>   In my shroud.
> Yet I hear myself bawling, castrated,
>   To the crowd.
> My shroud is torn off — how reduced I am!
>   Gauge my breadth!
> Like this how can I be of use to them
>   After death?

The Commandant's steps were sepulchral!
I resolve, why can't I, as of yore, then,
Walk abroad with a dull ringing tread?
In the alleys the scattered crowds skulk while,

Когда вырвал я ногу со стоном
И осыпались камни с меня.

Накренился я — гол, безобразен, —
Но и падая — вылез из кожи,
Дотянулся железной клюкой, —
И, когда уже грохнулся наземь,
Из разодранных рупоров все же
Прохрипел я похоже: «Живой!»

1973

РАЙСКИЕ ЯБЛОКИ

Я когда-то умру — мы когда-то всегда умираем,—
Как бы так угадать, чтоб не сам — чтобы в спину ножом:
Убиенных щадят, отпевают и балуют раем,—
Не скажу про живых, а покойников мы бережём.

В грязь ударю лицом, завалюсь покрасивее набок —
И ударит душа на ворованных клячах в галоп.
В дивных райских садах наберу бледно-розовых яблок...
Жаль, сады сторожат и стреляют без промаха в лоб.

Прискакали — гляжу — пред очами не райское что-то:
Неродящий пустырь и сплошное ничто — беспредел.
И среди ничего возвышались литые ворота,
И огромный этап — тысяч пять — на коленях сидел.

Как ржанёт коренной! Я смирил его ласковым словом,
Да репьи из мочал еле выдрал и гриву заплёл.
Седовласый старик слишком долго возился с засовом —
И кряхтел и ворчал, и не смог отворить — и ушел.

Having wrested my foot out before them,
My shattered stone fetters I shed.

I pitch forward, stripped bare, and disfigured,
And, falling, I strain every tendon
To extend my iron claw of a limb.
As I crash, from each sound-cracked loudspeaker
My choked voice is heard, the air rending:
"It seems I'm alive still!" I scream.

1973

APPLES OF PARADISE

I am sure I will die, for we all of us die — that's been proven,
But I'd rather be knifed than die peacefully in my own bed.
Murdered men are indulged, and provided with passes to
                                                    heaven:
We may care for the living, but take better care of the dead.

I will drop in the mud in good cinema style when it happens,
And my soul will drive two stolen horses, two lame jades
                                                    uphill.
In the Garden of Eden I'll want to pick rosy-cheeked apples...
But the gardens are guarded, and guards' orders are, "Shoot
                                                    to kill."

Whoa, horses! What's this? Was it worth all the living and
                                                    dying?
Just a vast barren nothing, no gardens, no flowers, no trees.
In the middle of nothing rose bleak-looking gates of cast-iron,
And a party of convicts, some five thousand, stood on their
                                                    knees *.

How my wild thill-horse shied! But I patted him, and cleaned
                                                    his fetlocks,
And I plaited his mane, and explained it was no use to neigh.
The grey-haired gateman wrestled suspiciously long with
                                                    the gate lock —
He kept grunting and grumbling, and gave up, and stumbled
                                                    away.

---

* This is a familiar picture from the times of Stalin's terror:
a transport of prisoners would be made to go down on their knees
and crawl, to prevent escape attempts, as during en- and detrain-
ment.—*Tr.*

177

И измученный люд не издал ни единого стона,
Лишь на корточки вдруг с онемевших колен пересел.
Здесь малина, братва,— нас встречают малиновым звоном!
Всё вернулось на круг, и распятый над кругом висел.

Всем нам блага подай, да и много ли требовал я́ благ?!
Мне — чтоб были друзья, да жена — чтобы пала на гроб,—
Ну а я уж для них наберу бледно-розовых яблок...
Жаль, сады сторожат и стреляют без промаха в лоб.

Я узнал старика по слезам на щеках его дряблых:
Это Пётр Святой — он апостол, а я — остолоп.
Вот и кущи-сады, в коих прорва мороженых яблок...
Но сады сторожат — и убит я без промаха в лоб.

И погнал я коней прочь от мест этих гиблых и зяблых,—
Кони просят овсу, но и я закусил удила.
Вдоль обрыва с кнутом по-над пропастью пазуху яблок
Для тебя я везу: ты меня и из рая ждала!

1978

* * *

Когда я отпою и отыграю,
Чем кончу я, на чём — не угадать.
Но лишь одно наверняка я знаю —
Мне будет не хотеться умирать!

Посажен на литую цепь почёта,
И звенья славы мне не по зубам...
Эй! Кто стучит в дубовые ворота
Костяшками по кованым скобам?!

Ответа нет. Но там стоят, я знаю.
Кому не так страшны цепные псы,—

And the grey worn-out crowd, it did not give a groan or
a murmur,
Only shifted a little on knees grown dead numb in the frost.
"Hear the ringing of bells? What a life, brother,"
sighed a newcomer.
It had all come full circle, again someone moaned on
the cross.

I do not want too much — though you mustn't say that I
am hapless —
Just my friends and my wife, let her fall on the coffin
and wail.
In the Garden of Eden I'll pick them some rosy-cheeked
apples,
Though the gardens are guarded, and guards' orders are,
"Shoot to kill."

Now I know this old man by the tears that he sheds as he
grumbles:
That's St Peter, he can let me pass through the gate,
if he will.
Here's the Garden of Eden, with millions of frozen apples,
But the gardens are guarded, and they've started shooting
to kill.

So I gallop away, from the cold wretched hell-hole I hasten.
Though the horses are tired, I can't stop, I'm running amuck.
I am bringing you apples, I lash at the jades, I am racing —
From the Garden of Eden you're waiting for me to come
back.

1978

*   *   *

How I will end, when I have sung my fill,
I cannot say, nor will I even try.
There is one thing, though, that I know full well:
I want to live — and I will hate to die.

I'm on a chain, the steel chain of esteem,
The links of fame are too strong for my teeth.
Who's there? Who's rapping on a hasp of steel
In oaken gates — a herald of more grief?

No answer — but I know who's standing there.
A watchdog they would simply kick aside.

179

И вот над изгородью замечаю
Знакомый серп отточенной косы.

...Я перетру серебряный ошейник
И золотую цепь перегрызу,
Перемахну забор, ворвусь в репейник,
Порву бока — и выбегу в грозу!

1973

Above the fence, I see up in the air
Familiar outlines of a sharpened scythe.

I'll twist my neck out of the silver collar
Or I'll bite through the gold-encrusted chain,
I'll clear the fence, fall on a thorn and holler,
Rip up my sides, and fly through wind and rain!

1973

БАЛЛАДА О ЛЮБВИ

Когда вода Всемирного потопа
Вернулась вновь в границы берегов,
Из пены уходящего потока
На сушу тихо выбралась Любовь —
И растворилась в воздухе до срока,
А срока было — сорок сороков...

И чудаки — еще такие есть —
Вдыхают полной грудью эту смесь,
И ни наград не ждут, ни наказанья, —
И, думая, что дышат просто так,
Они внезапно попадают в такт
Такого же — неровного — дыханья.

      Я поля влюблённым постелю —
      Пусть поют во сне и наяву!..
      Я дышу, и значит — я люблю!
      Я люблю, и значит — я живу!

И много будет странствий и скитаний:
Страна Любви — великая страна!
И с рыцарей своих — для испытаний —
Всё строже станет спрашивать она:
Потребует разлук и расстояний,
Лишит покоя, отдыха и сна...

Но вспять безумцев не поворотить,
Они уже согласны заплатить:
Любой ценой — и жизнью бы рискнули, —
Чтобы не дать порвать, чтоб сохранить
Волшебную невидимую нить,
Которую меж ними протянули.

      Я поля влюблённым постелю —
      Пусть поют во сне и наяву!..
      Я дышу, и значит — я люблю!
      Я люблю, и значит — я живу!

A BALLAD ABOUT LOVE

When the Flood's waters started to abate
And waves ceased over all the earth to roam,
Love crawled ashore, bedraggled and sedate,
Out of the muddy whirlpools and the foam,
And vanished into thin air to await
Its time — though who could say when it would come?

There are some people — very funny creatures —
Who will breathe deeply of this heady mixture,
Expecting no reward, nor bent on grieving,
Without a thought for anything sublime,
They suddenly begin to breathe in time
With someone else's quick, uneven breathing.

> I'll make lovers' beds of fields and groves,
> Let them sing, awake and in their sleep!..
> I am breathing, that means I'm in love!
> I'm in love, and that means I'm alive!

There will be years of wandering through hills
And valleys, for the Land of Love is vast.
It'll put its knights through rigorous ordeals
To test their love, to see how it will last.
It'll call for distances and silences, it will
Deprive them of their sleep and quiet and rest...

You cannot drive the madmen back — they say,
Just name the price, and we will promptly pay.
They'll pay the highest price — they'll risk their
                                              lives
To keep the thread from breaking, to prevent
The magic golden thread from being rent —
The flimsiest and the strongest of all ties.

> I'll make lovers' beds of fields and groves,
> Let them sing, awake and in their sleep!..
> I am breathing, that means I'm in love!
> I'm in love, and that means I'm alive!

Но многих захлебнувшихся любовью
Не докричишься — сколько ни зови.
Им счет ведут молва и пустословье,
Но этот счет замешен на крови.
А мы поставим свечи в изголовье
Погибших от невиданной любви...

И душам их дано бродить в цветах,
Их голосам дано сливаться в такт,
И вечностью дышать в одно дыханье,
И встретиться — со вздохом на устах —
На хрупких переправах и мостах,
На узких перекрёстках мирозданья.

      Свежий ветер избранных пьянил,
      С ног сбивал, из мертвых воскрешал,—
      Потому что если не любил —
      Значит, и не жил, и не дышал!

1975

* * *

Люблю тебя *сейчас*,
               не тайно — напоказ,—
Не *после* и не *до* в лучах твоих сгораю;
Навзрыд или смеясь,
               но я люблю *сейчас*,
А в прошлом — не хочу, а в будущем — не знаю.

В прошедшем — «я любил» —
               печальнее могил,
Всё нежное во мне бескрылит и стреножит,—
Хотя поэт поэтов говорил:
«Я вас любил: любовь еще, быть может...»

      Так говорят о брошенном, отцветшем,
      И в этом жалость есть и снисходительность,
      Как к свергнутому с трона королю,
      Есть в этом сожаленье об ушедшем,
      Стремленье, где утеряна стремительность,
      И как бы недоверье к «я люблю».

But oh, how many lovers must have choked
On love, and hear no calls, however loud!
They figure in malicious idle talk,
Their names, though, should be written down in blood,
And we'll light candles for the hearts that broke,
That loved not wisely, and were too well loved...

Their souls will wander among flowers, their song
Will fly to heaven in heavenly unison,
They'll breathe eternity, as if reciting verse,
And with a sigh for hapless golden dreams,
They'll meet on bridges across timeless streams,
On narrow crossroads of the universe.

    Fresh winds cheered the chosen like strong
                        mead,
    Raised them from the dead, and turned their
                        head;
    If you have not loved — you have not lived,
    If you have not loved — you have been dead!

1975

*   *   *

I love you *here and now,*
                 not secretly — for show;
I'm burning in your rays — neither *before* nor *after.*
I do not want the past,
               the future I don't know.
I love you *here and now,* with tears and with laughter.

"I loved you" is so sad,
              it's colder than the dead,
All tenderness in me it will hamstring and kill,—
Although it was the poet of poets who said,
"I loved you once: that love, perhaps, is still —"*

    They speak thus of the faded and the lost,
    There's pity here, a touch of condescension,
    As for a king long from the throne removed.
    There is a mild regret here for the past,
    A longing slightly marred by apprehension,
    A sort of faint distrust towards "I love."

---

* This is the first line of an immortal octet by Pushkin.—*Tr.*

Люблю тебя *теперь* —
                    без пятен, без потерь.
Мой век стоит *сейчас* — я вен не перережу!
Во время, в продолжение, теперь —
Я прошлым не дышу и будущим не брежу.

Приду и вброд и вплавь
                    к тебе — хоть обезглавь! —
С цепями на ногах и с гирями по пуду,—
Ты только по ошибке не заставь,
Чтоб после «я люблю» добавил я «и буду».

Есть горечь в этом «буду», как ни странно,
Подделанная подпись, червоточина
И лаз для отступленья про запас,
Бесцветный яд на самом дне стакана
И, словно настоящему пощёчина,—
Сомненье в том, что «я люблю» *сейчас*.

Смотрю французский сон
                    с обилием времён,
Где в будущем — не так, и в прошлом — по-другому
К позорному столбу я пригвождён,
К барьеру вызван я — языковому.

Ах, разность в языках,—
                    не положенье — крах!
Но выход мы вдвоём поищем — и обрящем.
Люблю тебя и в сложных временах —
И в будущем, и в прошлом настоящем!

1972

I love you *here and now,*
                                without a stain or loss.
This is my day and age — I shall not slash my veins!
At present, during, now and *in the course* —
The future leaves me cold, the past won't come again.

I'll swim or wade or crawl
                                to you — then come what may!—
Lugging my fetters and a heavy yoke.
Cut off my head, but never make me say
"I shall" after "I love", please, not even in joke.

     About "I shall" there's bitterness, alas,
     It's like a forgery, or some such disgrace,
     A hatch to use when it suits you to go,
     Clear poison at the bottom of the glass;
     A slap in honest present tense's face,
     A twinge of doubt about "I love you" *now.*

My French dream makes no sense,
                                I struggle with each tense,
The future is all wrong, and in the past I stammer.
I'm pilloried, it seems, in every sense.
I'm locked behind the barrier of grammar.

This barrier, I guess,
                                is worse than any fence.
But we shall seek and find
                                a way from this impasse.
I love you, dear, in every blessed tense —
Even the future, and the compound past!

                                                    1972

* * *

И снизу лёд и сверху — маюсь между,—
Пробить ли верх иль пробуравить низ?
Конечно — всплыть и не терять надежду,
А там — за дело в ожиданье виз.

Лёд надо мною, надломись и тресни!
Я весь в поту, как пахарь от сохи.
Вернусь к тебе, как корабли из песни,
Всё помня, даже старые стихи.

Мне меньше полувека — сорок с лишним,—
Я жив, тобой и господом храним.
Мне есть что спеть, представ перед всевышним,
Мне есть чем оправдаться перед ним.

1980

* * *

Ice down below, ice up above — I freeze between.
Drill through the bottom, or ram through the top?
There's always hope — I'll surface in the end,
Then wait for visas, plugging at my job.

Above me, ice will break up with a bang.
I'm sweating like a ploughman and his horse.
I shall return, like those ships in the song *,
Remembering it all, even old verse.

I'm half my age — a little way past forty.
I'm living, thanks to God and you, my wife.
I have a lot to sing to the Almighty.
I have my songs to justify my life.

1980

---

* The reference is to "Anchored Ships Lie in Port...", which
is in the present collection.— *Tr.*

VYSOTSKY ON HIS WORK

FROM A 1970 QUESTIONNAIRE

Your favourite prose writer: Mikhail Bulgakov.

Your favourite poet: Bella Akhmadulina.

Your favourite actor: Mikhail Yanshin.

Your favourite actress: Zinaida Slavina.

Your favourite theatre, play and director: The Taganka Theatre, *The Living,* Yuri Lyubimov.

Your favourite film and film director: City Lights, Charlie Chaplin.

Your favourite sculptor and sculpture: Rodin, *The Thinker.*

Your favourite painter and picture: Kuindzhi,*Moonlight.*

Your favourite composer, musical piece, and song: Chopin, *Study No. 12,* the song *The Sacred War.*

The countries you are sympathetic to: Russia, Poland, France.

The ideal man: Marlon Brando.

The ideal woman: That's a secret.

The person you hate: Not too many of them, but the list is significant.

The person that is dearest to you: Can't say at present.

The most remarkable historical personality: Lenin, Garibaldi.

The historical personality that is repulsive to you: Hitler and his camarilla. Mao.

The most outstanding person of the present times: I don't know of any.

Who is your friend? Valery Zolotukhin.

What do you love him for? If one knows what one loves someone for, that's not love, that's just a fine relationship.

What is friendship, do you think? It's when you can

tell someone everything, even the most repugnant things, about oneself.

The traits characteristic of your friend: Tolerance, wisdom, unobtrusiveness.

The favourite traits in a person: Ability to feel and act like one possessed (in a good cause only).

Repugnant character traits: Stupidity, mediocrity, baseness.

Your distinctive traits: The friends will say.

What do you lack? Time.

What sort of person do you think you are? All sorts.

What do you like life for? What life?

Your favourite colour, flower, scent, sound: White, carnation, the scent of sun-bleached hair, the sound of church bells ringing.

What do you want to achieve in life? I want to be remembered, and to be allowed to go everywhere.

What would your gift to your beloved be if you were omnipotent? Another life.

What would give you the most joy? Hamlet's first night.

What would be a tragedy? Loss of voice.

What was the reason for feeling fine the last time you felt fine? Just a good mood.

What made you grieve the last time? Everything.

Your favourite dictum: "We'll sort it out." V. Vysotsky.

A phrase that's characteristic of you only: We'll sort it out.

What would be the first thing you'd do if you became the head of state? Cancel the censorship.

What would be the first thing you'd do if you became a millionnaire? I'd throw a party.

Your hobbies: Poetry and lighters.

Your favourite spot in your favourite city: Samotyoka, Moscow.

Your favourite football team: No favourite football team.

Your dream: Of a better life.

Are you happy? Sometimes.

Why? Just so.

Do you want to be great, and why? I want to and I shall. Why? Well, I ask you!

June 28, 1970

The circumstances of filling in the questionnaire by Vysotsky are described by Anatoly Menshchikov, the author of the questionnaire who was at the time a scene-shifter at the Taganka Theatre.

His responses were not hasty or unconsidered: Vysotsky "worked" on the questionnaire for four hours — in the breaks between the plays. On that night, *The Fallen and the Living* and *The Antiworlds* were on, and Vysotsky played in both. I brought the questionnaire to Vysotsky; it was a sort of ledger with the questions glued on at the side. He snatched it up, full of curiosity: "How long is it until the beginning, about forty minutes? OK, time enough to fill it in..." When I came up to him before the beginning of the play and peered at what he had written over his shoulder, Vysotsky had answered just two questions, the simplest ones, at that, those in the middle — about colours and scents, which did not call for much thought. During the performance of *The Fallen and the Living,* in which Vysotsky played Hitler, Chaplin and Gudzenko, I sidled up to him several times. Wearing now a soldier's tunic, now the Chaplin gear, he kept working on the answers whenever he was not on stage... But he answered only four more questions until the end of the play.

There is a short intermission between *The Fallen...* and *The Antiworlds.* All the actors and actresses skipped away to the refreshment room for a snack, but Vysotsky retreated to an empty make-up room. Sitting there, he plugged away at the questionnaire. Each time I dropped in, he would say, "It's quite a job you've given me! I'm sweating at it like a slave..." He said it smiling slyly, and you could say he looked eager. Next time I peered over his shoulder, he rebuked me: "It isn't nice to peer." And he covered what he had written with his hand, like a schoolboy.

After the performances, the questionnaire was not yet filled in. It was past eleven already. We had dismantled the sets. The only make-up room in which the light was still on was Volodya's. He finished filling in the questionnaire in my presence, signed it, put in the date — 28 June 1970, closed the ledger and said that he felt as if he had acted in ten performances running.

I was glad to see that Vysotsky had put so much of himself into the answers. When I came home, I switched on the light and began reading, though it was quite late by then. To speak quite honestly, I was disappointed, damned disappointed! My impression was that the answers were much too simple. Indeed, already in those days Vysotsky was someone whom we worshipped, we followed him about like kittens follow their mother, and there he was, answering the questions so tritely: "Kuindzhi, *Moonlight*." Or: "Rodin, *The Thinker*." I thought he would write "Godard", or "Fellini", I mean, one of the film directors. He did not write anything like that, although he knew them very well, he had seen and admired it all.

The next day, Vysotsky sensed that I was disappointed, and asked, "Out with it. What was it you didn't like?" I said frankly, "Your favourite song, *The Sacred War*. Of course it's a fine patriotic song, but —"

Here he looked at me with a kind of anguish and annoyance, and, putting his hand on my shoulder, said, "You puppy. When this song makes you feel creepy all over, you'll understand that I'm right. You'll understand why I love it so much..."*

Time passed, and I realised how right he was. I also realised that his answers had been sincere. He was not afraid to be himself, he did not show off, like many of us, naming fashionable idols. *Moonlight* and *The Thinker*, they impress everyone; as do the war songs. Other artists may come later that will make one think — but they come later. Vysotsky did not reject his first sensations, he did not betray them. The things that impressed him once remained with him forever.

---

* The foreign reader is in much the same situation as the author of these memoirs, as far as the song in question is concerned. The postwar generations in this country see it as just another war song. The fact is, though, that it was written very soon after Hitler's assault on the Soviet Union, and for those who went through, or just remember, the war, it is much more than a song — it is a symbol of the whole unending horror of those four years. Vysotsky speaks of his flesh creeping, but people are known to have had heart attacks on suddenly hearing it, long after the war. Incidentally, an English version of the song by the present translator appeared in *The Great Patriotic War. 1941-1945*, Planeta Publishers, Moscow, 1985.—*Tr.*

In 1978, when I no longer worked at the Taganka Theatre, I showed the questionnaire to Vysotsky again. He reread it carefully and said, obviously surprised: "How rum. I've nothing to add. Am I really stuck in the rut?" True, only eight years had passed since the filling in of the questionnaire; ordinarily, it is a short period of time, but not for Vysotsky. His time was much more compressed than other people's: in a day, he did more than some other people managed in a year...

Who are your favourite writers and poets?

Above all, Pushkin...

Haven't we expressed our love for Pushkin, in recent years, much too often?

How is it possible not to love Pushkin? One can be indifferent to poetry, in general, Pushkin included, but if poetry has a fascination for a person, that means Pushkin first and foremost.

Of the modern poets, I like verse by Samoilov, Mezhirov, Slutsky, Yevtushenko, Akhmadulina, Voznesensky...

How about prose?

I like books by Fyodor Abramov, Vasily Belov, Boris Mozhayev — those whom we call "village writers". Also Vasil Bykov and Vasily Shukshin...

Isn't it very difficult to be the author of lyrics and music, and performer, all rolled into one?

I don't know if it is difficult or not. Never thought about that. In my view, this is in any case more natural than "triple" authorship of a song.

Doesn't song-writing interfere with your work as an actor? Don't they create a sort of intrusive image of their author, which it is difficult to get rid of onstage and on the screen?

I don't think so. They are an integral part of me, they aren't a hobby, it's all very serious, no less serious than work at the theatre.

Now you mention it, your hobby —?

I have none. No time for hobbies. Except books, maybe —

What's your attitude to the critical articles about your songs which appreared several years ago?

My songs, both in the early days and now, are very

personal, some of them were not intended for a broad public at all. I wrote them for myself, for my close friends, trying to find a new form of communicating to my coevals what concerns me most.

It's not very pleasant to be criticised, you know. Still, I now feel grateful to the authors of those articles, even though one of them analysed songs with which I had nothing to do whatsoever. At that time, I was only beginning to write songs; besides, the genre itself is fairly rare in this country. An exacting approach was therefore necessary, and it may well be that it played a significant role in the fact that several of my records appeared. There were things which I had to reappraise, others I just could not accept, and still others made me reconsider my positions.

FROM AN INTERVIEW GRANTED TO THE
PYATIGORSK TV STUDIOS (1979)

What is the human failing that you are most ready to forgive?

Physical weakness.

And the failing that you do not forgive?

There are many of these, and I would not like to list them all; above all, greed. And the absence of a clearcut position, which entails very many other shortcomings. A person without a clearcut position does not know what he wants to do with his life, he has no opinion of his own and cannot judge for himself, independently of others, he cannot make judgements on any subject, on persons, the meaning of life, you name it. This inability for independent thinking is both a misfortune and a defect.

What qualities do you value in men?

A combination of kindness, strength and intellect. Whenever I sign my pictures for teenagers, I always write, "Grow up strong, intelligent and kind." Just this combination.

And what qualities in women do you appreciate?

I'd write this: "Be intelligent, beautiful and kind." And beauty isn't just looks.

If you weren't Vysotsky, who would you like to be?

Vysotsky.

What question would you like to ask yourself?

How many years, months, days and hours of creative work I have left... That's the question I would like to ask myself, or rather that's a question I'd like to know the answer to.

What do you believe yourself to be?

Just what I am. The combination of artistic genres and elements that I handle and try to synthesise, that's what I am. It may well be that all of this will be named with one word some day in the future. I work on verse more than on anything else, of course. It is mostly here that I have this thing that is called "inspiration", which will come at night, alight on your shoulder, and whisper in your ear some time around six in the morning, when you have bitten the nails to the quick and believe that it's all no good — and suddenly it will come. That's it: above all, work on verse.

As long as I live, as long as I think, I shall, of course, write poems, I shall write songs. When a song is worthwhile, it can live longer, unlike a human being. A good person will worry and fret, and will die before his time. With songs, it's the other way round: the more it is sung, the longer its life, the more it will live.

SPEECHES AT CONCERTS: A MOSAIC

On My Song Writing

I write "author's songs" *, and I believe them to be a specific genre. Generally speaking, they are not songs even but poems on a rhythmical base. A very long time ago I heard Bulat Okudzhava sing his songs, and I saw that lines of poetry which I had previously read with my eyes became much more effective when he sang them to a guitar. It may very well be any other musical instrument. For instance, at the beginning I tried singing to the piano and the accordion, because when I was a small boy my parents forced me to study music. I can only thank them now: in this way, I learned the ABC's of music. But most people choose the guitar because it is the kind of a simple musical instrument which many can master. It is, of course, very difficult to learn to play the guitar as a virtuoso but much easier to learn to play by ear an accompaniment to one's singing.

I began with songs that were called by many street songs or even gutter songs, for some reason. I thus paid tribute to the urban romance, which by that time had been completely forgotten. The people must have had a craving for this kind of simple, normal conversation in song, a craving for simple — not simplistic — human intonation. They were unsophisticated, those first songs, and the one and only flaming passion that informed them was man's eternal

---

* The term is a literal translation of the Russian *avtorskaya pesnya*. Other terms in use are "guitar song" and "poem-song", but "author's song" is perhaps the most precise since the songs in question are "the author's" in every sense: music, lyrics, and performance.— *Tr.*

desire for the truth, his love for his friends, a woman, for his near and dear. It was all considerably changed and became much more complicated later, of course, but the essence remained the same. I believe that "author's songs" that we, several of us, are writing, is precisely this kind of talking to people — in the form of a song, of course.

We are often reproved for simplifying the melodies, it is said that I, for instance, deliberately write primitive songs. It *is* deliberate, but not ostentatiously so. I simplified many melodies on purpose even in songs meant for films. I believed that nothing should interfere with the perception of the text, with the meaning, with that which I want to express. I wanted the songs to enter not only the ears but the souls as well, right from the beginning, and I wanted the person who would care to sing them for himself to be able to do so easily.

Strange things have happened to "author's songs" in this country: they have been called "tourists' songs", "amateur songs", and what not, although all over the world "author's songs" are on an equal footing with what we call "concert songs". For instance, you watch TV programmes featuring Charles Aznavour, Gilbert Becaud, and other French *chansonniers* who write and sing precisely what we refer to as "author's songs". And no one doubts that such songs can be performed at concerts. On the contrary, they obviously offer great possibilities both for the authors and the people in the audience, for "author's songs" are no more than the possibility for, and a manner of, communicating with people in a normal, natural conversation. These songs call for a response from the audience, they call for an interlocutor. It is in this sense an eternal art whose roots go back into remote past — to Homer, the *akyns*, the troubadours... In Russia, too, singers wandered all over the land with their psalteries, singing songs and *bylinas*. In short, "author's songs" have their history and their traditions. And my preference is for "author's songs", with their modest means, and I would not like to change anything about those means, although I had offers to perform with all kinds of ensembles, orchestras, etc. I do that sometimes when I record LPs, for it is important for this kind of songs to have the effect of the audience's presence, which is quite difficult to achieve with an LP; in this case, that effect must be replaced with something to create a background.

I have never opposed "author's songs" to those of the variety show. They are different genres, each with its merits and defects. A pop song will have, as a rule, an orchestra with a powerful sound, a fine arrangement, a singer or singers with well-trained voices. I respect many of these singers. In this sort of songs, the emphasis is on performance and accompaniment, and if these are lifted, there's no muscle left. There are concert songs without a trace of poetry or information.

...You will please excuse my raising the hand all the time and interrupting your applause — there's never enough time, and I always want to do as much as possible... Because of this, people spread all kinds of legends about me — they say I don't like applause. That's not so. I'm a normal person, and I respect your attitude. I could even say that I need you probably more than you need me here on the stage. Believe me, these meetings give me more than they give you. The point is that "author's songs" give me a chance to tell you what worries me, what is of concern to me, that sort of thing. If I have someone to talk to, someone to share my ideas with, especially such a great crowd as here, you realise that that is my best reward. Not all people can enjoy this sort of experience, and I've been very lucky in this sense. I value these meetings very much, I love them, and try to inform my listeners as best I can.

Generally speaking, when I began to write my songs, I had no idea I would write for such giant audiences as now — in great halls, palaces, and stadiums... In those days, my songs were intended for a narrow circle of very close friends. We were a bunch of students then, and there were some very interesting people in the crowd. Some of them, I'm sorry to say, are no longer with us — like the writer Vasily Shukshin and the film director Levon Kocharyan. We met nearly every day, and even lived together some eighteen months. I would come home after acting in some film on location or some other kind of work, and I would bring back impressions and new songs. I was free, and I knew that people would listen to me with interest. The atmosphere was one of trust, complete ease and, what is most important, of friendliness. I saw that they needed my songs, that they wanted to hear what I was going to tell them in my song. In short, it was a way of telling my close friends something, of talking to them. And though so many years have passed, I'm still trying to revive, after so many years and many audiences, the friendly mood of those days. I even believe that these songs became so well known precisely because there is in them this desire that people should trust you, the desire to tell them about something extremely important. That is why people listen to them, that is why they are drawn to them. I have my guitar, your eyes, the things I want to tell you about, and nothing else. But that is quite a lot. If it comes into being, this thing that cannot be heard or smelt or seen, call it contact, atmosphere or anything you like — it's the most precious thing for me. That is why applause is not the most important thing. "Author's songs" don't have to have anything external — no stage, footlights or spotlights. I have sung in hangars, submarines, airports, fields, in giant stadiums, in ordinary rooms, attics, everywhere. None of it matters. The situation, the circumstances are not essential — the atmosphere is...

...People always ask me why I turn so often to the theme of war. In my view, that is an idle question. As long as people write music and poetry, they will always be moved by this theme. What people say here is serious, simple and clear.

My very first war songs were written for the film *I Come from Childhood*, and since then I have kept recurring to this theme, not only because I am commissioned to write songs for a play or a picture but also because of an inner urge. I would like to make one thing clear about these songs: they are in no way songs of retrospection — I cannot recall anything because I did not see anything of the war. They are associations, songs of association. They are written now by a person living in the present, for people most of whom have not been through the war, or people whose war is in a very remote past. But all the same, the war affected everybody: in this country, every family has someone who died or was wounded in the war, and my family, too, suffered heavy losses...

We must not forget that: and this is yet another source of my songs.

At our theatre, there is a play that I like more than any other — *The Fallen and the Living*. It's a play about poets and writers. We made an arrangement of verses of poets who fought and fell in the war — Kulchitsky, Bagritsky and Kogan. In the play, the poets walk along three paths from the rear of the stage, with a backdrop of black velvet, poets who were twenty or twenty-one at the time, and who only had time in their life to write a few fine lines, fight and die... One of them, Kulchitsky, volunteered for a reconnaissance patrol and fell in battle. He is buried in a common grave on Sakharnaya Golova Hill near Stalingrad (now Volgograd.— *Ed.*)... Then the poets go back, they file back into the black velvet, that's a poetic metaphor, the black velvet stands for the earth, they go back into the earth, into their common grave. Then the Eternal Flame flares up right there on the stage, poems are recited which were written by their friends who also fought at the front but survived the war, and songs are sung about the men who died in the war, and about that time in general. It is a requiem for them... I wrote several songs for that play.

But there is yet another reason why I write songs about the war. The fact is, I mostly write about men who risk their lives, men who may look death in the face at any moment, men in the most extreme situations. If we were to choose a symbol for all those songs, that would be *Unruly Horses*: "Along the chasm's edge, upon the precipice's brink..." You may have noticed that even in my comical songs I choose characters to whom something is going to happen this very next instant, not people who are taking it easy or chewing food — it's not interesting to write of the latter. In short, I'm interested in people to whom something has just happened or who are on the threshold of the unknown. Mostly I find such characters in the wartime, in the stories about the wartime.

For example, the song *All the War, to the End...* is dedicated to a friend of our family, twice Hero of the Soviet Union, pilot Skomorokhov. This song was written for the play *The Stars for a Lieutenant*; at concerts, I sing it, explaining in a brief introduction that the song is about the great air battle over the Kuban region in 1943, in which a great many planes fought on both sides. Among others, there was the famous German Udet squadron there, in which several pilots were awarded diamond crosses. One day our pilot, Skomorokhov, avenging the death of his friend, found one such diamond pair (he was allowed to go on individual sorties) and destroyed it in a dogfight... I was told this story by my uncle, who himself fought with distinction and was awarded Red Banner Orders.

In the numerous letters that I receive, one and the same question is often asked: Did I fight? Did I serve in the Navy? Was I a lorry driver? Was I a pilot? — and so on, depending on the kind of song that person had heard. There is this strange habit of identifying the image created onstage or on the screen with the person creating that image. Amazing things happen sometimes: I'm asked, for instance, "Why did you kill the horse in the film *Two Buddies Served*?" Or, to take another example: after the TV film *The Place of the Rendezvous Can't Be Changed*, many letters were sent to this address: "To Captain Zheglov, Interior Ministry." (Captain Zheglov is the hero of the serial.— *Tr.*). I mean to say, some people believe that such a person actually exists, and the actor Vysotsky simply observed him and then played the role. In the same way I am identified with heroes of my songs, so that I sometimes even feel hurt. If I sing, "I'm a YAK fighter plane...", that does not at all mean that I used to be a fighter plane. Or take this one, "I'm a sixth-class fitter..." — I've never been a fitter. The listeners are apparently misled by the fact that I use the first person singular in almost all of my songs, so they keep asking me if had gone through all the events of which I sing. Unfortunately, I cannot answer all those questions in the affirmative, for, although I have indeed been through a great deal, I'd need several lives to experience everything of which I sing.

You know, once a very well-known personality dropped in on a party, and the people there decided to count how many times he would say "I" per minute. He said "I" seven times in the first minute, and eight, in the second — by the stopwatch. I'm always afraid to fall into this extreme, but I believe that I can risk saying "I", because this does not come from egotism, but, first, from the fact that there is a great deal of my thinking and fantasy in my songs and, most importantly, in all these songs I express my own view, and my view only, of the world, of its problems, of persons and events that I sing of, all of them without exception express my opinion of and judgement on the theme of which I sing. That's what gives me the right to say "I". Second, unlike many of my brethren who write poems, I am an actor first and foremost, and I often play the roles of other persons, I often wear the skin of another person. It may be easier for me to sing from within another person's image, and that is why I always say frankly: it's more convenient for me to sing that way, on behalf of a certain person, a certain character. And you can always see that person. Perhaps that is the reason why some people ask if I had ever 'galloped like a horse? No, I haven't...

...I've been lucky in my life, for we all of us write poetry in our young age, and we all of us would like to go on doing that in the future, but then we fall prey to the worry and hurry, we start doing other things, and we drop writing poetry... I didn't, because I joined the Taganka Theatre and began to work. My comrades at the theatre respected what I was doing, and they suggested that I write lyrics and music for the plays. I think they suggested that because my songs were unlike anyone else's, because I did not imitate anyone. Indeed, I did not imitate anyone, and regard imitation in general an idle and fairly stupid thing to do, since the original is always better. Of course, there is the art of parody, but that is quite another thing. And people who simply imitate the manner of singing seem to believe that all they need do is breathe cold air at a window in winter, drink cold beer, and they will have mastered the Vysotsky style. It's all rubbish, I've never done anything like that to my voice, I've had it from the beginning, it only changed slightly over the years in which I made numerous appearances in the theatre and in concerts. I must say, though, that there are so many imitators now that I sometimes can no longer say myself whether it is I singing or not, except for a few intonations. In Odessa, for instance, I was shown someone standing behind a stack of tapes so high you could barely see him, and the records were marked "Vysotsky". When I asked him why the tapes were so expensive, all he said was, "Get lost". But then he recognised me, for there was my portrait on the boxes, and offered me ten per cent, if I provided him with several new songs. On each of those tapes, there were about 30 songs recorded, of which five were sung by myself and the rest by a fellow named Zhorzh Okudzhava. So you see, he borrowed Bulat's surname, sang with my voice, and the songs were sometimes mine, sometimes Bulat's, and mostly God knows whose.

So I always say that I categorically reject imitations. Imitation never yields good results. And I simply call on the people who have command of this unsophisticated instrument, the guitar: you mustn't try to imitate anyone, least of all myself. Even in ordinary life, the most interesting thing there is is talking to a personality, someone who has an individuality, an opinion and judgements of his own.

I want to state, and I insist on it, that "author's songs" require a great deal of work. A song lives side by side with you all the time, it worries you day and night. It takes just a few moments to record it, and very long time to work on it. If anyone should form the impression that it is easy work, then the impression is quite false. I often explain during my concerts that if everything I do apart from "author's songs", apart from the poems, is put on one scale — I mean my work at the theatre, the cinema, the TV, the radio — and my work on the songs, on the other, the second scale will outweigh the first, I believe. The reason is, I repeat, that the song keeps worrying you, it nags at your soul demanding that it be poured out on a white sheet of paper and, of course, in music. I work with a small tape-recorder, I start with a musical phrase, and if it's no go, I change the meter. But that's behind-the-scenes stuff.

* * *

...The theatre made a great impact on my songs. It all began with *The Good Woman of Sezuan*, with Brecht's songs. Brecht's theatre, the theatre of streets and squares, is very close to me. The thing is, I also began writing songs as a street singer, reviving the oldtime city romance. The source of those songs was the desire, shared by many of those who began life in those days, to fight against official art, against the dullness and uniformity of the musical scene. I wanted to sing for my friends, I wanted to sing something distinctly my own, something important and sincere.

Many believe that some of my songs are oldtime folk songs. There may be a kind of stylisation about them, especially in the tragic, grotesque, or marching songs. They vary in genre and theme; moreover, they were written on behalf of different persons — because I'm an actor, I played all kinds of roles (sometimes for myself only), and I believed that the same could be done in songs. It all turned out to be interconnected. The manner of reciting my verse, the meaning being emphasised by the rhythm, by the sound of the guitar, the manner of singing the songs from within a definite image — all this comes from the theatre. In their turn, the songs affect the roles I play.

The songs are born in all sorts of ways. Now a line will cross my mind, now a word, then a theme will loom, or some story will strike me, and will be remembered. But can one really explain how a song is born?

The songs I write for plays also emerge in all kinds of ways. Sometimes they exist by themselves, and, having heard them, people use them in plays. Other songs I write especially for the occasion, knowing beforehand where and when the song will sound in a play, and what character will sing it. Sometimes the need for a song is realised during a rehearsal, so we go through what I have, and if we don't find anything suitable, I write a new one. It's the same in the cinema. It also sometimes happens that songs written especially for a film or a theatre production are not included in the film, for some reason, or a theatre production may be suppressed, and then the songs live an independent life, going beyond the boundaries of the theatre. But then, they began beyond those boundaries. I have already mentioned that at first I wrote for our gang, and now too. I write for myself and my friends, as a rule. They are the first to hear my songs.

It so appears, then, that the songs did not go beyond any "boundaries", they were born outside the theatre.

As for the spreading of my songs, I don't play any part in it at all. The people themselves collect them. I believe that, just as there was not only printed but also handwritten literature in the 19th century, there now exists tape-recorded literature. The new technology produces a new kind of literature. If the great poets of the past lived now, I believe many of their works would be recorded on tape.

LPs can also be a kind of literature. For instance, right now they are going to release a new disc with my songs in France. There are city romances from ten years ago there, dedicated to my friends, and there are also some recent songs. I suddenly had a desire to go back to the fairytale style, to write something in the fantastic vein. I revived the old meanings of such set expressions as *nelyogkaya* (lit. "the heavy one".— *Tr.*) and *krivaya* (lit. "the crooked one".— *Tr.*), which became characters in a song — *Heavy-handed* and *Clubfooted*. Just imagine the scene: someone meets Heavy Hand, and it carries him God knows where, and the other one, Clubfoot, promises to lead him out of the swamp, only she can't because one of her legs is shorter than the other, and she goes round and round, in circles. So the fellow had to take up the oars himself, and row against the current.

Recorded on that disc is also a song which is very important to me — *A Parable of Truth and Lie* (in imitation of Bulat Okudzhava). Actually, it is not an imitation but an attempt to write something in the style of Okudzhava — I wanted so much to do something to please him.

There appeared in France an LP recording of my songs about the war years, which I sing to the accompaniment of several guitars.

And another one, with new songs that are·my tribute to folklore. I wrote them for the film *How Czar Peter Had His Blackamoor Married*, only they were not included in it...

An introduction to one of my LPs — a very fine, warm and professional introduction — was recorded by my friend Maxime le Forestier, a remarkable poet, composer and singer of his songs. I made friends with him here in Moscow, when he came to this country on a tour. Maxime sings in the tradition of the man whom I myself regard as my teacher in the art of the song, to some extent. That man is Georges Brassens. Le Forestier loves him very much, and he imitates him remarkably well. Unfortunately, I've never met Brassens, although he even translated one of my songs — *Stopped Mid Flight*.

Several times Le Forestier presented me to the public on French TV. I once sang on election day, choosing *Save Our Souls* for that appearance. The effect must have been very curious: there was this smooth entertainment, with very good performers, and it was all suddenly exploded by my hoarse, anguished voice. True, before I started singing, I translated in a few words what the song was about. I had the impression that the manner in which I work makes it possible to cross the language barrier.

Twice I sang at *L'Humanité* festivals. The first time was not quite a success, it seems. There was this audience of one hundred thousand. Before me, some idol had performed, and the public just wouldn't let him go. Then I appeared with my guitar, and that after a giant orchestra with drums rolling and electronic guitars going full blast. The young people naturally yelled for the previous performer, out of protest: it was a festival, after all, and they wanted to have fun. But, no: they announced a number by a Soviet singer... It's wrong to present me as a singer, generally speaking: I'm the author and performer of my songs, a guitar poet (incidentally, a genre that is traditional in France). In short, I was just someone out there on the stage trying to sing something to a guitar, in Russian, almost without translation. The audience was puzzled, and some started to drift off. After the first chords, though, they began listening — what was the chap making such a noise about? So they stayed...

The second time everything went well; they announced me properly. Besides, there must have been many people in the audience who knew me already. I sang one song in French and five in Russian. And I took care to do the translations of the songs myself. The response was marvellous, really marvellous, they wouldn't let me go, so I had to decide on the spot what else I should sing. It so appears that there are indeed no barriers to songs. The reason must be that the problems I raise concern everyone. After all, people are the same all over the world, suffering from the same illnesses and desiring the same things...

My Parts in the Theatre

...I spent a long time in search of *my* theatre. Before the Taganka, I had worked with different companies. It wasn't as if I had worked without particular pleasure, I love the theatre — but none of it became the content of my creative life, or half of that life. The other half is singing, and the cinema. And then I saw *The Good Woman of Sezuan* by Brecht, and realised that it was just the right thing for me. I cannot imagine even where else I could have worked. Nowhere else, I think... I would have dropped out of theatre, most likely, because playing, just playing, is of not much interest to me. When I am onstage, I want the people to think, to be excited, worked up. I want to entertain them. Why not? The public deserves to be entertained. During my concerts, I also make jokes, to give myself some breathing space. But I try to put some serious content in the jokes, too. Beyond the text, if not directly in the text. I prefer the Russian tradition, the Gogol tradition — laughter through tears, when you roar with laughter while your soul is sad, for none of it is so funny, after all. Now, Hamlet... I suggested my candidacy for the part myself. I had long wanted to play that role, and I had seen almost all of our Hamlets. I wanted to play it in a way different from theirs, but, more than that, in the way Shakespeare himself would want it played, as I then believed. But probably every actor thinks that way about it.

There was no special reaction in the company when work on Hamlet began — probably because right before that I had played Galileo. In our theatre, the person who plays the role is more interesting than the role itself: what is important is what that person wants to say, what his message is, and not just an actor who puts the role on like a costume. You put on a wig, change your voice, change your persona, but in the process you yourself may disappear.

That is why, when I began rehearsing, it was taken into account that Hamlet would be played by an actor already well known as the man with a guitar, a person who wrote songs and sang them, that is to say, someone who carried in himself some image. Before the beginning of the play, I would sit with a guitar upstage before a bare wall. In the prologue, I sang songs to Pasternak's lyrics which hold the key to the whole play: "But the order of acts is thought out, and the end of the road can't be changed." In our production, "the order of acts was thought out", and Hamlet knew much more than all the other Hamlets that I had seen. He knew what would happen to him, he knew what was happening to the country. He knew that he would not escape the fatal end. Those were cruel times that fell to his lot. I even wrote the lines:

> *I slept on skins,*
> *I ate meat off the knife,*
> *I always gave*
> *My vicious horse free rein...*

In our production, Hamlet is, above all, a man. A man brought up by harsh times. But he was also a student. And he was more intelligent than his playmates. He was trained for the throne, he was to reign in his country. But the throne had been seized by a regicide. Hamlet was intent on revenge, but he was against murder. And that tormented him.

At this point, I believe, I found the necessary inner move. The Hamlets that I had seen, and which you may have seen, kept searching, during the whole of the play, for proof of Claudius' guilt, in order to kill him and to justify himself, to justify his revenge. On the contrary, I keep looking for proof of the King's innocence. In the mousetrap scene, I hope to convince myself that he hadn't killed my father. I do everything for blood not to be shed. When Hamlet is told that the ghost of his father is wandering about everywhere (and that means that his spirit is not appeased), I nod as if to confirm that I could see him — and I can really see him whenever I want! My Hamlet loves his father so much, he is so attached to him that he can see him at any moment. He only has to call him for his image to appear. But all that happens only in Hamlet's mind. I believe that this is a very clear and comprehensible interpretation. And I also think that it is Shakespearean.

I don't think there are any roles which I would be unable to play, except, of course, for women's parts and those roles that do not suit my age, roles which I must no longer play. But I would never say that a certain role is heroic and some other one, comical, and choose one or the other: I'd play both with the greatest pleasure. I don't know how it would come out, but I never have a feeling that there are some roles that I cannot play.

On Work in the Cinema

My first appearance in the cinema was in the film *Girl Friends*, in which I said just one phrase, "A chest and a tub." Great stage fright. I repeated that phrase with dozens of intonations. In the end, I pronounced it with a strong Caucasian accent, in a high-pitched voice and with a stammer. That was my baptism of fire.

1960. The film *Dima Gorin's Career*, in which I played Sofron the driver. In the same year, *713 Requests Permission to Land*. Here, I played an American marine. The types were different, but neither of them was a "positive hero". Both of them accosted girls. Then came the payoff! I was beaten up in both films. That was a real introduction to the cinema: there were many takes, and the cinema is the most realistic of all arts. Everything in the cinema is realistic: the food is real, driving a car is real, the punches are real. In those days, I thought for the first time about abstract theatre or cinema seriously, and even with some tenderness. But— Anyone who has breathed the air of the sets even once will want to breathe it more and more, even if it reeks of smoke and paint and wood. Then came the film *The Penalty Kick* and, simultaneously, *Leave of Absence*. In the first film I played the gymnast Nikulin, who was mistakenly given a real horse to ride instead of the gymnastic apparatus, and in the second, a sailor from the cruiser *Kutuzov*.

So I had to mount a horse, to be "in the saddle" in more senses than one, and I had to do pretty difficult stunts. I also had to wear fatigues and scrub the decks. I have been riding horses ever since, and it came in useful in other films as well. I've never had to scrub decks anymore, but God moves in mysterious ways, and I may well have to recall the old days. Then came *The Cook*. Krasnodar Territory. The Kuban. New faces, new people, new places. Summertime. Summer heat. Beautiful evenings. Whenever I recall this, I wax lyrical. Even in these days. It is always sad to part with people with whom you have worked for six months or a year. A film is, after all, a whole chunk of life. And sometimes you never meet again people with whom you have gone through all kinds of things. This is sort of unjust. The theatre is better in this respect. Partings are not so frequent in the theatre. True, partings here are sometimes a source of real pleasure — a case of "Good riddance!" God forbid that we should meet again... In my case, though, such partings were rare.

It suddenly dawned on someone that I'm not necessarily a negative or comical character — I was selected to play the part of Volodya in the film *I Come from Childhood*. Volodya was a serious person. He had been through the war, he had barely escaped from a burning tank, and when he came back home at thirty, he was grey-haired, his face badly mangled. But nothing had soured his character, he remained a kind, gentle and sensitive chap. For the first time, I wrote several songs for the film then. They were war songs. That is why this part and this film are precious to me.

Then came *Vertical Line*. Mountains. The poetry and the hardships. Mountain-climbers. Here, too, I had to climb mountains, to practise on ice and rocks. I spent nights in the tent, listening to mountain-climbers' stories. I just couldn't help writing about these people and their life, in which such concepts as friendship, help, hope, faith, risk exist in pure form, and courage is not just a word but a way of life. Then there was the film *Brief Encounters*. Here I played a geologist who left a managerial office to dig in the earth with his own hands. He was a freedom-loving, jolly fellow, light-hearted and serious at the same time. Again I wrote several songs for the film.

After that, there was again a sudden return to "bad guy" parts — in *Two Buddies Served* and *Master of the Taiga*, where I played a White Guards lieutenant and a timber-rafters' foreman, Ryaboi. Both of them were strong men, but both used their strength and talent in the wrong direction. Lieutenant Brusentsov believed that he was saving his Motherland, but he was in actual fact fighting against it; even when he had lost all faith in the "White Cause", he continued to kill, blinded by hatred and anger. He died, when his last hopes died.

Ryaboi, on the contrary, had no delusions at all. He saw everything quite clearly, but he lived according to the laws of the wolves. According to the laws of the taiga, as he himself put it. It turned out, though, that the laws of the taiga had changed and he hadn't.

It so happened that the actors and film directors with whom I worked always became my friends. They are all different people, and each of them is interesting in his own way, although we are all of us engaged in the same important business of film-making.

At present, I do a great deal of acting at the theatre but, going back to the beginning of our story — he who has even once been "on camera", has been poisoned by the cinema for good. I have been so poisoned, and that is wonderful.

On Popularity

...During the first night *Hamlet* was played at the Taganka Theatre, I couldn't begin for some fifty minutes. I just sat in front of a wall, the wall was cold, the central heating was off. That was the way the play began: I had to sit upstage near the wall. It turned out that some young people, students mostly, had broken into the auditorium and refused to go. In their place, I would have done the same, I myself had climbed into a theatre through the roof when a French company came on tour, in my young days. That's the way I became aware of my popularity — I felt it with my back against the cold wall.

Now, about audiences: I prefer an attentive public, a well-disposed public, I'd say, regardless of the age. I would like the public to come precisely for the performances that they want to come to. I'm delighted that the people want to hear the songs that we call "author's songs". The listener and the performer are well-disposed toward each other, they are mutually disposed to listen and "tune in" to each other. When people come to see

Vysotsky in the flesh — well, I don't like that. One is likely to spend half the concert teaching the audience that everything is normal, that the person they see onstage is that very person — and only in the second half does the listener become free from this, and begins to react naturally to whatever goes on.

Audiences vary greatly. The age differences do not worry me at all, they don't impose any limitations. The young people react very well. It is no accident that the actors of the older generations are so fond of young audiences. I even like children's audiences, I write many songs for children — although children, strange as it may seem, like adult songs.

I like the atmosphere of encounters at which you have that sense of ease. When you work and work, there is no time to worry if you're more popular today than yesterday. There is one way of getting rid of cheap popularity, one way to avoid resting on your laurels, and that is doing your job. As long as I can hold the pencil in my hand, as long as all sorts of things run through my head, I shall go on working. It is a good antidote against self-admiration.

This prompts an answer to the question, why have my songs become so popular? The answer would be something like this: in these songs, there is a friendly mood, I address myself to my friends. This seems to me to be the secret of my songs: there is trust in them. I trust absolutely my audience, the listeners. I believe they will be interested in what I tell them.

It would be nice to switch on the lights in the audience, I would like to see the listeners' eyes; otherwise it'll be a bit of ordinary play-acting... "Author's songs" rule out any deception; here you have just one person with a guitar standing before you all night, face to face. There is one thing that "author's songs" take for granted: that the same problems, human fates and ideas worry you as they do me; that injustice and the people's grief rend your soul just as they do mine... That is what "author's songs" need: your eyes, your ear and my desire to tell you something, your desire to hear it.

"Author's songs" seem to be a really living thing, for one instantly becomes part of an organism that includes those who sit in the auditorium. The pulse of this organism is conveyed to me. It all depends on you and me.

If there are no people to whom you sing, it's the same as if a writer burnt a short story or novel that nobody had read. It's the same with me: once I have written something, I want everybody to hear it, of course. That is why, when you hear me say "Dear comrades", that is sincere. We have all learnt these two words by heart, they sound as a cliché. Everybody says "Dear comrades" or, say, "Comrade, will you give me a light?" That's the wrong sort of "comrades". Real comrades are friends, the people that are near and dear.

...I would like my spectators to see how hard and full of drama the path towards harmony in human relations is. In general, I regard human emotions as the main goal of my creative work — in the cinema, the theatre, and in songs. Only this force can lead to spiritual perfection.

POETS SPEAK OF A POET

THE RUNNER

There's no rest, no delay on the steep endless way;
Though the mouth may be dry, without fear or dismay
Push ahead, try to seek out the goal.
On your feet nearly dead, you are running ahead
Of the times — on your heels, gloomy shadows' tread.
Shadows fly where they want, but you want no reward
From the sinister ghosts which you've always abhorred,
Which you've judged and condemned in your soul.

Posts flash by, on the roadside, like omens of fate,
You're alone on the road, bent on some fearless feat,
Neither brothers nor friends, not through slander or praise,
None will help you — no force great enough can be raised,
And are you not, yourself, a born rebel?

Like a bullet in flight, hot winds whistle in the night,
But you sometimes feel cold as you run, as you fight
For a quick breath of air that's as brief and unfair
As your life without rest — not a moment to spare
In the battle against infinite trouble.
You, eternal unlucky luck's herald and friend,
Your perpetual race in the night — can it end?

THE DREAM OF A CENTAUR

We dreamed of him then as we mourned.
If there'd been humans on the moon,
They'd have had dreams of him — undreamed, uncanny.
That dream of mourning fell on all
Like an enormous pitch-black pall.
We're trying to forget it — but how can we?

The horse in *my* dream had his face.
The horse's bell rang like his voice.
He was a thoroughbred, that dapple grey.
The driver whistled — whipped the horse —
He did not know whose face it was.
There were deep potholes all along the way.

Life's like a driver — or a clown —
And in full stride the horse went down,
It was as if an apple-tree was felled.
And those who loved him, wailed aloud,
And those who did not, looked devout:
They also loved him now — for being dead.

THE POET

Don't call him bard, or any other
such thing: he was a poet by nature.
We all have lost our younger brother
Volodya — the entire nation.

He's left to us Vysotsky Streets,
a Lévi-Strauss tribe, and the stunned
land stretching from the bleak Far East
to blazing Black Sea shores, unsung.

All that Vysotsky left to us —
his songs and films and TV serials —
the people's loving, gracious hearts
save from the perilous leap year.

Now all around your turf-edged mound
keeps growing an eternal crowd.
You wanted ever to be known
not as an actor but a poet.

Right as you enter the Vagankovo
we dug for you your home in death.
So now you, Hamlet of Taganka,
are covered with Yesenin's earth.

The downpour puts the candles out...
And all that's left — Vysotsky's soul
packaged in tapes, the countless crowd,
like bandages off wounds, takes home.

You lived and sang and acted, grinning,
you Russia's love and Russia's pain.
You will not stay in black-box limits —
you will break out of all constraints.

You sang Yesenin and Shakespeare,
your soul in 10 *g* overload.
You spoke of things to Russians dear
so that we got lumps in the throat.

All scribes will be no more than scribes
living in lines on brittle paper.
A poet will live on in the sighs —
a million sighs of myriad people.

*   *   *

The poet's dead *. Thus Hamlet died once, tested,
By slander, sword — and then by poison slain.
The poet's dead — we are alive. With justice,
We have no right to speak of him in vain.

Words suck on poets' fame and name like leeches,
And gossip's deadly — can't you understand?
A poet's fate is — dying in the trenches,
While dreaming of the flowers in no-man's land.

Men of his reckless faith, where are you now?
Where are the friends for whom he so much cared?
The poet's dead — his ravaged heart gave out:
No heart could bear what his heart had to bear.

There is much gossip among knaves and sops
About the broken strings that ring no more.
The poet's dead, and we can no more hope
That this is just a rumour, as before.

He's free from his ridiculous renown,
He's gone beyond all borders, lands and skies,
He's sleeping buried in a mass grave now,
Where Russian poetry also buried lies.

The poet sleeps, with all his magic power
Intact, himself as silent as the night,
And Russia, voiceless since that mournful hour,
Is unaware yet of her hapless plight.

And on the earth, July's warm rains are ringing,
And sadly smoulders our lives' fragile thread,
And countless poets countless songs are singing...
They can't replace, though, him who now lies dead.

---

* The words echo the beginning of Lermontov's poem on the
death of Pushkin.— *Tr*.

THE BLACK SWAN

Night yet another star has stolen.
The light is gone.
I'll pick up the guitar that's fallen
And sing a song.

The words are sad,
And sadder still
The tune we hear.
A life
Cut in mid song, I will
Remember here.

Again we hear the raucous song,
It rings in us.
So many destinies were wrung
By that hoarse voice.

Defying death, in heavens soars
Your fearless soul.
You black swan, there's no voice like yours —
I can't sing so.

His films and tapes our memories rake.
Sad rings his song.
And on the record's glossy lake
The swan lives on.

The swan lives on...

THE SONG SELLERS

They're grilling kabob —
                    spitting coals and burnt fat.
Nearby on the beach
                    you can buy a cassette.
Here, loud from the booth a familiar voice sails.
An impudent poster:
                    "Vysotsky for sale."

Volodya,
        you're now so beloved by these hordes
of owners of cars with Hi-fi tape recorders!
Kabob-smelling fingers
                    push
                        tape-cassettes in,
and, though you're no more,
                    willy-nilly you sing.

You sing in a huckster's
                    dream of a car
for him and his chocolate-smeared
                            whore.
The huckster gives tongue —
                    it's the most he can feel:
"This feller is good:
                    I won't sleep at the wheel!"

Volodya,
        between
                sheer hell and paradise,
it's awful, to sing
                for those whom we despise.
But, fortunately,
                no cassettes or headphones
will ever steal our
                dying groans.

You spread
        among students in Paris
                the Word,
You sang to the back rows
            of all the world.
You flew in a chopper
            and dropped from the sky,
and sang for prospectors
            in swamps by the fire.

You were our Hamlet
          and our Chelkash *.
The hucksters won't get you,
           nor any other trash.
Your funeral was fit
        for a genius or hero.
A genius may flare
        for an hour or an era.
You were a poor genius of the '70s — which
were not in poor geniuses
        terribly rich.

There was Okudzhava —
        sad, gentle and wise,
but yours was a harsher,
        a more biting voice.
There is in your voice,
        soul-shattering, hoarse,
an echo of cries
        from old-time peasant wars...

Kiosks on the beach
        selling kabob and songs.
A brief life is over.
        The cheap sail is on.

---

* Chelkash — a freedom-loving smuggler in one of Gorky's stories.—*Tr*.

REQUIEM

The summer has flown.

The birds have flown.

You've flown away...

The wind bangs the doors
of telephone booths
near the Vagankovo Cemetery.
Maple leaves are burning
and smoke reaches out
towards heaven's face
with its long, dark, thin fingers.
It's as if someone there in the earth
were suffocating
and wanting to climb out
catching at anything that comes to hand.
Yes,
things are really cramped
down under the earth.
Tombstones
stand shoulder to shoulder,
crosses of stone and iron are crowding
like old women
queueing to buy immortality...
I did not see a single familiar star
except you,
my brother, Volodya,
Your Highness Vysotsky.
You are lying
out there
at the edge,
near the gates,
where passers-by
like to feed the pigeons.
You're lying there,
yourself a passer-by,
and a pigeon, and pigeon's feed.
Perhaps they made you a gatekeeper?
Well, if that is so,

I beg you:
do not be silent —
speak, sing, whisper (you can do it all).
Let them realise
that there should be no more dying,
that there is no more room
for the dead
either in the earth
or in heaven,
that there is no more room
behind this ancient fence.
Soon
death will spill over the fence
like milk boiling over.
It will all flow out
and get mixed with life.
And that will mean the end of the world.
Please stop them all,
Volodya!
Tell them that they *have* to live!
Tell them that they *have* to rise from the dead!
Tell them that you've left just a little room
underground —
only for me,
for we have to say to each other
something very important,
and we have to write yet another
ineffable song,
to appear in it,
to disappear in it,
when evening
comes.

Bulat Okudzhava

*   *   *

Of Volodya Vysotsky I wanted to make up a song:
Yet another will never back home from the journey return.
People say that he sinned, that he shouldn't have burnt out
so young...
He just lived as he could, and without sin there aren't any men.

We shall not part for long, very soon we shall also be gone.
Just a moment will pass, we'll be out of this, hot on his heels.
Let it soar over Moscow, his heart-warming, hoarse baritone —
We shall listen and cry, we shall listen and smile through
the tears.

Yes, I wanted a song of Volodya Vysotsky to write,
But my hand shook, and verse did not jibe with the melody
rightly.
The snow-white swan of Moscow flew up in the sky
spotless white,
And the black swan of Moscow on black, mourning-black
earth alighted.

REMINISCENCES

"Leave curiosity to the mob,
and take the side of the genius."

*From Alexander Pushkin's
letter to Pyotr Vyazemsky. 1825*

KINDNESS WAS HIS MAIN CHARACTER TRAIT

Talk between Nina Maximovna Vysotskaya and Ogonyok
Correspondents Sergei Vlasov and Felix Medvedev

When Volodya was born, we lived opposite the Riga Railway Station, in Pervaya Meshchanskaya Street, which is now Prospekt Mira. He was an amusing child; he began to talk very early. The first sentence which he pronounced, standing on the porch of our dacha, was, "There it is, the moon." (In Russian, the two parts of the sentence rhyme.— *Tr.*) By the time he was two he had learnt a great many poems by heart, and recited them with expression. Reciting, he would always climb on some kind of dais, mostly a stool. In July 1941, when Volodya was three, the Germans began to bomb Moscow. I took my son to an air-raid shelter, and there he would find something to climb on and recite poems, loudly and with expression.

After one such performance, a middle-aged man came up to me and said softly, "Thank you for your son," and kissed my hand.

Soon we left for Buzuluk, in Orenburg Region, and lived through all the hardships of the evacuation together. We lived in a village, and I sometimes brought him a cup of milk from work, which he shared with other children, saying, "Their mothers aren't here, no one's going to bring them milk."

People often ask me how come that my son knew wartime life so well, the war ended when he was not yet seven. He learnt a good deal from his father, with whose family he lived in Germany since the age of nine — his father stayed with the army there after the war. It was also important that Semyon Vladimirovich was a regular army officer, he fought in the Battle of Moscow, liberated Lvov and Prague, and took part in the storming of Berlin.

Volodya also loved to talk to his uncle, Lieutenant-Colonel Alexei Vladimirovich Vysotsky, a war veteran and writer, who undoubtedly made a great impact on him. He also learnt a great deal about the war from his father's wartime friends.

When Volodya finished school, the question naturally arose where he was to continue his education. Volodya stated quite resolutely that he wanted to enter the Theatre Institute. But none of us, I mean his relatives, wanted that. Besides, Volodya's friend, Igor Kokhanovsky, wanted to enter a civil engineering institute. They handed in their applications together, and soon became students of the Moscow Civil Engineering Institute.

I borrowed a drawing board from some friends of mine, proud that my son would soon become an engineer. But the drawing board was mostly used by Igor, a diligent, industrious boy, while Volodya was constantly distracted; he would drink coffee, or just pace the room, deep in thought.

I closely remember one evening, or rather late at night, when they worked at their drawings at out place. That was in the middle of the first year. Suddenly I heard my son shout: "That's it! No more of this for me! I'm not studying at this institute any more!" Entering the room, I saw Volodya pour Indian ink on his drawing. I still keep it.

"I've had enough engineering activity," he said laughing. "Can't stand it any more."

I went to the Dean's office. The Dean summoned Volodya and told him in my presence: "Vysotsky, you mustn't make a rash step. You have a distinct talent for mathematics."

"That's as may be," Volodya said confidently, "but I don't want to be an engineer, and I won't. It's not my cup of tea, don't you see? So why should I occupy a place that is meant for another, someone who needs it more than I do."

Back home, Vladimir told me: "Don't worry, Mother, I know the time will come when I'll be onstage and you will be sitting in the audience, and you will want to whisper to any stranger sitting next to you, 'That's my son'. I'll be an actor, a good actor, and you won't be ashamed for me."

Somehow, I believed him, and did not worry as much as I had.

He must have worked hard that six months before he joined the drama studio?

Yes, he worked very strenuously all that time. He studied at a drama circle run by Vladimir Bogomolov, a Moscow Art Theatre actor. One day I dropped in at the studio when they were rehearsing. Volodya was playing the part of a peasant who came to the railway station to buy a ticket, they told him at the booking-office that there were no tickets, but he was going to get one all the same. It was the first time I saw him on the stage, and I can still remember how amazed I was to see the completely unexpected actor's devices he used. After the rehearsal I came up to Bogomolov and asked him (although I knew the answer already): "Can Volodya devote his life to the stage?"

"He can and he must! Your son has talent," he replied.

Volodya would stay at the studio until late at night. He told me how they rehearsed, how they built the sets themselves, how they made the costumes. That was a time of totally devoted apprenticeship. Volodya devoured book after book; true, he loved books all his life, and he collected them assiduously."

Did Volodya write poetry in those years?

Volodya and Igor Kokhanovsky began writing verse when they were still at school. Igor still has a thick notebook which they filled with their poems. They chose themes from school life, and the verses were really funny, as far as I can remember.

When did your son begin to sing?

It all began during the first year at the drama school. He must have borrowed something from the boys from our street he mixed with. But he began to sing his songs when he graduated from the theatre studio. He had a remarkable memory, he could recall almost totally a story he read just once, or a long poem he heard once. When he was only a child, he could recount the story

234

of a film or a play he had seen in great detail and with considerable expression.

Did he find it easy to enter the theatre studio?

No, the exams proved very difficult. The situation was complicated by his hoarse voice. I remember hearing someone refer to my son: "Which Vysotsky is that? The one with the hoarse voice?" Volodya went to a professor, a throat specialist, who provided him with a certificate to say that his vocal cords were in order, and that his voice could be trained. He was prepared for the exams by Bogomolov, who can be said to be Volodya's first teacher in the art of theatre.

The artistic director of their year was Pavel Massalsky. Volodya worked with great enthusiasm, he spent whole days at the studio. I remember going to the Yeliseyevsky foodshop right before closing time to buy a few buns, sausages and butter, and taking it all to my son and his friends. Volodya spent a great deal of his time on parties, friendly satirical sketches, that sort of thing. He had the gift of grasping other persons' nature and expressing it through action and words, and he fearlessly parodied his teachers — Massalsky, Tarkhanov, Kedrov. Radomyslensky, the rector of the studio, once called Volodya an incorrigible satirist. He also loved mocking at himself. He didn't like to speak of himself in any but the joking vein.

Do you remember your impression of his first song? What did you think of it?

You know, I didn't like his earliest songs, which were far from elegant. They are now referred to either as underworld songs, or as gutter songs. Frankly speaking, I did not take his song-writing seriously in those days, and neither did he, I believe. Later he realised that verbal art called for a different attitude, and he began to work in earnest. I realised for the first time that my son was writing real songs after the film *Vertical Line*. After that, I listened to his songs avidly, and that was the only way to listen to them: whether he sang for an audience of thousands or to just one listener, someone who simply dropped round, he put his whole soul in the song, as if he were singing for the last time in his life.

Which is your favourite song?

Wolf Hunt. Incidentally, when that song was born,

Yevgeny Yevtushenko (a Soviet poet.— *Tr.*) sent him a telegram from the North, where he was on a visit to the Navy: "Heard your songs twenty times running. I go down on my knees before you."

All of Volodya's songs were a continuation of his life. He would often come to me at night and say, "Ma, I've written a song." So I would be his first listener. If it wasn't too cold, he threw the window open, as if the room was too small for him, and then belated passers-by would invariably gather below in the street, and they would sometimes argue if it was a tape-recorder or an LP being played. Later he would more and more often sing his freshly written songs to Marina Vlady, his wife, although she'd sometimes be thousands of miles away. The bills for his telephone conversations, or rather telephoned concerts, sometimes ran into three-digit numbers, but he took it all in his stride. "Mummy", he would say, seeing that I was worried about his expenses, "we earn money to spend it." With his impatience, it was at first difficult for him to have to wait for the connections to be made before he could speak to his loved woman, and the song *07* (the digits you dial to get an inter-city connection.— *Tr.*) was written one such evening when he was waiting for his call to Paris to come through. Later the telephone girls came to know him well, they put him through at once, and sometimes listened in on those extraordinary concerts.

Where did he find the time to do it all? He acted in the theatre, played in films, travelled all over the Soviet Union and many countries of the world, wrote screen plays, prose and his countless songs. There are hundreds of them...

Volodya wrote mostly at night. That was his habit since his youth. When he moved here, to Malaya Gruzinskaya Street, I almost never stayed the night here, for he would pace the rooms nearly until morning, pencil in hand, "chasing the rhyme", as he said. He never went to bed before four in the morning. And by 10 o'clock he had to be at a rehearsal in the theatre. In the morning I would sometimes come and wake him; he would ask what time it was; if I said, five to nine, he would say, "Oh, I can sleep five minutes longer". And he would fall asleep at once.

Generally speaking, he believed that sleeping was a waste of time. His favourite phrase was, "We got to work!" (the original is in broken Ukrainian.— *Tr.*). Of course, this excessive strain undermined his strength. How often did I tell him, "Volodya, you can't go on like this, you're heading for a fall." The fact was, he had heart trouble in his childhood.

Did he know that?

He did, and still he worked as if bent on wearing himself out. He hurried to get things done... Several days before his death, fate seemed to give him a sign, or a warning. He was driving a car with some friends; suddenly he felt ill, he went pale, the hands became damp; he got out of the car and realised it was the heart... Still, he continued to work in the same way as he had. Apart from everything else, he had a duodenal ulcer...

Did he take any treatment?

He didn't! Although we did our best to talk him into it... Only once did he go to the hospital to do something for the duodenal; even then, they intended to keep him for forty-five days, and he ran away after less than two weeks — he begged Marina to bring him his clothes. She would come to the hospital in the morning and stay there until lunch, and in the evening she'd go there again, to make him stay there. If she hadn't, he wouldn't have stayed there even those two weeks. Marina brought him all the latest medicines, and the ulcer became better after the treatment, but the heart —

What did Vladimir write his poems on? In notebooks, or on sheets of paper?

He never had a special notebook. He mostly wrote on sheets of paper, but he would write on anything that came to hand — theatre programmes, a box of cigarettes, a bit of wrapping paper, or carton.

During his lifetime, there was not much of a hurry to publish his work — putting it mildly. How did he take it?

Once I overheard a telephone conversation of his. They called him from some editorial office to say they couldn't publish his verse. "So that's that," he said, "excuse me for troubling you." He then walked to the window, stood there awhile, and then suddenly said in a sharp voice,

237

"They'll publish me! After my death, perhaps, but they will!"

Even during his lifetime, though, his poems were "published" in "publications" that were dearest to him — on the tombstones of mountain-climbers.

You knew his character well. What was his main character trait?

Kindness. This was obvious in his childhood already. He would gather the children from our house in Pervaya Meshchanskaya and feed them all, or give away his things to them — toys and books and shirts. This remained his main feature throughout his life. When friends struck by some misfortune came to him, a well-known actor, he would often go to the wardrobe, produce a sweater or a jacket and give it away. I saw many people wearing his things. He believed it his duty to help others. He might have his hands full, but he would always drop everything and hurry to help someone who needed his help. One day he brought a box of fruit home — that was in winter — I asked him, who is it for? It turned out that he was going to a hospital: a son of a friend of his fell ill, and he needed vitamins. Another friend was involved in a car crash, so Volodya dropped everything and rushed far away from Moscow; he spent days and nights by his bed, and then took him to a hospital in the capital, all by himself.

He had many friends; still, whom did he regard as his closest friends?

As I said, at school he was friendly with Vladimir Akimov and Igor Kokhanovsky; at the theatre, Valery Zolotukhin and Ivan Bortnik were closest to him. Towards the end of his life, he told me once himself that his best friends were Vsevolod Abdulov and Vadim Tumanov, the well-known geologist.

One day he was sitting here on this sofa, where you're sitting right now, and he suddenly said, "You know, Mother, I just discovered that I have not less than a thousand friends — and I have brotherly, open relations with all of them." I believe he spent about three-forths of his free time on his friends, on helping them. He had a very special gift — he could help people when it seemed impossible to help. He often said, "Folks deserve to live well." He said it with a lower class accent, to make it less highflown...

THAT'S WHAT MY SON WAS LIKE

An interview granted to Vladislav Starkov, editor-in-chief of the Argumenty i fakty *weekly, by Semyon Vladimirovich Vysotsky*

It would be interesting to know in what environment your son grew up, what he saw of the world, what his interests were. All sorts of legends are current about all this.

Volodya was born in Moscow. Till the age of nine, he lived with his mother, Nina Maximovna; between 1941 and 1943 they lived in the Urals, where they had been evacuated. As for me, I was at the front until the end of the war.

Since January 1947 Volodya was brought up in my second family; he lived with us in the town of Eberswalde, Germany, where I was stationed. Volodya had the best of relations with my second wife, Yevgenia Stepanovna Likhalatova. My wife and I were eager to teach Volodya to play the piano — he had absolute pitch, as his German teacher of music said. He was a diligent pupil, but between school and the music lessons he was guilty of boyish pranks that were a matter of great concern to us: now he would explode a grenade in a neighbouring forest and come home with his eyebrows singed; now he would swim alone across the river Finow, which was not yet fully cleared of mines and shells. We resorted to a stratagem: Yevgenia also began taking music lessons. The ruse was a success: Volodya did not play as many pranks as before.

Soon we returned to Moscow, all three of us; we settled in Bolshoi Karetny Lane, where Volodya went to the fifth form of School No. 186, which was next to our house. He finished school in 1955. During the whole period when Volodya lived with us his upbringing, both in Germany and in Moscow, was mostly in my wife's hands, as I finally returned to Moscow in 1953.

In 1955 Volodya moved, together with his mother, to a new flat at 76, Prospekt Mira, which she then received. Even afterwards, though, he very often came to Bolshoi Karetny, to our place in Flat 4 to see his friends who lived in the area of Samotyochnaya Square. After 1960, when my wife and I also moved to another flat, the one in Kirov Street, Volodya kept coming to 15, Bolshoi Karetny, to see his friend Levon Kocharyan; in the latter's flat in the third floor he became very close friends with Vasily Shukshin and Andrei Tarkovsky. There is a questionnaire which he once filled out; under the section "Your favourite place in a favourite city", he wrote, "Samotyoka. Moscow."

Did it ever occur to you that your son would be a musician or an actor?

Frankly speaking, never. When he finished school, I advised him to enter an engineering institute, confident that my son must become an engineer by profession. He passed the entrance exams easily, finished his first term successfully, and then suddenly dropped out. That was quite unexpected to us.

At that time Volodya must have realised what his calling was?

Yes, he soon joined the Art Theatre's drama studio, and from then on he followed his own path. He learned to play the guitar using a self-instructor book, and he sang not only his own songs but also those of Bulat Okudzhava and Yaroslav Smelyakov. He complained that the musical education he received in his childhood was not enough. The fact is, he was very exacting in his demands on himself.

Vladimir was a very purposeful person; he did not spare himself at all. He had a remarkable memory, and this helped him greatly in his studies, and was later especially useful in his poetic and artistic creativity. I sometimes compared myself to him: in the army, especially during the war and during manoeuvres, the strain is also terrific. I believe, though, that his style of life was much more strenuous and intense than mine. Volodya sometimes slept not more than four hours at a time, and wrote songs mostly at night, because in the daytime he rehearsed at the theatre or worked at film studios. Incidentally, there were no stunt-men to stand in for him in films. He rode wonderfully, he swam, he was a fairly good boxer, and he knew the basics of karate.

What was your attitude to your son's songs when they were so unjustly criticised?

Frankly speaking, I always liked his songs. I refused to agree with those who saw them as "manifestations of decadence", "advertising anti-social elements", that sort of thing. Sure, there was irony and sarcasm in his songs, but my son always studied closely man and the soul of man, he always wanted to find the grains of the good in that soul; he sought for, and saw, the ways for perfecting that soul, and he was deeply aware of his responsibility before the country and the people.

You are a military man. It is apparently no accident that war themes are very strong in your son's creative work. Please, tell us a few words about your friends, about those whom Volodya met in your home.

My friends from the war years often came to our place both in Germany and later in Moscow. They always remained to him "Uncle Sasha", "Uncle Lyonya", "Uncle Kolya". Volodya dedicated his *Ballad of the Dead Pilot* to one of them, twice Hero of the Soviet Union Nikolai Mikhailovich Skomorokhov, now Air Marshal.

I saw that Volodya always listened with great attention to the veterans' stories of heroic feats and everyday life at the front. Conversations with myself and with my brother Alexei Vysotsky, awarded seven orders during the war, of which three were Red Banner Orders, were the source of many of his poems and songs about the war. My brother and I fought from the beginning of the war to the end, fighting for the liberation of our own land and of the peoples of Poland and Germany from Nazism; I also fought in Czechoslovakia. I served in the army until 1971, when I retired with the rank of a colonel. My brother died in 1977.

We know that Volodya saw something of the world. What did he tell you about his travels?

He visited many European countries, the USA, Canada; he particularly liked Mexico; he even went to Tahiti. Naturally, he often talked to members of the bourgeois press, who eagerly looked for hints at oppression in the USSR. Although certain officials, who had a say in the publication or nonpublication of his poems, in the matter of recording LPs, and so on, could be said to have been guilty of a kind of oppression, he was always above these intrigues. He had nothing but fine words to say about his Motherland. He missed his home and his friends even in the most interesting, exotic countries. You can find confirmation of this in his poems and songs. The whole people knows them.

How early he died! How did it happen?

After we returned to Moscow from Germany in 1949, a heart murmur was discovered during a medical check-up at school. It disappeared by the age of sixteen. In the last years of his life he kept secret his heart trouble. He lived a very intense life. He flew to Tahiti when there was danger of an infarction. On the last day of his life he intended to give a concert. He did nothing by halves. But he had no strength left. The doctors were powerless to help him. His first heart attack proved his last.

Our grief will not be cured by time. We are comforted now by official recognition of our son's work and by the love for him shown by the people. It also gladdens our hearts that Volodya's two wonderful sons have grown up. They have also followed artistic professions. The elder, Arkady, has graduated from the Cinema Institute, the younger, Nikita, has followed in his father's footsteps—he has also graduated from the Moscow Art Theatre's drama studio. He has recently returned from the army, and is now working at the Sovremennik Theatre, the young actors' studio (Sovremennik-II). They have children of their own: Arkady has a daughter, Natasha, and son, Vladimir; Nikita has a son, Semyon.

So life goes on...

Iza Vysotskaya

LIFE WAS WONDERFUL
WHEN VOLODYA WAS ALIVE

I do not remember what date it was, or what day of the week. It was 1956. We had been to the virgin lands in Kazakhstan on a concert tour. We had cruised the steppe in a lorry, chasing tumble-weed. We came back to Moscow chock-full of impressions, having gone through a baptism of fire at the hands of very young, very boisterous and extremely varied audiences. We rehearsed *Hotel Astoria*. Freshman Vovochka Vysotsky appeared among us, third-year students; he played the tiny role of a soldier. He was a very funny, very amiable and kind boy. He had an innate readiness to like anyone, a readiness to help anyone, to make a gift of himself.

In the spring, we celebrated the official approval of *Astoria*. A noisy student party was joined by the teachers; there were the famous speeches by Veniamin Radomyslensky; we split at dawn. But Volodya held on to my hand and wouldn't let me go. Everybody had gone, but we stayed back; we walked to Trifonovka. Later, we would often walk about Moscow, along the boulevards, at night and in the grey hours before dawn, quarrelling and making it up. I would keep running away, and he would pursue me. One could be capricious with him, one could play the fool, taking nothing seriously.

Later that boy with the hurried, slightly jerky walk, that naughty and funny boy became my own one, my loved one. It seemed then that he would always be at my side, cheerful and loyal.

Long yet fast years would pass, and Volodya would become drier, his face harsher, but he would stay loyal to the end — loyal to the inner core, to the dream, to comradeship. There would be pain breaking through the laughter. But when we saw each other, we would again laugh easily, and I never noticed the years that had passed.

...We had a whole half of a room, the left side. It was our youth whispering, laughing and crying there on the vast bed behind a screen in Prospekt Mira. Volodya was like a gust of wind, but he would stop in mid flight when I moved towards him, he would become all ears, the pupils would distend, absorbing all, taking in the pain and increasing the joy. How often I laughed softly, for it was too late at night, as Volodya told me so many stories from the life of the street! Little by little these stories became polished miniatures, funny, comical, but never malicious.

He also recited Mayakovsky wonderfully. Especially *The Bedbug* and *The Big Clean-up*. It was as if all the characters came to us behind the screen, they felt quite at home there, quite free and easy, and they would act each in his own manner.

We were engrossed in Remarque. The silence of total immersion came upon us. Somewhat later, it was Hemingway—*To Have and Have Not, The Sun Also Rises, The Old Man and the Sea*. It all sounded like an incantation.

Volodya would wake up at once—joyous and amazed. He would receive a clean shirt, a cup of tea, any little thing, as a wonderful gift; he would run away to the Pushkin Theatre, leaving a store of joy behind, and I would wait for him to phone—it was all interesting to me, whether he'd got to the theatre in time, whom he'd met, what they'd said, when he'd be back, or where I'd have to meet him, everything. The orange cigarette-packs lay on the window-sill like bits of the sun, funny nonsense on bits of paper, a ringing street outside.

* * *

A sunny summer. We are returning to Moscow from Gorky on board a real ship. The ship's huge wheels slap against the dark water, working it up into snow-white froth. The tiny cabin smells of hot wood. We watch out for the sunsets-and dawns, and we listen to the damp silence of the night.

That summer, we were shooting *Foma Gordeyev* in

Gorky [1]. Zhora Yepifantsev (he was in the same year as Volodya) played Foma, Alla Lyubetskaya, a year older, was Lyubov Mayakina. We went to my parents' place, and, of course, ran off to see our friends. Alla was badly ill. There was a break in the shooting. We decided to go to Veliky Vrag—a place where the right bank was very high with great many ravines sloping towards the Volga and the left bank smooth and endless. I knew and loved this place, wild, empty and of an ill fame, for many drowned here: the Volga ran deep and wide here, with a strong current.

Enchanted by the view, the boys decided to swim across the river. I was awfully frightened and, sobbing, rebelled, but my little sister Natasha and I were strictly told to sit quietly, to keep our eyes open and not to obstruct the husband in performing feats of valour.

We could no longer see the arms swinging, the two heads moved farther and farther away. A long barge lazily drifted by. Where were the boys? Ships passed, the time dragged interminably. We felt frightened and cold. Natasha was quite small then, she was hungry. "Do we have to die of hunger, if they're drowned?" she asked. I was in a stupor. Suddenly I saw the boys. They had swum across the Volga. They had been carried too far downstream, and had travelled back by boat. There they were, walking along the bank, absolutely tired out and absolutely happy. The world was beautiful again.

...I have just seen a TV programme on Oleg Borisov [2], and again I became immersed in the past. Right after the drama school, I had the great luck of working side by side with the great actors of the Lesya Ukrainka Theatre in Kiev. Volodya often visited me. One day he crept into the auditorium during a rehearsal of *Uncle Vanya* [3]—Mikhail Romanov never allowed strangers to be present at rehearsals. Suddenly, sensing someone's presence in the balcony, he asked sharply: "Who's there?" "Nobody—so far," Volodya replied, and was allowed to stay.

Life was wonderful when Volodya was alive. Everything was bright, everything sounded fine and smelt fine, the joy was greater and the tears, sweeter. One day, a guitar appeared back there in my wonderful life,

245

and it at once became my tormentor. Volodya sang as much as he could and whenever he could—even when he shouldn't have. There were three of us now.

In the spring of 1981, I ran to the Hermitage losing my way in the back streets and lanes. The boys were waiting for me there, Volodya Akimov and Arkasha Svidersky, the friends of Volodya's childhood and of our youth. The Hermitage (a theatre in Moscow, not the museum in Leningrad— *Tr.*) was our regular meeting place, of course; memory is wandering there, and I fear going there alone. We are three. We soon get over the changes we observe in each other. We are young again, we feel fine again, Volodya may come up to us any minute and say, "Here I am!"

THE FATHER THROUGH THE EYES
OF THE SON

An interview given by Vladimir Vysotsky's son Nikita to S. Bogdanov, cadet of the Lvov Higher Military Political School

Nikita, to what extent was your decision to work in the theatre motivated by your father's example? Can we say that there may be a sequel to Vladimir Vysotsky's work in the theatre?

My father's example most certainly played a role in my choice of a profession, but it mustn't be exaggerated. When my father died, I was only sixteen. Of course, he took my brother and me to rehearsals, to performances at his own theatre and the Art Theatre, he talked to us of his work. Largely, my decision was made already in those years. But I failed to enter the theatre institute first time round. For a year, I worked at a plant. In 1986 I finished the Art Theatre drama school. I was invited to work at Sovremennik-II.

Many say that my acting is much like father's. Of course, one cannot escape comparisons, but I want to be myself.

Did your father talk of his problems and failures with you? Did he discuss his plans with you?

I was quite small in those years, and my father did not, of course, let me in on everything. Even in these days I keep learning various facts from his friends and colleagues. There were very few people with whom he discussed his plans, not more than five persons. He trusted his friends. But he never spilled his difficulties and his anguish before them. He was more likely to bear their share of pain himself.

Many people felt amazed that he should have sung so much. Was it to entertain people? Hardly. That was his testing ground. He often created things while we relaxed.

Vsevolod Abdulov, one of my father's closest friends, once told me a characteristic episode. My father came to his birthday party after a performance at the theatre where he had worked as if it was his last performance—as usual. He came there exhausted, yet he sang all night. When he finished singing, he looked out of the window: dawn was breaking. A whole night had passed... This kind of little things are valuable in that they put the finishing touches to the portrait. Some people, those who do not know many of the intimate details, are sometimes puzzled by various, sometimes controversial, facts from my father's life. That is the drawback of many publications about my father's life: they show details of his life out of context. Thus a reader may learn from a publication like this that Vladimir Vysotsky gave five concerts in one day. The natural conclusion that he will form will be that Vysotsky raked in money by the shovelful. Hence the fantastic gossip about his millions, about his dachas... Yes, he did sing a great deal, especially in the last years of his life. But people begged him to, they phoned him, they came to him, they tore him to pieces.

We are saying now that he worked at a difficult time but remained true to himself. He was one of the few who dared to say that attempts were made to stop his mouth, who dared to speak of the things he did not accept — and he said this not just among his close friends but for the whole country and the whole world to hear. The creator's courage is not only in saying something but in saying it before audiences and in terms that count. To speak out clearly, and with talent; above all, to speak honestly and truthfully.

I always feel a sort of mistrust for Vysotsky's thoughtless admirers or fans. Inadvertently, they fritter away the main thing about his work — his thoughts. These people have nothing in common with him.

What sort of a father was he?

There were times when we wouldn't see him for months. But he was always very attentive to us, he remembered us and took care of us. In general, he was very tactful in his relations with people; he always tried to see their point of view, to see how they felt.

What do you feel when you see films in which your father played?

What can Shukshin's relatives feel when they see him on the screen? Or Dahl's relatives? There are a great many people who simply reject Father, his very appearance irritates them. For me, he is like a breath of air. He was a unique actor. He had excellent technique, he moved marvellously on camera, and had a great way with the spoken word. In all his parts, he played himself first and foremost. He never did slipshod work. There were failures, of course, but film-making is a collective art. I don't believe there is a single failure that could be attributed to him personally.

Did he lend an attentive ear to those who discussed his work? What was his attitude to criticism?

Father knew how to listen to people. He was very attentive when his work was seriously analysed. But such attempts were too few. There was no debate as such. Access to publication was forbidden him, and he therefore developed, through his work, a very strict editor within. My father knew what he was worth, he was never a thoughtless self-made man in art.

After Father's death, there were several publications in the national media in which he was openly denigrated — as in S. Kunyaev's article "From the Sublime to the Ridiculous". They said that father's verse was illiterate doggerel, and that his orientation was all wrong. We realise now that it's all nonsense. Whatever they may say, the people will never cease loving him.

How did he take the rejections over all these years?

Outwardly, with great humour, but in actual fact he was pained and embittered. During his lifetime, he was not even called a poet or a bard — merely an "author and performer of songs". But there are many people in this country who are called that, and there are great distances between separate individuals. He felt it, he saw it very well. He applied several times for membership in the Writers' Union. After Father's death it became known that his last application was not even considered, as there were no grounds for it — he had no publications to his name, although his songs were performed in films and in theatre productions, that is to say, they were seen as literary productions. He was not in need at all of the Union's privileges, all kinds of "Holiday Homes", writers' titles, etc. What he needed badly was the main thing —

recognition of his personality. Many writers, including well-known ones, are now proud of their acquaintanceship with Father, of the fact that he visited them and sang for them, but it was these prominent writers who stopped him from joining the Union.

I believe — and I'm not alone in thinking so — that the whole point here is the stature of his personality. Dullness in art — and not in art only — finds it hard to survive next to a great talent, for the talent makes the insipidity obvious.

We know only too little about his concerts abroad, including the concerts he gave for the emigrants.

During his concerts here, he sometimes discussed his tours when answering notes from the audience. His concerts for the emigrants were not a kind of political statement or anything like that. He realised that these people were uprooted, torn away from their Motherland, and he sensed the tragedy of their position. He had no intention to emigrate — he even wrote a song about that. He ruled that out, although he was offered several chances of which I know for sure. He was offered everything — official recognition and money. But he would not sell out his Motherland.

The last question now. You begin your career at Sovremennik? Why here, and not at Taganka?

This was a distinct possibility. It was even discussed. Everyone was well-disposed towards me there. But, firstly, I want to have an independent career of my own, although I haven't changed my name, nor do I hide whose son I am. Secondly, the experiment at our drama studio is interesting and promising. As we see it, our theatre must be acutely socially relevant, with special emphasis on conflicts. Very interesting young actors are working here. As for my father's themes — they're close to me, they will be my life and my pain.

I'M LIVING THANKS TO YOU...

A talk between Marina Vlady and Leonid Pleshakov, an Ogonyok correspondent

"Marina, the longer the time since Vysotsky's death, the more we want to know about him. He has left us his songs, his parts in films. His friends have published memoirs. Still, one wants something more — details that would tell us of his character, his habits, likes and dislikes, all those trifles that make the image of a person three-dimensional. You were at Vysotsky's side the last twelve years of his life. You observed him in situations in which no one else saw him. He wrote his last poem for you."

"I understand it all — Volodya's vast popularity in the Soviet Union, and the interest of his admirers for his life and work. But my story of life with him would hardly satisfy those who expect something breathtaking. It was really an ordinary family life, just like everybody else's."

"Do you remember the way you became acquainted?"

"It all happened a bit romantically and at the same time, one might say, quite simply. In the summer of 1968 I played a part in Sergei Yutkevich's film; I brought my two older sons, Igor and Peter, to Moscow. The younger one, five-year-old Vladimir, remained in Paris with his granny. Over here, I sent the sons to a Young Pioneer camp near Moscow. After a week of shooting, I would go on Sunday, quite early in the morning, like all parents, to visit my offspring, loaded with bags, some treats, everything as it should be. We parents would come at the time of the solemn hoisting of the flag and morning parade. We would stand aside, waiting for our children to be free, to have time for us.

"One day the boys ran over to me in great excitement.

"'Mama,' they cried, 'the boys here sing a song, and there is something about you in it!'

"And they sang a few lines from the song about a fancy-dress ball in a zoo. You remember that one?"

"Certainly. Only I thought that Vysotsky wrote it when you already knew each other."

"No, his name said nothing to me at the time. In short, my chaps were delighted that someone's written a song about their Ma, so far away from home, a song that was so popular with their new friends. So I heard of Vysotsky's songs before I came to know their author.

"We met like this. At that time, an old acquaintance of mine, Max Léon, was *L'Humanité*'s correspondent in Moscow. One day he invited me to the Taganka Theatre, which was then at the height of its success. On that night, they played *Pugachov*. Vysotsky played the part of Khlopusha. I liked everything—the production, Khlopusha, everything. After the play, we went to the restaurant next to the theatre for supper—Max Léon, myself, several actors from the company, quite a large crowd, in fact. Later, Max Léon invited everyone to his place. We had tea, we talked, and Volodya sang his songs, of course."

"What precisely?"

"All his songs. He sang a lot, he sang willingly, and he charmed us all, of course. He was a charming man, generally, he could win anyone over. That night, he was really in superb form. And I sensed that he sang especially for me..."

"Which of his songs did you like best then?"

"All of them, especially the fairytales. In short, he began dating me after that night. I saw all the plays in which Volodya had a part. He turned out to be a remarkable actor and a very interesting person. In short, I liked him, and he liked me. We became friends. We became husband and wife. Our marriage was officially registered on December 1, 1970. It was witnessed by Max Léon on my side and by Volodya's friend Vsevolod Abdulov, the actor, on Volodya's. At first we lived in hotels, where I stayed in Moscow, and in Volodya's mother's flat in Noviye Cheryomushki. When a journalist, acquaintance of ours, went abroad for a long time, he left us his flat in Matveyevskoye, and we moved there. In 1975, we bought this cooperative flat in Malaya Gruzinskaya. It became our home."

"The notion of home covers a great many nuances. It is not just a shared roof overhead, it is also the family, certain relations between husband and wife, their mutual obligations, their friends. But you lived in Paris, Vladimir here. Long-distance family life, that's not quite easy to understand."

"It wasn't long-distance all the time, not by a long chalk. When I didn't work—and that was not at all rare—I always lived here in Moscow. Sometimes several months at a stretch. But even when I was working on a film or at the theatre, I came over to my husband whenever I could. So did Volodya.

"You ask what I did here? Kept house. Went shopping, cooked meals, I did everything any wife does."

"Volodya used to say that he liked to cook himself."

"That happened—sometimes. Not too often, though. And then, there was little he could cook—fry a few eggs, or a piece of meat, say."

"And you? I hear that you know recipes not only of the French cuisine but also Italian and even African ones. You used to live there..."

"Oh, I'm a famous cook. I love to cook, and have some ability that way, only I prefer my own cuisine, not some national one. I invent recipes myself, and the result is OK. Volodya liked whatever I cooked. Although, I must say, he was no gourmet, he wasn't at all fastidious about food. He could be happy with bread-and-butter and tea. Still, I did my best to please."

"Did you have—how should I put it—difficulties?"

"Of course. We both had a temperament, a strong character."

"Do you believe you have a strong character?"

"Oh yes!"

Marina said this in a tone that left no doubt that she was not in the habit of changing her views. That was why I asked:

"Did Volodya obey you?"

"On the whole, yes..."

"And you?"

"You see, it never happened so that he had to tell me to do something one way and not another. I tried to work things out in advance, to anticipate what he would say. After all, I have a simpler personality, with greater plasticity of a purely feminine nature. Besides, he had a much better head than mine, so listening to him was nothing to be ashamed of."

"You often lived apart. Did you write to each other?"

"The first six years, when Volodya could not come over to me, and I had important business in Paris, we wrote to each other nearly every day. I have kept all his letters. Our private life is in them. I shall leave them intact. After my death, they may read them and even publish them, if that is of any interest to anyone, but for the present it is just my life and his, and let it remain so, for the time being. Besides, frankly speaking, there is nothing special in them — just normal letters of someone in love. They are purely personal, intimate, and they have no literary value. Incidentally, it has been noticed by many that even great writers' and poets' personal correspondence is much less interesting than their literary works. There must be a law of a kind here."

"If you had to describe Vysotsky in one word, which trait would you stress as the most important?"

"That is impossible. His was such a rich, generously gifted nature that it would be impossible to describe him briefly."

"Was your life with him always interesting?"

"Naturally. If it hadn't been, I wouldn't have lived twelve years with him. He was much more than a husband. He was a good friend, and I could share with him everything that was in my mind. He too told me everything about his affairs, about his plans, I was the first to hear him recite his new verse and sing new songs. He would come home after a night at the theatre, exhausted, worn out, but all the same we would spend half the night chatting of the theatre, of life, of everything."

"For this, one had to have retained intact the feeling of being in love, in all those twelve years..."

"We were lucky in that respect. Part of the reason may have been that we did not live all the time together. Partings always help to keep the freshness of feeling and to forget the trifling hitches of everyday life. Although, even when we parted for a very short time, we talked literally every day on the phone, so there was no time to start missing each other... Yet, this feeling of being in love remained."

"How did you spend your holidays, when you had them together?"

"Travelling, seeing new places. Volodya tried to show me as much of his favourite places as he could, everything that was precious to him. We went to the Caucasus, to the Ukraine, and sailed on the Black Sea aboard the SS *Gruziya*. Once, when they were shooting a film in Byelorussia, he took me along. We travelled all over the republic. We stayed in a village with some granny, and slept in a hayloft. That was wonderful, there were woods and lakes all around. You see, those were not tourist trips, when you take a look at something and roll on. Wherever we stopped, Volodya would be surrounded by friends and acquaintances, so the most important thing was always meeting people, interesting people.

"For me it was, apart from everything else, learning all about my Russian roots, a discovery of the motherland of my parents."

"When someone is dear to you, you always want to introduce him to everything that is precious to you. What was most dear to Vysotsky, as far as you could tell?"

"He loved Moscow, and he knew it very well. Not the traditional sightseeing musts which are always shown to tourists, but the city in which he was born, where he grew up, studied and worked. The city with all its intimate nooks that were near and dear to him. He often sings of this in his songs."

"He must have taken you to that house in former Pervaya Meshchanskaya, where the Natalis furnished rooms had once stood, which became after the revolution ordinary communal flats where, as he has it in one of his songs,

> *There was just one amenity —*
> *One loo to forty cubicles...*

True, there is only a part of that three-storey house still standing, and even that part is hidden in the backyard of a large house on the corner of Prospekt Mira and the Riga Railway Station square..."

"Yes, he did take me there, and also to the house in Bolshoi Karetny, where he used to live at one time..."

"Were you interested?"

"Of course. I learnt better not only Vysotsky's Moscow but also his own character, the sources of his creative work.

"In the evenings, we loved to roam the streets of Moscow. There was one thing that always struck me and amazed me—you could say it won my heart, you could hear Volodya's songs nearly out of every window."

"How did he take it? In general, what was his attitude to his fantastic popularity?"

"He was very well aware of it. Fortunately, he knew great success both as an actor and as a singer during his lifetime. He realised that the people loved him, that his work was known to all, and that it was dear to most. He would sometimes write a song, and three days later you would hear it everywhere, everyone would know it. The most amazing thing was that it was not broadcast on radio or TV, it would spread like wildfire simply because it was a song of Vysotsky.

"What was his attitude to his fame, you ask? He was certainly proud of it, deep within, but he never gave himself airs, he always remained a simple, easily accessible person, just one of the boys."

"This 'being one of the boys' was not always correctly understood, not by all people. I have met people all over the country who swore that they were Vysotsky' friends, but when you pressed them for details, it turned out that they had met Vysotsky on one or two occasions, and only in passing..."

"The explanation is easy, Volodya had such an easy poise, he behaved so naturally, that even after a single meeting a person might regard himself or herself a close friend of his. He was a very charming person, and this produced a natural response in the others. I have often observed, not only here in Russia but also abroad, how quickly he found a common tongue with extremely diverse people. I don't know even now what his secret was. I just state it as a fact.

"Towards the end of his life Volodya spoke both French

and English fairly well, so that he could do without me as an interpreter on his visits to Paris. But being able to speak and to understand others is by no means all. Establishing contact with absolute strangers, making them want to keep up a conversation with you — that is an art. Volodya did it easily and naturally. The reason may have been that he loved to talk to people, he always took an interest in them, and that was why he was interesting to them as well. Not to mention those who knew his work even a little.

"My sons simply adored Vysotsky. The middle son, Petya, began to play the guitar — not without Vysotsky's influence. Volodya then gave him a guitar as a present. He had a lucky touch: my son's youthful enthusiasm later grew into a professional occupation. He graduated from the guitar class of the Paris Conservatoire, and he now gives concerts and plays at competitions.

"All my relatives loved Volodya, and so did all my Paris acquaintances—strangely, even those who had never been connected with Russia and the Soviet Union in any way, either in language or political beliefs. People would listen to his singing for hours, entranced..."

"That's something that I cannot really understand: there are so many purely Russian idioms and nuances in Vysotsky's songs that in my view cannot be translated into another language. Without them, the whole meaning is lost. Apart from the purely linguistic difficulties, such as slang, there are so many details from our history in his songs, so many features of the national character, specifics of our way of life, if you wish—and none of this is amenable to translation. You have to be born among all these things, you must know them, in order to understand and feel them."

"Naturally, his songs can be fully understood only by those who have lived in Russia. But, apart from the lines, the songs are also marked by Volodya's temperament, his expression, the timbre of his voice, the charm of his personality—all those things do not need a translation, they can be understood by themselves.

"But we seem to have drifted away, slightly. Where were we?"

"We said that Volodya had a great many friends..."

"It would be more correct to say that he had many

acquaintances who could say that they were his friends. But if we are speaking of his closest friends, those with whom he liked to talk, to be together, not just those with whom he was on friendly terms — there were not more than a dozen, probably fifteen, but not more. They were people from different walks of life — poets, writers, a merchant captain, actors, a director, a radio engineer, a geologist. Their occupations were a reflection of the interests of Vysotsky himself. He loved them all, and they loved him, only not as Volodya's usual admirers did, but as a person, as a comrade."

"What was it that he valued more than anything in them?"

"I cannot speak for him. The circle of his friends automatically became my circle. I had it all given to me readymade, so to speak. I only know that they were interesting people, that they and Volodya were always glad to be with each other, that they have remained true to his memory. I see them rather rarely now, but even if we meet just once a year or once every five years, I'm sure that I can fully trust them, with my eyes closed, and I can rely on their support."

"What did you like most of the things he did?"

"In the theatre it was Hamlet, of course. Although he played other parts superbly, too. The parts of Svidrigailov or, say, Lopakhin. I still cannot understand why no video recordings were made of those productions. It is so simply done, given modern technology: you just set up a camera and make a record. How many people could have seen the plays for which it was impossible to get tickets! These records could have been left to the future generations, too. There was so much waste in all this...

"In the cinema, his best roles were those of Don Juan in Pushkin's *Little Tragedies* and von Koren in a film after Chekhov's *The Duel*. I believe that no one could have played them as he did. But that is a matter of taste. Other people may like other roles he played."

"How did he write his poems, his songs?"

"Everybody asks me that, but it is so hard to answer this apparently simple question. Volodya had great capacity for work, and great love for it, you might say. The stage, rehearsals, acting in films, solo concerts — it was all an endless race that took up 18 hours of his life a day.

Even at rest he could not just sit around doing nothing. He was always busy doing something, speaking to people, learning something, writing something down. But I cannot say how or why a rhyme or an image came to him. He could leap from the bed in the middle of the night and write for several hours running, like one possessed. But that is a purely external observation — I cannot say what the inner spring of his creativity was."

"I was surprised to see that there are fewer books in his study than I had expected. Quite a few, in fact, but not as many as I had expected. And what an elegant desk..."

"There is nothing peculiar about this. Volodya never wanted to collect books simply to boast of a large library. There's only that on the shelves which he loved, that which he kept rereading, and wanted to have close at hand at all times."

"Which books did he read again and again?"

"Above all, Pushkin. Volodya adored him. I don't know anyone else who would read Pushkin just as well as Vysotsky did. He liked very much Pasternak's poems, too.

"You were struck by the desk. We were once told that they were selling the furniture that had belonged to Alexander Tairov and Alisa Koonen *. We went to see it, and we liked it very much. It was fine old furniture, not of great value or anything, simply it had a soul, unlike this modern trash. It was also precious to us because it had belonged to the people of the theatre. There was quite a lot there, but we chose what we liked best: a bureau, some chairs, a desk. The heirs were in such a hurry to sell that they left a few postcards, drawings and notes written by Tairov. Volodya loved working behind this desk."

"I heard that he wanted to put in a wall or screen in his study, right behind his back."

"There was some talk of it. In his childhood and youth Volodya lived under very crowded conditions. He

---

* Alexander Tairov (1885-1950) — director, one of the most radical reformers of Soviet theatre, founder of "synthetic theatre". Alisa Koonen (1889-1974) — Tairov's wife, and a great actress (at the Moscow Art Theatre and the Kamerny Theatre).— *Tr.*

only had a tiny corner to study in. Even in Matveyevskoye, where we had a large flat, his study was wery small. This became a habit, apparently; he felt more comfortable at work when there was something behind his back. But I noticed at the same time that he did not require any special conditions to write. He could work anywhere: at hotels, on a ship, at his friends' dacha, visiting friends — anywhere."

"Is it true that he wrote down his verses on anything that came to hand: on a bit of paper, cigarette packet, anything, and that a great deal has been lost because of this?"

"That is not quite so. Indeed, when the long-sought-for rhyme or word came, he could write it down on anything, but he'd never lose it. Anything that he wrote down in a hurry would be typed at once. He was in general a very tidy person, and especially in everything that had to do with his creative work."

"We have grown accustomed to the fact that in his songs Vysotsky responded to all sorts of events in Soviet life, to extraordinary manifestations of human nature, to anything that broke familiar stereotypes or, on the contrary, was a highly characteristic feature of a certain stratum of society. It did not matter much what or who he wrote of: one could feel that the subject was of great concern to him, that it did not leave him indifferent. It is strange, though, that you have travelled with him all over the world, you've been to so many countries, and none of it has left any trace in his work. There's so much about our life here and almost nothing about life 'out there'. Perhaps it didn't move him? Didn't excite him?"

"I don't believe that this is correct. Vysotsky wrote not only songs, as many of his admirers believe. Apart from songs and poems that did not become songs, he wrote prose (excellent prose, in my view), scripts, sketches of travel. I read them—they're fine pieces of writing. Some of them describe our trips."

"Do you remember how his last poem was written? 'Ice down below, ice up above—I freeze between...'"

"Of course. In the summer of 1980 Volodya was in Paris with me. Time came for him to return to Moscow, I couldn't join him—my sister Tatiana was dying of cancer. She had had a long and terrible sickness, she had attempted all kinds of cures, and the doctors seemed to have done everything to save her, but she had only several days to live. I had to stay by her side. Then there was a part in a film. You can imagine what I felt.

"It must have been a day or two before he left for Moscow. Volodya saw a bright picture postcard, the kind that is pushed in one's letterbox over here to advertise something. He fiddled with the card awhile, then began writing fast between the lines of the advertising text and on the margins. When he finished writing, he read it to me. I liked the poem very much, and said, 'Give it to me.' 'No,' he said, 'it needs some rewriting. I'll send it back to you from Moscow by telegraph'.

"Indeed, he rewrote a few lines and sent it to me.

"After the funeral, I turned the flat upside down, trying to find that advertising postcard. I knew he would never throw it away. And I found it. I now keep it as the most precious thing he left me."

I first heard lines from that poem during the civil funeral service for Vysotsky at the Taganka Theatre. "I'm living thanks to God and you..." That was said about Marina, One could have hardly recognised her then, in the last minutes of parting with Vysotsky. She was always so sure of herself, always cheerful — and there she was, struck down by grief. There were grey hairs never seen before. I would never have dared to bring up that terrible day, but, since she had mentioned it first, I asked:

"I'm sorry, Marina, but had you expected that so many people would come to pay their last respects to Vysotsky?"

"I knew there would be many. Very many. But I had no idea, of course, that the gathering would be so vast. I remember all Paris coming to the funeral of Edith Piaf — there was a great crowd. She was very loved by the people. But a great many more people came to Volodya's funeral, although it was not officially announced. The people learnt of it themselves. I'm saying all this now because so many years have passed, and I have seen documentaries, photographs, I can now look at it from the outside, so to speak. At the time, though, I could hardly take in anything. It was all in a fog. There was just one thing thudding in my head: Volodya is dead, Volodya is dead..."

"There was a great deal of talk over here about a memorial for Vysotsky. I'd be interested to know your opinion."

"There were very many designs for a memorial sent in for the competition. It was all organised on very democratic lines, and any sculptor could take part. Of all the designs suggested, I liked most of all the monument in the form of a slab of granite sunk in the earth and struck by a meteorite with bits of stone sent flying. With just one word carved on the stone: VYSOTSKY. Everyone knows when he was born and when he died. Those who don't know — well, they just needn't know. That would be a symbolic memorial, it would say laconically much more than those memorials that intended to convey facial resemblance. I'm sure that no sculptor, even the most talented one, will be able to convey this resemblance. He was too varied and many-sided a person. If anyone should see what sort of person Vysotsky was, they can go to the cinema. But — a memorial? And anyway, in his song about it Vysotsky stated precisely what sort of a monument he would not have liked to see on his grave. He laughed in advance at any attempt to achieve a portrait-like resemblance."

"What are you engaged in in Paris now?"

"I play at the theatre. Films, too. But mostly I'm busy with myself. Trying to pull myself up—"

Marina gestured, as if pulling herself up by her hair. I did not quite understand.

"Where are you pulling yourself from?"

"The bottom..."

"What bottom?"

"You know what. Just live through what I have, and you'll understand. In one month, I lost two persons that were closest to me — my sister and my husband."

"You still cannot come to?"

"No. And I shall probably will never come to. Right now I'm trying to work a great deal, to soothe the pain somehow. I was very lucky—I had a lot of work both in the summer of 1980, and after."

"What have you at home, to remind you of Volodya?"

"A book of his poems. His photographic picture from

Galileo. It has been with me since the first days we met. A very interesting portrait. A severe one. Volodya stands, in profile, leaning over a burning candle...

"And his songs, of course. Our friends have searched out and recorded everything that he has ever sung in the theatre, the films, on TV, at concerts, and even what he sang for his friends only."

"Do you often listen to these records?"

"No. I don't listen to them at all. I cannot hear his voice when he is no longer alive. It is unbearable."

Vladimir Akimov

VOLODYA (The Years of His Youth)

The peace that we had awaited so long still reeked of the war.

The German prisoners of war were clearing Moscow of the ruins, and building houses. They built them solidly and thoroughly. Just the way they had killed.

There was not enough bread for the children in the devastated country. Not enough for the POWs, either.

A family of two — and there were very many of these—redeived less than a loaf of rye bread per ration, plus a bit as a makeweight. The third member of the family, the father and husband — was lying in a grave in a place where he had defended them from those who were now smiling so ingratiatingly near bread-shops.

The less-than-a-loaf of rye bread had to be brought home in its holy intactness, the makeweight could be eaten on the spot. On the other hand, it could be exchanged for any one of incredibly beautiful things: a ring made of a three-kopek piece with bits of coloured glass made to look like semi-precious stones, a penknife, a lighter made of an empty cartridge shell or transparent plexiglass. And the children traded their bits of bread for all these things, staring, fascinated, at the pocket of the alien uniform stained with whitewash and the blood-red brick dust, in which the makeweight disappeared. The prisoners of war were excellent artisans.

The thunderstorm had passed, but the thunder still rumbled — in the souls and in the fates.

The same steel ballbearings were used in home-made wheel-carts of the legless and in children's scooters. District public education department still issued soldiers' underwear to the children once a year—the undershirt and pants that their dead fathers could no longer wear.

...On a cold October day of 1949 Volodya and me were sitting in the square opposite the Screen of Life cinema eating a watermelon we chipped in to buy. We nibbled at the rinds until they were white.

The feeling that we talked of something extremely important on that bench always stayed with us. The point, of course, was not what we talked about in any precise sense. What was, or could have been, so special about the things that two fifth-formers who had only recently seen each other for the first time might talk about?

We must have talked of what we had read and seen, of what we knew. It had so happened that I stayed in Moscow all through the war, while Volodya was evacuated, together with his mother Nina Maximovna, in 1941, and then, since January 1947 had lived in Germany, where his father, Semyon Vladimirovich Vysotsky, a Signal Corps officer, had served after the war. We must have talked about those POWs, of course, and about bread — the bread-shop was across the road, on the corner of Karetny Ryad, where now stands the house in which actors of the Bolshoi Theatre and variety actors live. But none of this was important. Frankly speaking, we did not remember ourselves later what we had talked about.

But even many, many years later, one of us (it was mostly Volodya) would say — no matter whether we would be alone or amid the hullabaloo of a party:

"Remember that watermelon we ate?"

And we would be plunged back into something really intimate, sitting on a bench holding in our freezing hands the icy watermelon. In the evil October wind. In which we felt warm.

We counted that day as the first day of our friendship.

When we were older, we set a date to that event—19 October. Or rather, one day when we recalled that watermelon for the umpteenth time, we fell to thinking: what date it was? Unable to recall anything definite, we decided—let it be 19 October. After all it was the Lyceum day, when people remembered their friends (19 October was the day Pushkin and his circle met to celebrate their graduation from the Lyceum. See Pushkin's poem *19 October.— Tr.*). After all, it may have really been 19 October. God alone knows. We were both eleven at the time, and we were pupils of the Fifth E Form of

Secondary School No. 186 of the Komintern District of Moscow, in Bolshoi Karetny.

Excellent pupils were disliked in those times. "Underachievers" were not respected. Average pupils evoked no feeling at all, as if they were nonexistent. The normal thing was something on the swing pattern: an excellent mark followed by a bad one, or the other way round. Of course, no one kept to this norm consciously: it all happened that way by itself, as there was a very rich life outside school, and an interest for that life was literally tearing us apart: we had to be in time everywhere, we had to see and take a hand in everything, there were a thousand and one things we had to do in one day, and no time to do them in.

Volodya's progress at school was smooth and easy, no effort at all, even somehow cheerful, and that cheerful spirit ran over the edge, producing all kinds of small miracles.

When the school door was firmly blocked by a shell-shocked watchman who had the Headmistress' orders not to let anyone with a schoolbag until classes were over, who was it thought of a way out? Vovka Vysotsky. Our well-worn schoolbags, officers' bags, gas-mask bags went flying out of the third-storey windows like missiles from ancient catapults, dropping heavily under the feet of scrawny old women mincing towards the Central Market-place. The old women, who had seen, in all the hard times that had fallen to their lot, much worse things, found the dead zone in no time flat, and dived for cover by the school fence as quickly and smoothly as old foxhole troopers. In the meantime the watchman, mumbling something, we couldn't understand what, opened the door before a tidal wave of boys rolling down the stairway. The watchman was a well-disciplined old soldier: no boy with his schoolbag could get by him; without the bag, it was OK; could be a physical training lesson, or something; none of his business.

It was spring. Those first precious days. The grey-black snow lay shrinking in the corners of the school grounds, but the asphalt was drying already. Moscow's old-timers, the sparrows, deftly pinched the crumbs from under the noses of the clumsy dirty-grey doves which had recently appeared in the capital—no one knew where they had been brought from and for what purpose.

The guard on the tower of the prison separated from our school by a narrow asphalt pathway watched, with good-natured curiosity, our boyish games near the brick wall warmed by the sun. Someone would be kicking a tin, someone else would drop on the asphalt in a spectacular save, ripping his only trousers and bruising the long-suffering knees. No time for French irregular verbs, no time to find out which of the two travellers would arrive first at point A from point B. Life was the subject! And we studied that subject diligently and purposefully, learning each day a bit more of its infinite wisdom. There were strict rules here, and a mistake cost much more dearly than a mistake in a dictation. "Never hit him when he's down", "one fights one", "fight till first blood", wear a knuckle-duster or a lead weight, and you might be bashed by the friends until your enemies took pity on you. Picking a fight with a boy accompanied by a girl was regarded as indecent, still more so, picking a fight with a grownup. Cowardice, selling out, stained you for life. Universal contempt. There were all sorts of other unwritten street laws, but they were LAWS, and any transgression against them was never forgotten by the boys' community of freemen.

I'm sorry to have digressed, though, rambling in the groves of childhood, leaning over its pure springs, unmuddied despite everything, over its waters with all kinds of beetles and spiders, lilies and the rest of the botanical nonsense.

Speaking of botany: the subject was taught by a teacher who, like everybody else, had a nickname. Children of all peoples and ages are experts at bestowing nicknames, it's just the sort of eye they have, ironic and wise; taking offence at those nicknames is both silly and sinful. Some do take offence, though — and how! One day that teacher gave us a homework assignment — we had to grow mould on some object and bring it to school. The assignment was very difficult for those times, next to impossible, for anything that was remotely edible was eaten long before it could be covered with mould. On the appointed day, Vovka Vysotsky seemed to be the only one (except for a straight A crammer who brought some garbage in a tidy jar) to bring a mouldy carrot.

I refuse to describe the events that followed. Let the reader imagine them for himself, bearing in mind that that was the teacher's nickname — The Carrot.

After that, no one dared call Vovka The American—a hickname that *would* crop up from time to time ever since the first day he appeared in our form on his return from Germany. Certainly he was an American: a ginger-coloured suède jacket, almost wearing a tie, proper footwear, while we all wearing God knows what, just rags somehow patched up; soldiers' high boots were seen as a hardly conceivable luxury. Sure he was an American.

Mama Zhenya, as Volodya called his stepmother, told me many years later that, running back from school on that first day, Vovka howled a long time demanding that they dress him "like everybody else"!

There were all sorts of people among our teachers — just as anyone else's I suppose. I shall mention only some of them, if that is of any interest.

Mikhail Petrovich Martynov. Our physics teacher and head of studies. Tall, solidly built. He was handsome, that special handsomeness of courageous, strong and intelligent men. A war veteran. I never heard him yell at anyone. A stern look was enough. He had a phenomenal memory: he remembered all the classes that graduated in the years of his teaching at our school and headmastership at the neighbouring girls' School No. 187 (No. 30 now). When we learnt that Mikhail Petrovich — that was the respectful way we referred to him, even among ourselves — was going to transfer to another school, we felt sincerely dismayed.

Nikolai Timofeyevich Kryukov, nickname Walrus — for his thick grey moustache. An excellent mathematician. A rough but effective sense of humour. He fought in the First World War, an artillery lieutenant. Awarded the Order of Lenin for his service as a teacher.

Mirra Mikhailovna Fischer. The teacher of literature in Form 10 D to which I was transferred during our last year at school: after Mikhail Petrovich's departure, the teachers at last decided to break up the Vysotsky-Akimov-Kokhanovsky threesome.

Unlike the absolute majority of literature teachers of those times, Mirra Mikhailovna taught us, above all, to think. Just as a teacher of music would train the pianist's hand.

Nadezhda Mikhailovna Gerasimova. Headmistress and teacher of history of the USSR.

At the beginning of 1953, Volodya and myself skipped classes one day to see a film at the Hermitage cinema—*Let Freedom Ring*, one of a number of Hollywood films. We had been told that there was a fantastic sequence there in which the noble hero fought a gangster boss. The fight was all it had been cracked up to be.

In the two days that followed the temperature was below 25° C. It was the law that schools did not work on days like this.

When it grew warmer and we began studying again, our escapade was forgotten. We ought to have stopped there, but we must have sounded so enthusiastic in our account of the action-packed film that our class-mates could not stand the temptation. We joined the crowd. First, we couldn't very well abandon our comrades, and secondly, we were fired by our own eloquence. We weren't fifteen at the time.

The following day, the whole form was told to go home and fetch our mothers. The interrogation was conducted by Nadezhda Mikhailovna.

"Why did you play truant?"

"Everybody went, so I went along."

"Who was the first to give the call?"

"Dunno. Someone yelled. Someone behind my back."

"So," Nadezhda Mikhailovna would sum it up. "Supposing your friends wanted to blow up the Kremlin, and you were told to blow up Lenin's Mausoleum, would you go along?"

A frozen tableau. It was, I repeat, January 1953: the consequences were only too easy to imagine. Struck by horror, our mothers stopped crying even.

She was a curious person, was the headmistress of School No. 186. She treated our class with the greatest suspicion and ill will—she even vetoed our graduation ball. Shilly-shallying wasn't her style.

But that was all in the future. At the time of the watermelon, we were at the very beginning of our friendship.

There were pill-boxes sitting heavily in the Hermitage Gardens—a leftover from 1941: Moscow had been ready to fight in the streets, if need be.

The black narrow slits of the pill-boxes frowned, like dead eyes, on our children's games.

A thin woman in a red beret could often be seen walking in Sadovo-Karetnaya Street. If she saw any teenagers ahead, somewhat older than we were at the time, she would overtake them and peer in their faces. Then she would drop behind...

We were growing up. There were neither TV sets then nor tape-recorders. People danced in the dusty stone wells of the backyards to gramophones. An electric motor would sometimes be attached to a gramophone, it would be plugged in someone's flat on the ground floor, becoming a sort of electric gramophone. That was better than nothing: you didn't have to crank the handle all the time. It is curious to remember it now, but boys danced with boys, and girls danced with girls. Separate education of the sexes was making itself felt. Volodya would come to our yard, about five hundred yards from his house in Bolshoi Karetny, and shuffled, with great abandon, to such tunes as "Baron von der Pschick", and the like, either with Mazepa, or with Bulba, Cat, or me (my sheet nickname was Kim Il-sung). At school, everybody called everybody else by their nicknames, mostly derived from surnames. Volodya was called Vysota ("Height").

Ah, those courtyards... Each had its own mood, laws and legends, its heroes and pariahs, its dramas and comedies. You could write a novel about each and every courtyard of Moscow.

The terrible rows of the communal flats over a misplaced refuse pail or washing done out of turn spilled over into those courtyards. The living quarters were cramped and crowded, which in no way helped to assuage the tempers. Weddings were rare, funerals frequent. The people who died were mostly not old at all—they had just had more than their share of war and other troubles.

The boys tore about on self-made scooters or played football, or else, having seen *Sea Hawk* or *The Sign of Zorro* for the fifteenth time, they fenced fiercely with rapiers made of packing boxboards. In the heat of the fighting, they'd shout themselves hoarse; the ballbearings of the scooters rumbled endlessly; in the corner of the yard, on the swings welded out of plumbing tubes, an enthusiastic chorus would bawl *Ships Came to Our Harbour*, the indispensable *Murka* (a song beloved by the underworld.— *Tr.*), *It Struck Twelve*, and suchlike. I still wonder how the nerves of the grownups, no longer strong for obvious reasons, could stand it all. But they did, and no one broke up the crowds of children—a fatherless lot, they just didn't know any better, and they were entitled to a bit of fun. But if an adult saw that the kids' fun and games or conflicts were getting dangerous, he was honour bound to interfere—also according to the unwritten law of the street. And interfere he did, often with little concern for the type of language he used. There would be cuffs all round, or the culprit would be dragged by his ear to his mother.

There weren't many toys in the shops, and somehow the adults never got around to buying them. The finances of many families, especially those left without the provider, were hopeless, money was scarce and too badly needed for more essential things. So the kids acquired the things they needed through barter, and kept exchanging their valuables for something more attractive.

The things that kept changing hands were scooters; toy soldiers; magnifying glasses extracted from filed binoculars and telescopic sights; zip-guns made out of brass hunting cartridges and rubber strings cut out of gas-masks; self-made pistols fired with a match, which frequently blew up, crippling the shot; all sorts of cartridges and caps; signal lights; knives and penknives; details of uniform and insignia, mostly captured from the enemy. And there was a great deal else, leftovers of the war, which often held the menace of death or maiming, unexpected and thus all the more meaningless and bitter.

One day late in May (it must have been some time in the seventh year of school), Volodya, myself and some other boys went for a swim to a place on the Savyolovskaya Railway, somewhere beyond Yakhroma.

On a high sandy bank, in a little ravine overgrown

with scrub, which we used for a loo, we discovered a box of artillery shells. Volodya, who had seen plenty of German weapons and ammunition while in Germany, stated authoritatively that those were German light howitzer shells. That was all right with us, we didn't care much if it was a howitzer or something else, the main point was that the dark-green shells contained compact noodles of cannon powder, which could be exchanged for God only knows what valuables. It would have all ended really sadly if it hadn't been for Volodya's heated arguments: one of his friends in Germany had blown himself up in precisely the same situation. However, having given up, with great reluctance, the idea of taking the shells apart, we could not stop tempting fate: a cave was dug in the steep sandy slope, a couple of shells were put there, and a fire made over them. We settled on the edge of the bluff and began to wait, mouths open and hands over ears. We waited so long that we got bored; we started a rhymed counting game: someone had to climb down and see if the fire had gone out or not... Thank God, we didn't finish the rhyme: there was a tremendous bang and stench of explosives, and we slid into the river along with a huge chunk of the bank. Which was exactly what we wanted. At first, all we could do was hiccup with fear. Then we felt elated.

The following Sunday, Volodya and myself went there again, deciding we'd leave the shells strictly alone, but there had to be something much more valuable there.

I should mention that Volodya was in general rather inclined to all kinds of mysterious searches for God knows what—but the search sometimes brought unexpected results.

There was a closet over the corridor in the communal flat where I lived, crammed with all sorts of dusty rubbish. I was too lazy to rummage among the trash, and I somehow forgot about the closet.

After my mother's death I lived alone; we were fairly grown-up already, about eighteen or nineteen. One day Volodya said:

"Look, let's dig around in the closet. Maybe we'll find something there."

"Find what?" I was taken completely aback.

"Gold," Volodya blurted out.

"You must be crazy. What gold can there be there?"

"Look, Volod, let's just dig around, OK? There must be *some*thing there, gold or whatever."

In short, we climbed up into the closet. We found no gold, of course, but we dug up the folding easel of my father, who had died back in 1947. In the paintbox, there were beautiful French oil paints, from pre-revolutionary times. Volodya was in raptures. I worked at that time at a plant and at the same time took lessons at the amateur studio for railwaymen's children; I wanted to become a professional artist. Only I never had any oil paint, let alone paints like this: they were beyond any dream. There was gold for you!

Volodya had these kind of strange insights, as if he absorbed some sort of essence through time and space, whether through the subconscious, the imagination or intuition, I cannot say, I'm no specialist here. You take this apparently meaningless phrase in the funny song "I will Be Now Like Marina Vlady..." You know what happened after he'd written it: Marina came to the Soviet Union to make a film, she heard that song, she then listened to all of Volodya's songs, she was interested in the author, they met — and hey presto! Chance, as we know, is but concealed law.

But let us go back to that day which nearly became our last.

There was a bit of unpleasantness at the Savyolovsky Railway Station: while we were buying icecream, the electric train left, and the next one would only leave in two or three hours. The big gap. So we waited.

On a dirt-track, very close to the spot where we had been the last time, we were stopped by a military patrol and literally booted back. As far as we could make out from the spate of soldierly swearwords, four kids had been blown up by a mine just an hour before.

We didn't like to remember any of this in the years to come...

We read a lot: at school, holding the book under the desk on the lap; at home, sometimes one book for two, nearly knocking our heads together: the most interesting passages would be read out loud. We read everything that came to hand, but on closer scrutiny there was a kind of selectiveness about our reading. In Pushkin, Volodya preferred the epigrams; in Gogol, the horror tales like "The Terrible Revenge" and "Viy", and these had to be read before going to sleep, for heightened effect. *Notes from the Madhouse* and the brilliant play of adventure, *The Gamblers* [1], were read many times over. *And Quiet Flows the Don* [2], *Peter the First* [3], *Port Arthur* [4], *Yemelyan Pugachov* [5], which were then printed in Leipzig—the Germans were still paying the reparations—were swallowed in no time.

Like all boys, we had a weakness for books of thrilling adventure, but there were vexingly few of these.

We then decided to make up for the shortage of thrillers through our own literary efforts. Our source of inspiration was, frankly speaking, *Engineer Garin and His Death Ray* [6].

In the eighth form, we filled four notebooks, each 24 pages long, with something that we called *Apparatus IL*, the IL standing for *ispepelyayushchiye luchi* (annihilating rays). We were in no way worried over the discrepancy between the abbreviation and its possible foreign equivalent. The notebooks have long since disappeared: we must have given them to somebody to read, or something. I am naturally hazy about the details of the plot. The action was set in France and the USA.

The daughter of the professor who invented the IL apparatus comes to a villa near Paris and, seeing her father's arm dangling from a window, realises there must be something terribly wrong with her Dad. It is only too true: Dad's rubbed out, the apparatus pinched. I remembered this well, because we were terribly proud of the arm detail.

Later, reports come of nightmare heists of banks in the USA. The daughter realises that the apparatus is over there. She flies across the ocean. The chase is joined by a policeman, the brave Sergeant Smith. Knowing absolutely nothing about the USA, except for the fact that Negroes were continually ill-treated there while the whole country was shaken by mass demonstrations for peace and socialism, we were still right about the policeman's rank — there are fewer policemen of the officer rank out there than over here.

The shoot-outs and chases took place entirely amongst skyscrapers. The sergeant and the professor's daughter naturally fell in love with each other. We believed that we had a real thriller on our hands and saw no reasons why it should be rejected for publication; we therefore decided to write an ending the way it should be, the way it was accepted among real, grown-up writers: having caught the bad guy, Sergeant Smith would quit the police and join the demonstrators. We started writing it several times, but each time boredom stopped our pen dead. So we dropped the idea. We hadn't yet heard the term "time-serving", but we felt that there was not much joy about the thing. And we couldn't stand boredom.

Time passed. The pill-boxes in the Hermitage Gardens were dug up and taken somewhere.

Stalin died. For three days the Hall of Columns was open to the public. The whole of the city centre was cordoned with troops and mounted police, the streets blocked by lorries filled with sandbags and by trams, in order to avoid the tragedy of the first day, when an uncontrolled mob in Trubnaya Square trampled to death a great many people, mostly schoolchildren.

Getting into the Hall of Columns was regarded as an act of particular valour among us kids. Volodya and myself, we got there twice — through all the cordons, sometimes begging, and sometimes lying; climbing over roof-tops, attics, and fire escapes; through strange people's flats whose back stairs opened onto other streets or communicating courtyards; under lorries; under the bellies of horses; up and down again, getting out of the most varied scrapes: we ran and we crawled and we climbed and we jumped and we somehow got through. That's how we paid our last respects to the Leader.

Vladimir Vysotsky's first appearance on the boards, so to speak, dates from that time, too. It happened in the neighbouring girls' School No. 187. The senior forms from our school were traditionally invited to their parties. When the girls' amateur theatricals were over and the long-awaited dances could at last begin, Volodya burst onto the stage and reeled off several Caucasian stories. They were absolutely decent, almost sterile. But very funny. Later, though, there was little fun for the performer. Volodya couldn't explain himself what had possessed him, especially as there had been no talk then of an artistic career for him.

We were growing up. It was us now whom the woman in the red beret caught up with in the street, peering into our faces with quick, somehow birdlike, eyes...

As for Nikolai Gogol, there hangs yet another tale by that name. In the spring of 1962, Volodya, myself, and our friends Levon Kocharyan and Artur Makarov went to the Arbat where Artur's friends, husband and wife, both teachers, lived. Zhenya Urbansky beautifully sang to a guitar. His striking, manly voice was in perfect harmony with his looks and talent. We were sitting in a fairly large room with a low ceiling, crammed with old furniture that was also low: all kinds of cupboards, chiffoniers and bureaus. A long narrow chest stood by the wall, covered by something old and patchy — that was an exhibition piece in this house, and an old lady, the host's relative, introduced newcomers to that chest as if it was a living being. "Gogol used to sleep on this chest," the old lady solemnly announced, and she was so ancient that no one would have doubted had she said that she had personally heard Nikolai Vasilyevich saw wood on this particular chest. The more so that it all took place in an ancient nobleman's mansion which could easily remember not only Gogol but also Napoleon.

Volodya forgot all about the party, he kept prowling round the chest, gazing at it this way and that. The old lady got terribly excited and, shielding the relic with her body, kept telling us that we ought to go and dance. We walked down into a hall with white columns and two tiers of windows; here, there was a concert piano, gymnastic parallel bars, a vaulting horse covered with leatherette: the mansion now housed some kind of school in which our friends taught.

Volodya soon quit the dancing, and when he reappeared, he looked like someone who had done a very difficult job now happily concluded.

"We are staying here for the night," he told me, his eyes shining with excitement.

"What for?" I was surprised. "We live nearby, and it's inconvenient, after all."

"Inconvenient nothing. I have settled the matter."

I don't know how he had got round the old crone, but he slept on Gogol's chest — though earlier she hadn't let anyone touch the thing, let alone sleep on it.

"Well, how was it?" I asked, when we returned from the Arbat on the following morning, blue and wintry.

"The devil only knows, Volod," he replied. "There was *some*thing!"

"What?"

"I don't know. We'll sort it out."

Zhenya Urbansky died three years later, in the summer of 1965, doing a car stunt for the film *The Manager*.

Lev Kocharyan died in 1970. The first and the only film he directed was called *One Chance in a Thousand*. He himself wasn't given even that much of a chance. The picture cost him dearly: it couldn't have cost more dearly. Cancer. He did everything to grab that chance. Doctors gave him a month, but he made himself live a year and a half. I'm sure he'd have lived longer, had the then bosses of the cinema, and his colleagues, given him a chance to do another film.

The influence of Lev on Volodya, and on all of us, cannot be exaggerated, as they say. It was immense. Lev could do *everything*: he could gallop on a horse, he could drive a tank—the first time he ever was inside one, he could navigate a ship out of a port, he could sew, sing, play the guitar, and fight, when there was no other way of protecting somebody; he could do tricks, like putting a needle and thread through his cheek without a drop of blood, or eating razor blades; God only knows what else he could do, in diverse areas of human activity. Apart from all this, Lev had the gift of bringing people together. In his novels, Yulian Semyonov often turned to this personality. It is to these novels that I refer those who are interested in him for lack of space in these brief notes.

There are just a few more things I would like to add. Lev was our senior by eight years. He graduated from Moscow University's Law School but later chose the cinema as his career; he began it as an assistant director in Sergei Gerasimov's *And Quiet Flows the Don*. In 1958 he married I. A. Krizhevskaya and moved to the same house, 15, Bolshoi Karetny, in which Vladimir's father lived — three floors below. At Kocharyan's, we made friends with Andrei Tarkovsky, Vasily Shukshin, Artur Makarov, Edmond Keosayan, Yulian Semyonov, Grigory Pozhenyan. There was a continuous stream of people passing through Lev's flat. Not a stream — a cataract, more like it. Actors, actresses, policemen, beginning writers (so far as I know, Lev was the first person to whom Yulian Semyonov brought his *38, Petrovka Street*), artists, directors, lawyers, officers, doctors, sportsmen, stunt-men, and people of a quite different mould — no one asked any questions about their occupations. It was all there — a black pistol (mentioned in one of Vysotsky's songs.— *Tr.*), a guitar, tall stories, taking pot luck, and a good deal of leg-pulling. Neither promotion nor well-being were valued here, especially as most could not boast of either, but there were other values — a desire to help, courage, a sine-qua-non decency in the relationships, ability to stand on one's dignity under all circumstances and in any environment, ability to hit back at a cad or a scoundrel.

Volodya brought to Lev his new songs, and the first recordings were made on Kocharyan's Dnieper-10 (a really ancient make of tape-recorder.— *Tr.*).

To avoid any impression of nostalgic embellishment, I must say that at first Volodya's songs were received in exactly the same way as all the others'. They had currency just like everybody else's, so to speak. The reason may well have been that Volodya was one of the boys, and his songs were meant strictly for the gang. Not more than that, though not less, either; no one could predict, of course, his fame in the not too distant future throughout the country and throughout the world. But gradual recognition among friends, though it wasn't either final or speedy, gave Volodya strength, it helped him to pull through a really difficult period in his life: his career at the Pushkin Theatre did not run smooth, and only the writing of songs kept him afloat. Also his friends.

Lev worked in the film *Leave of Absence* — and Volodya got a part in it. Then Lev worked in *The Living and the Dead* — Volodya got a part, too. It was not the sort of string pulling that is so common in the cinema — it was faith! And faith, as we know, can move mountains.

Volodya justified that faith, improving his acting all the time.

Who knows — the fairytale jinni may have developed his magic strength by pushing at the walls of the vessel in which he was cooped up. He pushed! He did not lie there like a chrysalis. Water bursts dams, talent breaks through the harsh circumstances of his life precisely at the moment when all paths seem to be barred. The breakthrough, in my view, came with Volodya's war songs. They were immediately perceived as something new — and that was precisely what they were — different from anyone else's, unlike anything else.

...One day we were sitting at Kocharyan's, Volodya and me. We were just chewing the rag, as usual.

"Look, Volod," Volodya asked suddenly, interrupting what he was saying in mid sentence. "Do you know which German army group advanced on the Ukraine?"

The question was unexpected, and it was asked in a tense tone of voice completely at variance with the previous talk. I had long known that Volodya could appear to be absolutely engrossed in a conversation while actually thinking his own thoughts.

"There were two. Army Group South, the main one, and Army Group Centre, which was moving from the north through Byelorussia."

"'Centre'!" Volodya said after a moment's silence, the way one speaks when making a choice.

He took the guitar and stepped into the next room. He returned almost at once — we had hardly had the time to exchange a word.

"Look, Levchik, Volod... I've put together something here..."

He never said, "I've written" but always "I've done," "I've put together," "I've invented," "I've concocted," with a kind of shy self-irony. He sang:

From victory to victory and step by step,
Army Group Centre rips across the steppe.
They will return as jolly, as merry as they come,
So just you wait you lovely, sweet buxom gals at home!

That song was especially written by Volodya for

the play *The Fallen and the Living* at the Taganka Theatre. Volodya owed his move to Taganka to his "author's songs" rather than actor's gifts, which were at that time undivined either by himself or, still less, by the directors. The period, fortunately, did not last long.

"Why did you choose 'Centre'?" I asked some time later.

"It's a better word. Just listen to it. Like a bolt snicking!" he made a movement as if working a rifle bolt. "'Centre'! Well, and South — South is South... Just a beach."

Volodya was remarkably sensitive to the music of the word.

Volodya studied music when he lived, together with his father and Yevgenia Stepanovna, in Germany. To be more precise he was taught the scales and all kinds of ABCs. But being taught and studying, you will agree, are quite different things. Studying means learning to express oneself in some new mode. By studying what was, one teaches oneself the future. How? No one knows how — everyone has a theory.

There were always plenty of people in the two small rooms the Vysotskys occupied in the communal flat in Bolshoi Karetny: his father's and step-mother's relatives and friends. Leonid Kaufman, a pianist from the Utesov jazz band famous in the 1950s, sometimes played there. Kapitolina Lazarenko, one of the most popular variety stars of those times, wife of Colonel Lazarenko, a friend of Semyon Vladimirovich's, used to drop in. His brother, Lieutenant-Colonel Alexei Vladimirovich Vysotsky, with his wife Shura, would come over. Shura had been badly wounded in the war, she had lost an arm, and wore an artificial limb of very fine craftsmanship. With this mutilation, and with her amazing, perfectly beautiful face — believe you me, perfect is the only word to describe her — she aroused a piercing and bitter feeling, although she was always cheerful and fond of company: those who did not know of her disability did not notice anything.

When Uncle Lyosha and Aunt Shura came, Volodya followed them about everywhere. And he listened to them.

The heroes of many of his war songs have living prototypes.

The capacity to listen is a gift. Volodya's gift was of the rarest quality.

He also used this gift in Pervaya Meshchanskaya, where his mother Nina Maximovna lived, and where a great many lives, badly mangled by the hard times, huddled together in what used to be furnished rooms. He listened to his distant relative Kolya, who sometimes appeared there. One day, when we were still mere boys, Kolya showed us how cards were made in labour camps out of newspaper and potatoes. The suits are painted with soot from a burnt heel and with brick pounded to dust and mixed with saliva. They were fine cards — the stuff felt like satin to the touch. Volodya kept them a long time, although we never, in fact, played cards much. Kolya was released after the 1953 amnesty, after quite a long term in the gold mines of Bodaibo.

The attitude towards former inmates of labour camps was at that time mostly sympathetic. In a world broken up and lacerated by the war, no one could safely say that hunger or some other inhuman cause wouldn't drive him across the boundary of law. And then, the boundary was so vague that a person might find himself beyond it without noticing it. And, as we know now, and as many people knew even then, he need not trespass at all — the law would trespass against him.

Underworld songs, or, as they were also called, "gutter songs", with their simple plots, were concerned precisely with fatal circumstances, broken up lives, broken hearts, lonely mothers and orphans. This kind of misfortune was all around us, in every family. Misfortunes sought the listener. The best listener was he who had himself suffered. Herein lies, I believe, the secret of the popularity of street folklore in those years. It expressed more than it seemed to be saying.

The fact that Volodya began with contributions to street folklore was, in my view, quite natural and organic — it couldn't have been otherwise. He had plenty of misfortunes both in his work and at home, in his private life. Enough and to spare. He had no home of his own. Only in 1975 did he get one — his first home, and his last, in Malaya Gruzinskaya. On the wall of that house, admirers of his talent who thought it best to remain anonymous put up a modest plaque, on the night of July 25, with this inscription: "Here the poet Vladimir Vysotsky lived between 1975 and 1980."

But, if truth were to be told, it was a good life, the life we led in those years, now so remote. Not in any material sense, of course: the purchase of a new pair of trousers was a very serious move requiring long preparation and rejection of certain pleasures of life. It was just a good life, cheerful and friendly. And we were not afraid of anything or anyone.

In about 1956, Alexander Vertinsky sang in Moscow for the first time after many years. A concert at the Lenin Komsomol Theatre. The very idea of getting tickets seemed absurd. But it was even more absurd to miss a concert by Vertinsky. So we went, eight of us, our gang from the school years.

One look was enough to tell us how the land lay: the entrance was besieged by an eager crowd, mounted police towered like unconquerable icebergs. Trying our luck there would be utter idiocy. Next to the theatre, though, all was dark and quiet — that was our chance. Volodya was the first to see the fire-escape: all experience comes in handy, some day. We climbed onto the roof and then down, past some people with red armbands, who froze with fear. We went through it all like a hot knife through butter. Not only did we get into the auditorium — we even found seats, as if they had been especially left for the eight of us. The curtain rose, and Alexander Nikolayevich appeared, very tall, in black tails and an impossibly white shirtfront. He was slightly hunched — he was getting on, and he looked a little like an ageing griffin... We wouldn't have missed it for worlds.

And then there was "Baikalov", who helped us so often over tickets to the cinema and all sorts of concerts to which tickets were not to be had for love or money.

> *The car is driving fast,*
> *The car is carrying us —*
> *Two Vovkas, Mishka, Garik, well, you know —*
> *Along the tidy streets;*
> *My heart, excited, beats:*
> *My friends and I, we're driving to a show.*

It's time to disembark —
Go, attaboys, go!
No tickets! What a lark!
Yo-ho-ho-ho-ho!

"Your tickets!" the attendant cries.
"No tickets? Go home, boys, go!"
But here Akimov replies:
"My Dad phoned a minute ago!"

If memory serves, this was Volodya's first song, a sort of rhymed account of our adventures, to a meddley of tunes from Utesov. The year must have been 1956 or 57.

We never clapped eyes on Baikalov, the circus manager. He was not acquainted with us, either, but there were minutes when we enjoyed ourselves hugely — all thanks to him.

It would all begin with Volodya's telephone call to the business manager of the establishment at where the spectacle for which our hearts pined was taking place.

"Baikalov here. Manager of the Moscow Circus. Look, my son and a couple of his friends will drop in on you —"

Then it was my turn, for I had the most respectable-looking mug in the crowd: I would go straight to the business manager. In winter, everybody would chip in, to make me even more presentable: one would give me his new fur hat, another, a coat, Volodya had a foreign-looking scarf. It never failed: the name of the circus manager and the smooth performance were a magic combination.

Somehow we had time for it all — playing the fool and doing what had to be done. Everyone in our crowd has made something of his life.

Arkan Svidersky is a doctor; Yasha Bezrodny, assistant manager of the Taganka Theatre; Volodya Bayev, a police officer; Lev Eginburg, an artist; Volodya Malyukin, an engineer, Misha Gorkhover, a musician; Grisha Khmara, business manager in the cinema; Lyosha Akimov, a scholar, State Prize winner; Garik Kokhanovsky, a poet, author of well-known songs.

At that time, we were only at the beginning of our path — which was, frankly speaking, far from clear. We were only groping about for that path, and everybody did his best to help the others. Volodya retained that trait for the rest of his life.

Lying before me is Volodya's letter to Grozny, where Lev Kocharyan, then assistant director, and myself were with the team which made the film *The Cossacks*. I was then making my first steps as assistant designer.

"Hail, Volodimir, light of my eyes, Volodimirovich! It has come to our attention that you have become a menace to all the Circassian and Ossetian girls of Grozny, not to mention Odessa. And that you are chasing the stars of our Soviet cinematography.

Vasyok and me, we are certainly villains, for we, the sons of bitches, have not yet written you a single line. So let's take it from the top.

We have been in the city of Riga. It is an ancient city, but life is expensive, so the Vasyoks have sold their souls there, not to mention their clothes, just to survive. Me, I sold my shirt, and Garik his watch and nylon swimming trunks.

Vasyok left for the capital with a rouble in his pocket, and had to sell his fountain-pen at a side-station, to get himself the bedding and to coddle thus his tender drunken body.

I stayed in Riga to play an extra and to rehearse. Later, I returned to Moscow, too. Iza, that's my wife, is OK, so you needn't worry overmuch.

As for your flat in 20, Sadovo-Karetnaya, we settled two knights there for a short time. The knights are from my theatre, and they have nowhere to live, except railway stations. They are very quiet kids, they sleep with their clothes on, they leave without washing their faces, no raping of girls, no drunken orgies. The neighbours dote on them. When you come, we'll kick them out, those knights. If you're against, we can tell them right now, but my heart bleeds for them. Hungry and homeless, they are. Then again, they are ever so quiet, and come only for the night. Your neighbour Zinaida, our wet-nurse, watches over them ceaselessly.

There is nothing new in Moscow, the weather is grey, the Hermitage functions but we never go there, for I work nights, and Garik seeks employment. A bunch of Georgians called Rero are making the scene there.

Me, I rehearse a play called *Pigs' Tails* from morning till night. The title seems impressive. Not much success so far, but what the hell—

Grisha pampers his Granpas and Grannies in the country, Misha does a job of work on TV; he pushes about props in a cart and knows everything.

Kisses on your sugar mouth. Your friends, ever, the Vasechoks.

7 Sept. 1960."

Garik, alias Vasechok, that was Igor Kokhanovsky; we made friends with him in the eighth form. Why Vasechok? There was some joke, which ended with the words: "That's it, Vasya! So long!" Volodya liked that phrase very much, and he pronounced it cheerfully and vigorously. We liked it too, and that's how we addressed one another—Vasya. This didn't stick to me, for some reason, but Volodya and Garik used that tag over many years. In the gang, Volodya was known only as Vasyok.

Garik then lived in Neglinny Lane, next to the Sanduny Public Baths.

The doors of what used to be furnished rooms opened onto a long corridor, where the kids whizzed on their bikes and the girls did their rope-skipping. In short, everybody amused themselves as best they could.

Naturally, playing the guitar on a bench in the corridor was regarded by the neighbours as an innocent and even pleasant pastime.

Garik played well. He had a repertoire of his own: Alexander Vertinsky, Pyotr Leshchenko, Vadim Kozin, and some songs by Sergei Yesenin, forbidden in those times. He played very few street songs. With great gusto, as he did everything that carried him away, Volodya learned from Garik the chords, the keys, the flourishes, all kinds of guitar technicalities. Then Volodya set off on a road of perfection and self-perfection leading towards high art.

In those years we seemed to be growing one from the other, nourishing our souls on each other's gifts. I believe that this is the law of all friendships, of which the other side is selflessness—when you give more than you take.

The thunder of the war rolled away into the distance. In the early 1960s, the woman in the red beret disappeared from Sadovo-Karetnaya Street. She died. People said that she came from Kiev, where her two teenage sons were killed by the Nazis right before her eyes. She went mad, and she kept looking into boys' faces in a strange city in the insane hope of seeing her children...

The years of the war receded into history, but the people who had fought in it suddenly became closer to us, to the generation of the war children.

1965. The 20th anniversary of the Victory. We were twenty seven or twenty-eight, and the veterans, forty odd, or not yet forty. At that age, the gap of 10 or 15 years doesn't show much. We now worked side by side, and we met as equals at parties. We chased the same girls. The two generations merged, the younger and the older ones, the generations of brothers. We had things in common that could be recalled and shared.

In the summer of 1965 Volodya and me, we lived in the Cossack village of Krasnogvardeiskaya near Ust-Labinsk, on the Kuban.

Edmond Keosayan, a friend of Lev Kocharyan and ours, was shooting the comic film *The Cook* there. Volodya had the part of Pcholka, and I went there for my practical studies as a student of the Cinema Institute.

Simultaneously, Volodya played in the film *I Come from Childhood* (script by Gennady Shpalikov, director Victor Turov) and worked on songs for that film, which are now so well known: *Common Graves, The Height, In the Cold, in the Cold;* the high officials of the film industry forbade him to sing these songs. Although he was naturally hurt, Volodya was already in a state when injustice merely excites pride and a desire to prove that he is right, to strike out at the powers that be. It was no longer possible to stop him, to intimidate him, to break him.

Besides, models of courage, daring, and strength of spirit were, as in our childhood, right at our side. The owner of the house in which Volodya and I lived had been a prisoner of war, he had been through Buchenwald. In *The Cook*, the lead was played by Vanya Savkin, a huge good-natured Siberian. As an eighteen-year-old scout, Savkin had been taken prisoner. Unconscious, he was dragged into a house; when he came to, he decided to show that he was not afraid of torture (which, as Vanya told us, he was in mortal fear of), so he put his leg in a burning Russian stove. His calf burnt out. Realising that a conversation just wasn't on, the Germans dragged him outside and shot him. During the night, Vanya came to. And crawled all the way to our lines.

Another actor who had a part in *The Cook* was Zhora Yumatov, who had served in a torpedo boat and had been awarded the Order of Nakhimov.

Here too, Volodya listened to people talk, absorbing it all like a sponge. But now he was also listened to — by the soldiers on whose behalf he now began to speak.

Serious educationalists and psychologists say that all children, with the exception of certain sad medical cases, are born geniuses, with amazing capacity for perceiving and expressing the essence of the world. It is only later that we, the adults, put in a great deal of effort to nip that capacity in the bud, so that later stages in life might be completely free of it.

The secret of child perception, when one and the same film can be seen ten or fifteen times, lies in the little person breaking through the conventionality towards the hero, acting together with him and becoming a hero himself — during the hour and a half at his disposal.

The secret of art also comes from childhood: it's in seeing and being seen at the same time.

Volodya retained the child's genius for seeing and entering what is seen, of becoming part of the action that is observed. That is the secret of his Truth.

To complete these notes, so far from perfection and completion, I would like to draw attention to the following fact: what was extremely important for Volodya was not only the attitude to his songs as such but also the attitude to their essence, to the themes, the subjects dealt with in them.

When we were on the Kuban, we talked one day of my future term project at the Cinema Institute. I had some ideas for it, but nothing definite yet.

"Look, Volod... Just imagine: Gorky Street. Fine weather. Ninth of May soon. And there is this pilot in parade dress. All those medals!" Volodya gestured to show how many there were. "Plenty of foreign ones, too. A crowd all around him. Pushing and jostling, almost fighting. All that. You'd think they're staring at the pilot, right? Not bloody likely: It's a Great Dane sitting by the wall. The master dropped in at the shop, and tied the Dane to the door handle. The dog is just huge! And he also wears plenty of medals—that's why everybody is gawking at him. Bastards."

The ashes of the war knocked at Volodya's heart. To the very end.

I never made a film about the pilot. I didn't get a chance to. And I was sorry about it even then.

I have said here a good deal about the realities of the times, probably more than about Volodya. But the subject of Vladimir Vysotsky's work was the times, which he expressed in a most striking and original way.

The times are the people. They are created by the mosaic of their feelings, thoughts and actions. But only a great artist can build a picture of an epoch out of these pieces of smalt that seem unmatched either in size or in colour. Volodya could.

It is no longer there, the bench opposite the cinema where something happened to us, something elusive and inexpressible in words which pertains entirely to the life of the spirit, when two human souls find EACH OTHER, mutually penetrating each other. The square garden isn't there either, just a small island in the middle of the roaring Sadovoye Ring. The cinema itself has long been pulled down—nothing but a vacant lot there. The mansion in the Arbat, where Gogol's chest used to stand, has disappeared, too. As has the chest, most likely... The wooden variety theatre in the Hermitage Gardens has also vanished; Volodya and I never missed a single programme there in summer; it was pulled down in 1974, lest it should burn down. And it hadn't burnt down either in the street fighting of 1917 or in the Nazi air raids. It went down, though, before attacking bulldozers.

In Bolshoi Karetny, we no longer see the house of the great Shchepkin [7], where Pushkin, Gogol and Griboyedov used to come. The cobble stones under the asphalt here are polished by the footsteps of the great ones.

The house has disappeared in which the incomparable Yermolova [8] was born; in the 1950s, the lane in which it stood was renamed after her — and became a street, not a lane, for some reason.

School No. 186 (No. 186 of the Guards, as we used to

call it) is no longer there, either. The building, after reconstruction, now houses the Ministry of Justice of the Russian Federation. Here at least there is some logic, a sort of continuity by contraries.

So many are no longer here...

There's something left, though. Volodya's handwriting on an old notepad which I have kept by chance, just as the letter to Grozny. He was "inventing", "concocting," or "putting together" something there:

"In a blue limousine
                              (struck out)
In a yellow

The most beautiful
The most desirable
                              (struck out)
The happiest one
The most unexpected one."

In the lower part of the scrap of paper, the letter-head: "Classified".

And, in Volodya's hand, a girl's telephone number: D-O- etc.

Igor Kokhanovsky

THE BEGINNING

In these notes, I shall not touch on the errors and exaggerations (and sometimes pure inventions) of the people who worked or frequently came in contact with Volodya. God forgive them their involuntary errors or complacent fantasy. A single phrase, which Marina Vlady dropped, in joke, in the TV film made by Natalia Krymova and Å. Thorsteinsson — that Volodya was very much like a character in one of his songs, "a fibber, a gas-bag and a merry fellow" — washes away the textbook gloss that many memoirists try to cover him with. Volodya was too much of a man "in and for himself", despite his openness and accessibility — qualities which were often merely a kind of shield for very intimate and very private things jealously guarded. One had to live years and years side by side with him to learn the true man. For about twenty years our lives were closely interwoven, and only some time about 1970 did they begin to split. But this last is a different matter altogether.

We developed an enthusiasm — serious enthusiasm — for literature, particularly for poetry, in the last year of school. The teacher introduced us to Velimir Khlebnikov (I remember that we were struck by the line "Russia, you are all like a kiss in the frost"), Igor Severyanin, Nikolai Gumilyov, Anna Akhmatova, Marina Tsvetaeva, Boris Pasternak, Sasha Chorny, Isaac Babel; we would go to the Lenin Library, get things by these writers, read them, copy certain passages and learn them.

One day Volodya brought into class a thin volume of Sasha Chorny, and we were so carried away by the poem *The Situation* that we immediately wrote some doggerel imitating his colloquialisms and the alliterations of Igor Severyanin: "I squeeze you, I tease you, the fire of desire..." Fortunately, that is absolutely all I remember of that poem of ours.

Later a book of Gumilyov's poems fell into our hands for a few days, and we learnt a few things from it, in particular "The Captains" and "The Worker" — these two I remember for certain. When Volodya somehow laid his hands on a collection of Babel's short stories (we had this book for nearly a month), we were so charmed by the Odessa stories that we began to speak in the language of Benya Krik and Froim Grach, peppering our conversation, often without much rhyme or reason, with passages like "you have a pince-nez on your nose and autumn in your heart", "do not let these stupidities worry you", and so on and so forth. Many years later I realised that many of the things that we read and learnt by heart in those years, sifted through our world perception, found echoes in Volodya's songs. For instance, Gumilyov's "pensive giraffe" became the prototype of the hero of the song *In Yellow Hot Africa*, while Babel's line "I sense, in fatal fervour" became part of a small masterpiece *Unruly Horses*. But all that would come later. In those years, though, life did indeed seem to us "to be a green meadow in which women and horses wander", and our craze for literature prompted us to try hand, timidly, at composition. At first these were stupid epigrams about each other or about our class-mates. On the last day of school, though, on the day of "the last bell", we took it in our heads to write a sort of account about the ten years of school, to write about our school life and about all our teachers, and in the space of four periods we wrote a jocular poem of twenty Onegin stanzas. Unfortunately, that "masterpiece" was later lost, but I'll quote here the connective stanza that Volodya wrote to integrate what we had written separately.

> *Well, is this boring, reader dear?*
> *I'm sorry if I failed the test,*
> *But it should be completely clear*
> *That I did here my level best.*
> *The rhymes like flies all fly away,*
> *And it would seem that near's the day*

When I will switch from verse to prose.
It may be for the best — who knows?
Our story's funny, if unlikely.
I want to make you laugh and grin,
For laughter is indeed no sin,
As says the great Arkady Raikin.
But now, dear reader, we must hurry:
I should get on now with the story.

Later we entered the same Institute of Civil Engineering. But Volodya stayed there only one term.

The turning-point in his decision to leave that college was the Eve of the New Year 1956. It was our favourite holiday, but this time we celebrated it in a highly unusual manner: we decided to dig in in the kitchen of Volodya's flat in Pervaya Meshchanskaya and concentrate on certain drawings, in order to hand them in on January 2. Otherwise we wouldn't be allowed to sit for our exam in Chemistry on January 3.

We bought a bottle of champagne (it was the New Year's Eve, after all!), laid in a store of coffee to drive away sleep, and started on the job.

At midnight, we uncorked the champagne, filled our glasses, clinked them, said "Happy New Year!" and, barely wetting our lips, returned to our drawings.

We finished them some time around two in the morning, so tired that we were not even sleepy. We decided to make some more coffee and finish off the champagne. I must say that we were so sore about celebrating the New Year in this way that we did not even talk about the ill-fated drawings — we ignored them, as it were. We finished the champagne, drank a cup of coffee, lit cigarettes, and it was only then that I looked at Volodya's effort. I just couldn't help laughing. The drawing sheet was divided into eight sections, and in the last of these we were supposed to pen samples of all types of lettering used in the drawing. What Volodya produced there could well be used to illustrate how lettering must *not* be done. He laughed, too, but sort of sadly, as if he was seeing the work of his hands for the first time. Then he began slowly pouring what was left of the Indian ink over the drawing.

"That's it. I'll start cramming, I have some six months —

try to enter the Theatre Institute. And this stuff — it's not for me."

He entered the Moscow Art Theatre studio and, since the course lasts only four years there, we graduated from our respective colleges simultaneously. Volodya joined the Pushkin Theatre company and immediately left for Riga with them, on a tour. Several days later he phoned me, asking if I could come over: there was a chance of taking a thorough rest at Riga's beaches. He had plenty of free time on his hands (studying for three tiny parts only), so we could swim and lie in the sun as much as we wanted. I thought it would be great, and left for Riga in a couple of days.

Volodya and several other young actors (two or three of his former mates at the drama studio, who were also invited to the same theatre) lived in the Metropole; here, there was a small cosy restaurant on the ground floor. We modestly supped there nearly every night (we were solidly hard up), but often stayed there until very late, when the musicians stopped playing and, gathering their instruments, vacated the dais. For us, it was the beginning of the most interesting part of the entertainment.

One night Volodya asked the headwaiter permission to strum on the piano, the more so that the restaurant was by that time half-empty. The permission was granted. But, before I describe what happened next, I'll make a small digression.

I cannot say that Volodya played the piano in any accepted sense of these words, but he did it often, and when he did it, he was oblivious to everything around him. Humming some tune, he would play an accompaniment, a few chords, over and over, and he would sit for hours at the piano like this. He would often play the fool, singing funny and often idiotic songs like, "You would come home, and wave your hand, and marry Vasya the dispatcher, and I'll kill whales by twisting tails, or they will make me a dog-catcher"; or he would sing some of Vertinsky's songs (which we both loved), but again not quite seriously, changing the lines, guying them (remember the episode from *The Place of the Rendezvous Can't Be Changed*, where Zheglov/Vysotsky sings "Where are you now, who kisses your fingers?"). When he came to my place (we had a piano), he would sit down at the piano at once and begin to strum. In the mid-1950s we caught the jazz bug, and Volodya's strumming was mostly free variations on popular jazz songs. Our favourite singer in those times was Louis Armstrong. Volodya began to sing "like Armstrong", at first rather timidly, as if groping for the right intonation and timbre, and later more and more boldly. In the end, he became so skilled in imitation that the impression that it was the great black trumpet-player singing was complete. It should be added that Volodya did not know English, I mean he did not know it at all, not one word, except "yes" (he studied French at school and later at the drama studio). But what an imitator he was! Those who knew English were completely at sea when they first heard him: the impression was that here was someone singing in English, yet they couldn't make out a single word. When they realised what the trick was, they would laugh to distraction.

After his marriage to Marina Vlady, he mastered not only French, which was apparently not very difficult, with his previous experience at school and the drama studio — he also learnt English. But that was much later. For the present, let me return to the summer of 1960, to Riga and the Metropole.

So the maitre d' allowed him to "strum on the piano". Volodya stepped on the dais, sat down at the piano, played a few chords and began singing *Kiss of Fire,* one of Armstrong's most popular numbers. I knew it all very well, so I started to watch the public, automatically rather than deliberately. Some curious things happened in the room. The people behind the tables first stopped eating and drinking, then talking, and then a hush fell on the restaurant as if it were a conservatoire. The waiters froze where the singing caught them, the customers moved their chairs so that they might see and hear better, and we played along, silently smiling and even shushing people when they wanted to say something. When Volodya finished the song, the public cheered loudly, applauding as if at some wonderful concert. Volodya was taken aback by this response from the public, but only for a few moments — he made a gesture, as if to say "no ovation please", and smiling at us, again started singing something in Armstrong's voice. About half an hour later he rose and wanted to step down, but the dais was surrounded by a crowd, each shouting some name, the title of some song they would like to hear; in short, the public wouldn't let him go... Volodya was clearly flattered, and he consented to do one more number. A few minutes later the whole scene repeated itself, and one of the regular customers even held out a hundred-rouble note, in the old funny-looking currency. Volodya smiled understandingly, but shook his head implacably; he politely declined the money, said, "That's it for tonight," and finally sat down at our table.

In the days that followed, whenever Volodya and the whole of our gang appeared on the threshold of the restaurant (which was situated in a sort of semi-basement, with several steps leading from the door down; anyone who entered the restaurant was visible to everyone), the waiters started running faster, reminding one of the silent pictures, so that by the time the "concert" began no work should spoil the enjoyment from hearing this unusual singer.

Having written this last word, I suddenly caught myself thinking that it has nothing to do with Volodya. He always performed songs, he played them out, not just sang. At the time of which I'm writing (and later, probably until the autumn of 1961), he had no songs of his own, and nothing seemed to indicate that he would write any. When Volodya was in his second or third year at the drama studio, I can't remember exactly which, the students decided to arrange a party, with satirical sketches. One day Volodya came to my place (I lived in Neglinnaya Street on the former premises of the Sanduny Public Baths, that is, a walk of some five or seven minutes from the Arts Theatre and the drama studio, so that we saw each other almost daily, and even several times a day, he would sometimes drop in at my place between rehearsals) and said there was going to be a party, he would like to write something funny, but nothing came out of it. Would I try? I said I would. A day later I wrote a Charlie Chaplin number for him. Volodya loved imitating Charlie Chaplin, and he did it marvellously: the walk, the gestures, the facial expressions, the eyes — he played it all so well that the likeness was amazing even without the moustache and the stick. And when he wore makeup and the costume (we even found Chaplin's bowler hat for him), that number was absolutely the hit of the party, not to be too modest about it. The more so that the theme of the sketch was extremely topical, a burning issue, one might say, for the drama students. The point was that they were only permitted to act parts in the cinema in their last, the fourth year, or was it in the third, I do not remember exactly. Since the grants were tiny, every student would jump at the chance of making some extra money (when one is young, there is no such thing as "extra" money, I believe), and of testing one's acting talents in the cinema, into the bargain. But the pundits of the studio believed that the cinema could damage the as yet shaky individuality of the actors. For all these reasons, Volodya's performance of a sketch ridiculing this state of things was cheered wildly.

So Volodya had no songs of his own at the time — but how he sang those we all of us sang at the time! They were mostly takeoffs of underworld songs. And, of course, Vertinsky. This combination, so strange at first sight, of gutter lyrics and the sophisticated and elegant subjects of Vertinsky was in actual fact quite natural, for the two elements contrasted with and complemented each other: the former could have absolutely none of the worshipful and at the same time somewhat condescending attitude to woman which made itself felt in nearly every song of the "poor maestro" and which was so much in keeping with our perception of the fair sex in those distant years. Incidentally, the word "sang" does not quite fit what our circle, which was beginning to take shape already, used to do. Of course we were simply full of pranks, as people are in their youth, we were simply playing the fool, attaching no importance whatsoever to all those "spivs" and "dens" and "narks" and suchlike words, whose only value was that they were funny and mysterious (this explanation is only for those much too serious people who see these songs as threatening the "formation of the young people's worldview"). Only those songs brought from the outside took root which were in tune with our lifestyle in those times — careless, slightly crazy and hussar-like. Any song was performed like a sketch rather than as a song, there would always be someone joining in the perform- ance — by chipping in with a word or a question. Inci- dentally, there were two singers, Volodya and myself. At first (before Volodya's songs appeared), it was mostly myself, for I played the guitar better, and Volodya was only trying to master it. Now as to who "we" were. Our "narrow circle" began to take shape already in our school years. Apart from the two of us, there was Volodya Akimov, then Yasha Bezrodny and Arkady Svi- dersky (from the other forms at school), and two or three other boys who split off from us soon after we graduated from school. Those whom I mentioned here stuck together for quite a while.

Anatoly Utevsky, or Tolyan, as we called him, went to the same school as we did, only he was a couple years our senior. He lived in the same house (opposite the school, across the street) in which Volodya's father lived. So they knew each other not only as pupils of the same school but also as neighbours. Tolya was one of those older boys to whom one is attracted at a certain age. He belonged to the "golden youth" of the mid-1950s Moscow — a circle that was to us unattainable and seemed to us to be mysterious. We naturally imitated this member of the "young avant- garde" in everything, wearing tight trousers, haircuts à la Tarzan and thick-soled shoes. When one of the national newspapers published an article under the title "The Scum", which scourged some of Tolyan's friends for a "depraved" way of life (their vices consisting mainly in that they danced boogie-woogie and spent many eve- nings at the Cocktail Hall, now the Moskovskoye Cafe, in Gorky Street, which was then known as Broadway among young people), he became a legendary persona- lity in our eyes. Alas, those were the years when the width of the trousers and the fashionable haircut were identified with an alien worldview, and those who practi- sed this lifestyle were contemptuously known as teddy boys. Tolyan was also a teddy boy, and this merely enhanced his reputation with us.

Lev Kocharyan, Tolyan's old friend, lived in the same house. At the time when Volodya and myself graduated from our colleges, Tolya worked as an investigator (he had graduated from a Law College), while Kocharyan left the legal profession for the cinema, and was trying his hand as an assistant director in Sergei Gerasimov's film *And Quiet Flows the Don*. It must have been at that time that Lev made friends with Artur Makarov, the adopted son of Gerasimov and Tamara Makarova, the actress. Artur (now a prose-writer and scenarist, the author of the short story "Home", which made quite a stir when it was published in the 500th number of *Novy mir*) and Lev soon became close friends, and later Akimov and myself joined them through the Utevsky-Vysotsky link. That was how the "narrow circle", closed to most outsiders, took shape.

The heart and soul of the gatherings of that circle was Volodya Vysotsky. Never in my life have I met another such witty joker, raconteur, and buffoon — anything, to cheer our lives. No one could ever understand where he dug up all those stories about Kostik Kapitanaki or Mario del Monaco, not to mention the endless jokes and puns. Or take his star number — the way he played a real earnest madman talking to a lamp post. He held the public spellbound until a crowd of some thirty or forty gathered to watch him (we would stand slightly apart, playing spectators, too, but careful not to spoil the fun, not to make him laugh), or until a vigilant guardian of law and order began to push through the crowd to find out what the matter was. Then Volodya would tell us, "Well, come on, boys," and the whole crowd would burst out laughing, realising it had been taken for a ride.

In the autumn of 1961, Volodya began to write songs. At that time I lost sight of him for about a month, as I was in the process of moving from one job to yet another and could not find anything suitable for quite a while, the more so that I quietly hated my profession of engineer. When we met, he sang to me five or six of his songs.

Many years later Volodya Akimov told me how the first of them, *The Tattoo*, had appeared. He and Vysotsky went to the Kursky Railway Station to see off Inna, the wife of Lev Kocharyan. She was leaving for Odessa, where Lev was preparing to shoot, or already shooting, I can't remember which, his first and only independently directed picture *One Chance in a Thousand*. They put Inna on the train; Volodya (Vysotsky) had his guitar with him, and he decided to sing "for the road" a song he said he had written in the morning. He sang *The Tattoo* and complained bitterly that no one to whom he had sung it believed that it was his song (Inna seemed to believe him at once), so he asked her to tell Lev all about it, stressing his authorship...

I remember feeling amazed when I heard, one night in the autumn of 1961, *The Tattoo*, *The Red, the Green, the Yellow and the Lilac, But They Were Eight, The City Plugged Its Ears and Wished to Sleep, You Bitch, Why Did You Shave Your Eyebrows*, and I believe a few more from the same series. Nothing in the past seemed to indicate such an "explosion of creativity". True, a year before he had written a comical song (which, however, remained just a funny episode) about the four sailors whose barge was tossed about for nearly a month in the Pacific Ocean (remember Kryuchkovsky, Poplavsky, Fedotov and Ziganshin?). But that, I repeat, had passed almost unnoticed. Mostly he wrote fairly funny epigrams about his friends, like this one:

> He's handsome like a Mosfilm star,
> The luckiest devil that we know.
> He says he's been called to the bar —
> What bar in town would have him, though?

This one is about Tolya Utevsky, who became a lawyer and worked on probation at 38, Petrovka Street (where the Moscow Criminal Investigation Department is situated.— *Tr.*) and was terribly proud of the "black pistol" (mentioned in one of Vysotsky's songs.— *Tr.*) that he was sometimes entitled to carry.

...So now Volodya began to write songs; he wrote them feverishly, sort of going on song-writing binges, and there were times when he showed us something new nearly every week.

Now, why was it that the subjects of his first songs had to do with underworld romantics and not something else — say, lyrical poetry, as in Bulat Okudzhava (whose name, incidentally, we — I mean Volodya and myself — heard somewhat later, at the end of 1962)?

The first reason was that Bulat Okudzhava, Alexander Gorodnitsky or, say, Novella Matveyeva took their song-writing seriously from the very beginning. As for Volo-dya, all he wanted at first was to have fun, and for others to have fun, too.

Second, I have already described what we had sung before Volodya's songs appeared, and the songs he wrote now were a continuation of those earlier efforts. And why had we sung *this* kind of songs? Simply because they were the forbidden fruit — which is always so sweet.

Thirdly, what sort of life experiences could a 23-year-old actor have, experiences that would prompt him "nobler" themes? What had he seen in life? In the words of Isaac Babel, "a couple of trifles": secondary school and drama school. (I hasten to soothe the overserious: these are not trifles, of course — yet not enough, obviously, to write about serious things.)

And we must not forget, of course, that Volodya was an actor — an actor by his very nature and, as they say, to the marrow of his bones. Acting was his element, his true nature. Underworld songs became one of the hypostases of this play-acting, which for quite a while remained unconscious and uncontrolled.

When he joined the Taganka Theatre in 1964, he grew more serious. Incidentally, the wave of underworld themes began to recede at that time. "I'm sick and tired, I'm tired and sick, I am too tired even to sing," he would write in January 1965. This sort of thing was no longer funny, and it was therefore no longer interesting. It was about then that he realised that what he had done in play became work, creative work demand-ing considerable effort.

"Vasechok, do you know that my songs are sung by Portuguese guerrillas?" he asked me one day in the winter of 1965. "A fellow has returned from Portugal, he says he heard it himself..."

His *Submarine* was already something serious indeed. And I believe that it was this song that marked the end of his youth as a song-writer. Everything before that had been merely a beginning. I have tried to explain here why his beginning was the way it was.

Vadim Tumanov

LIFE WITHOUT LYING

Flowers hit against the glass of the hearse like clumps of earth. They came flying from every side, thrown by thousands of hands. The car could not start, and not only because the whole square was packed with a crowd. The driver could not see the road. The flowers covered the whole of the windshield. It became dark inside. Sitting next to Volodya's coffin, I felt as if I was being buried alive together with him. The thuds against the glass and the roof of the hearse were endless. The human wall stood solid before the funeral procession. Police cars, with their sirens shrieking, could not clear a way for it.

The square and all the streets adjoining it were flooded by a human sea. People stood on roofs of houses, even on the roof of the Underground station. Later, I couldn't get rid of the completely extraneous thought: "How did they get up there?" It still seems strange to me to see Taganka Square different — routinely bustling. On that day in July it seemed as if we would stay there forever.

Cries of thousands of people merged with the shrieking of the siren. The flowers kept sailing through the air. I saw frightened faces around me. Total confusion. No one had expected anything of the kind. Marina's hand convulsively pressed my elbow.

"I've seen the funerals of princes and kings — I couldn't have imagined anything like this."

And I recalled Volodya's cheerful "A big crowd!" Those were the words with which he anticipated my usual question, returning after a concert: "Well, much of a crowd there?"

"That's me. A big crowd!"

Later, Yuri Trifonov would say, "How is one to die, after Vysotsky?"

It would be false and cowardly to write about Volodya

301

without referring to his relationship with well-known figures who are still writing. Many have changed their views about him. Some tend to alter them through addition of "new" impressions, or to drop inconvenient details.

The reader learns from Andrei Voznesensky's recent book *The Foremen of the Spirit* how particularly close were the two poets. That is, of course, true, and the truth is supported by quotations — which do not, however, refer to the last period of Vysotsky's life. But it did exist, that last, difficult period. It was a time when the Writers' Union considered Vysotsky's application for membership. The application was rejected. But the formalities are unimportant. Volodya realised with bitterness that all talk of invariable support — words that he had heard in plenty before — would remain mere words.

He was a thorn in the side of many, during his lifetime. His courage caused some people considerable headache — and continues to cause it.

You take for instance just this anonymous verse, which somebody took great pains to spread:

> *And he was told, in easy style*
> *to spread miasma everywhere,*
> *to go through every refuse-pail*
> *in search for themes for noisome airs.*

If only it were a mere epigram! A poet may dislike the verse of another poet — countless examples of this, in the history of literature. But this doggerel is no epigram, it is an epitaph. Someone who speaks of himself as a poet wrote this on the occasion of the poet's death...

His relationships with contemporaries were not easy. To some, he was obliged to say, "Leave all hope — I will never go."

He loved his native land, but his love was not blind. He never flattered his people, he taught them no gospel and did not see himself as a messiah. But he was very sensitive to the times.

Diametrically opposed assessments are proof of the great scope of a phenomenon. No one remained indifferent to his work. Passions are still running high, ranging from adoring acceptance to angry rejection.

Emotions, as we know, are incompatible with restraint, still less, with strict balance. The perception of Vysotsky is largely determined by the listener's life experiences. Volodya was told, for instance, that the Pope laughed uproariously as he listened to his song about himself.

And Bobby Fisher, who also understood Russian, failed to see the humour of the line "in a canteen closed to lesser mortals".

Unfortunately, appraisals are often determined by orientations. In France, Vysotsky's performance of Hamlet was recognised as the best ever. Soviet press has managed to overlook the fact.

I often observed one and the same picture at previews in the House of the Cinema and in theatrical foyers. "People's Artists" would stalk about, sleek, accustomed to signs of attention, conscious of their importance, wearing their insignia. When Vysotsky appeared, they'd be left nowhere, as if they did not exist at all. That was annoying, of course. That made them want to study the phenomenon of "mass culture".

People say that he liked to behave provocatively. That is not true. His fame was not notoriety, and he did not believe that fame was happiness. At one time he was my guest in Pyatigorsk, and he gave an interview to the local TV studio. Ordinarily, he avoided public interviews with journalists. On one occasion he responded to their reproaches with a reproach of his own: "There was a time when I would have liked to speak through you, but you wouldn't listen. Now I have the right not to want to speak."

This time, though, he unexpectedly agreed. He thought the questions would be of the lightweight variety, and was not disposed to give serious answers at the beginning. He grew more serious after the second question.

"Do you ask everyone that sort of questions?" he asked in surprise, and then replied: "Happiness is like travelling. It needn't involve movement in space. The travels may be through the soul of another person — through the world of another writer or poet. Only you mustn't travel alone, but with someone whom you love and whose opinion you hold dear."

He loved to travel through the world of Akhmatova, Pasternak, Gumilyov, Trifonov, Akhmadulina. He regarded Yevtushenko as a major poet. He knew the poetry of Mayakovsky, but his attitude to it was all his own, far from the generally accepted.

He could not complain of lack of public recognition. The whole country knew his songs. He wanted to see his poems published. That's a poet's natural desire. But no latter-day Nekrasov [1] came his way. (Nekrasov, the great Russian 19th-century poet, was also a publisher and a discoverer of poetic talent.— *Tr.*) And Nekrasov's *Sovremennik* (Contemporary) was not, alas, revived in *Nash sovremennik* (Our Contemporary) [2]. I recall in this connection Volodya's sad words, "They regard me as a cleaner."

I'm still uncertain whether I correctly understood the sense in which he used that word. But I knew who "they" were: he listed them, name by name.

At the Ministry of Culture, a certain high official asked him:

"Have you brought your records for me, from Paris?"

"What do you need them for? You can produce them here."

Then the man walked to his safe, took out records of Vysotsky's songs made in France, and boasted:

"I've already got them from others."

Vysotsky did not want success at any price. Thus he could not write on orders or from newspaper materials, unless he felt the theme through and through and knew the details of the situation by heart. That was the only reason why he refused to write songs for Roman Karmen's documentary about Chile. He was afraid of triviality and repetitiveness.

Volodya's heart was filled with joy at other people's success, and he did everything he could to help talented but unlucky people. He did not know what envy was, absolutely.

Always kind to other people, he was amazed at, and suffered from, any lack of kindness in response. He was a sensitive and therefore a very vulnerable person. I remember an episode from 1978, when he came from the theatre late at night, after a preview of some films. He roused me from sleep.

"Can you imagine the picture? The actors see each other on the screen, they recognise each other, all is joy and lightness. When I come on the screen, there's dead silence. What have I done to them, stolen their moon? Or taken away the Mercedes?"

Yes, he had his Mercedes, a status symbol — for the snobs, not for Vysotsky. He was in general indifferent to material expressions of success. His desire to see his work published in no way contradicted that indifference. His spirit thirsted for materialisation, for material consolidation in records and books. His personality was not reflected in the glossy surface of the Mercedes.

He valued kindness, honesty, sincerity and openness in people more than anything else. More than intellect and talent. He had nothing but disgust for falseness, and could sense it a mile away. A worker of our embassy met him at the New York airport, and launched at once into a lecture on honourable conduct and good manners abroad. ("Tell them we have put an end to all drinking long ago..." as a character in one of Vysotsky's songs says.) He also hurried to announce that a return ticket for Vysotsky had already been bought — a week before the planned date, so that six of the already announced concerts would have to be cancelled. Then he ritually embraced his duly instructed compatriot and kissed him — out of his sense of duty, most likely.

"Several days after that unpleasant episode," Volodya told me later in Moscow, "I suddenly felt an irrepressible desire to wipe my cheek, but I couldn't, because of the guitar in my hands."

It wasn't always that he could avoid these false embraces. He was sometimes caught unawares. His good manners, too, cut his chances of expressing his real attitude towards such people. On one occasion I met a certain well-known film actor at Vysotsky's, talking of himself in the cocky manner so common among film stars. Volodya was mostly silent, his replies were tepid and curt. The visit obviously depressed him, but the laws of hospitality bound him hand and foot. After the visitor left, Volodya sighed: "A talented and clever scoundrel is more dangerous than a talentless one. There are people that make one want to wash, after one's talked to them."

Volodya had a great many acquaintances, which was hardly surprising in view of his popularity. But he was close to only a very few, which is hard to believe when

305

one hears and reads reminiscences about him. You could count on the fingers of one hand the people who felt free to come to his place at any time. We all know that guests are stealers of time. Unbidden guests are in addition guilty of breaking and entering. Vysotsky's one wish in such cases was to close the door behind them as soon as possible. He was also unwilling to open his soul to anyone except his friends. He disliked lengthy effusions, and was usually reticent and silent. But what an interesting raconteur he was in moments of sincerity and openness among people whom he liked! He would give himself up completely to good humour and friendly revelry. Then the sunny days would give way to gloomy ones.

The endless talks and arguments with him are unforgettable. There was never enough time. The talk would often begin in the kitchen. I would mostly sit on the windowsill, Volodya would stand by the gas-cooker. Then we'd bethink ourselves: it would be morning already, and Volodya would soon have to go to a rehearsal. Of all the people that I met in my life, Vysotsky was the most interesting.

He suffered a lot over his failures, especially when he was not to blame for them. He went through screening tests for the role of Pugachov. But then he had to shave off the beard which he had grown: some influential personage had interfered. He was then invited to play in the film *Sannikov Land*, for which he had already written many beautiful songs. *Snow Without Mud's Like a Long Life Without Lying...* was one of those songs.

Someone said at the Mosfilm Studios, though:

"Aren't there any other actors here, except Vysotsky?"

His attitude towards work was not just serious — it was fervent, although he was often late for rehearsals at the theatre — and his relations with the theatre, I must say, were not of the best in the last years of his life.

He went on leave, for a year. He wanted to write a screen play and make a film about the Kolyma, to play the lead in it. He began collecting materials about it. To do this, he rejected an offer to take part in a foreign film, although they tried to lure him with high fees.

One day I told him about a certain Alexei Ivanovich, a person who really fascinated me. Try to imagine someone with all the external marks of an intellectual, as he is portrayed by the hackneyed imagination: fine facial features, polite, cultured, quiet, and tastefully dressed.

On the Kolyma, he looked very much to advantage against a highly contrasting background. Sitting next to him on the podium at a conference of front-rank workers of prospecting teams, I saw, by chance, that he was an excellent artist. I heard people say that he loved, and had a fine knowledge of music, and played himself.

My descriptions of people's appearance sometimes seemed hilariously funny to Vysotsky:

"Somehow all good men in your stories are blue-eyed, and disgusting types are invariably pock-marked."

Now, Alexei Ivanovich was not pock-marked. He was an elegant wearer of suits, and preferring conservative tones, mostly greys. In short, he looked fine. But one day, many years before the meeting on the conference podium, I had seen him kick a man in the face as the man was bending down. Alexei Ivanovich then held a high and awesome office, I must note, and he did not need to fear that the man would hit back.

Vysotsky recurred to that episode several times, he wanted to know the details, all the particulars about the Kolyma official's appearance.

"So what do we have here?" he tried to reason it out. "Does a person change with the circumstances? With his position? Do these people care about their reputation in the eyes of their own children? Suppose they would be ashamed for their fathers?"

That was how the poem *My Black Man in a Grey Suit* was born.

Black men came into his life in various guises. But he recognised them, without mistake. In France, he was struck by the so-called *gauchists*.

"They invited me to sing at their rally. I saw their faces, their provocative manner, I heard their wild speeches, I read their slogans, and I was horrified. It was a drugged mob thirsting for violence and destruction. Their social bravado was emphasised even by the clothes they wore. In vain did my confused interpreter try to talk me into singing; she was puzzled by my refusal to sing before these young people ready'to hit out without warning or reason'."

Some time later he read to me a poem he had just written — *The Brave Boys: The New Left*:

Please do not fuss, Madame, stop nagging, pray,
I do not feel like singing today.
I do not think they will listen to me —
And they'd do better to read History.

He rejected violence so totally that he was suspicious of people building muscle.

"I have a feeling they are going to beat up somebody. And it's sure to be someone weaker than themselves."

This echoes his well-known line: "I couldn't hit a man in the face even in my childhood." It is appropriate to recall here that at one time Volodya did boxing. In the interview in Pyatigorsk I have already mentioned he thus defined the human shortcoming which he was most ready to forgive:

"Physical weakness."

Volodya himself, though, was very strong, a good sportsman. And his attitude to sports was in general positive — he valued it. But he placed physical strength infinitely lower than moral one.

Volodya grew up as a street arab, he knew the laws of the street (someone may even say, the gutter):

And I grew up like all the mod grew up...

In his childhood, he shared the fate of the wartime generation, with its trauma of fatherlessness and neglect.

And the brother of Tolya Rvany
Came back home from Goldfield Zhelanny...

(Incidentally, Zhelanny was a goldfield in the Kolyma where Alexei Ivanovich was at one time boss.)

Vysotsky made himself, he built his personality all by himself, he built his own spiritual world. Having suffered a great deal in early childhood from aggressive caddishness, he would not stand even the slightest signs of it in his mature years.

One day we were walking along the Arbat; a couple of hulking young men, insolent and slightly drunk, came up to us, with the usual "Give me some fire". Slightly frowning, Volodya produced a lighter. He always had one with him, and they would light up at a touch. This time, though, he clicked and clicked, but there was no fire. The fellow recognised him.

"Ha, Vysotsky! Looks like you've become awfully bold lately."

Volodya flared up, and his response was dignified and devastating.

On another occasion, he was to sing at a writer's anniversary. At the last moment, he learnt that the people he had invited to the 'do' were not even given invitation cards. Vysotsky could not stand it when people were slighted, whoever they might be. He realised at once that what lay behind it all was the writing mob's elitist arrogant attitude towards outsiders. So he expressed his feeling to the hosts and organisers of the banquet at once, and in "oral Russian". He sang one song and left.

He might say of himself in the words of Hamlet, "Though you can fręt me, you cannot play upon me..."

I often hear people say, "They asked Vysotsky to sing, and he did. He was invited to a party, a banquet, a high society reception, and he went."

In actual fact, he was highly selective about his personal acquaintances. And as for singing, he only sang when he wanted to, never otherwise. Here are several episodes.

A tipsy major, who happened to be in Vysotsky's company, decided to order a "programme of cultural entertainment", on top of everything else:

"Sing us a few songs, Volodya!"

Vysotsky could not stand any familiarity in others, and permitted no familiarity in his own attitude to others.

"Look, Major," he said, when he'd had enough, "fire a few shots, eh?"

The secretary of a very highly placed personage phoned Vysotsky:

"Such and such persons would like to have you for the weekend."

"I have no time," Volodya replied in a restrained tone.

"You what?!" The secretary, unaccustomed to refusals,

could not believe his ears. "Are you going to say so to THEM, too?"

(He pronounced "THEM" in a respectful whisper.)

"I repeat that I have no time. Please tell them so."

In the song, it sounds a little bit different:

> *I am invited by some real big shots*
> *To sing my* Wolf Hunt — *though I'd rather not.*

He had a highly developed sense of personal dignity. In Irkutsk, he listened to toasts in his honour silently and glumly, and soon left, pleading indisposition.

"I was afraid I'd explode," he explained later. "There were several people there totally alien to me in spirit. I couldn't sing for them."

This sort of impressions were later compressed into verse:

> *There he is, arrogant like Richelieu,*
> *Like a noble Daddy in an old sketch...*

> *...You mustn't come to other people's tables*
> *Or answer anyone who hails you...*

In Siberia, he spent half the night talking to an old grey-haired woman from the village of Bolshaya Glubo-kaya, on the Kultuk highway, near Lake Baikal. Here, admiring the purity of the air, he said:

"It would be fine if Demidova could live here awhile."

He remembered that she was not feeling well at the time.

He liked travelling in company. And the people who were close to him in spirit lived in his soul all the time.

At the Leningradsky Railway Station, Yulian Semyo-nov, the writer, came up to Volodya and tried to talk him into going to his birthday party, at his place in Pakhra outside Moscow. Volodya declined the invitation politely, saying he was pressed for time, although at that parti-cular moment we were entirely free, we seemed to have been hungry in Leningrad already and, stepping off the train, had just been discussing where we could drop by. Why didn't he go? I cannot say exactly, but there seemed to have been something about the invitation, about its form, that had struck Volodya as incorrect. He was very sensitive to nuances.

In a hurry to get to the theatre, Vysotsky refused to give his autograph to a couple of young soldiers who stopped him at his car. There were three of us. We quarrelled, saying a great many unpleasant words to each other in the space of a few minutes. Volodya braked abruptly and, leaping out of the car, ran to find the soldiers. But he returned downcast.

"Seems like they've stepped off the earth!"

We parted in silence, and in the middle of the night someone rang at the door of my flat. It was Volodya.

"Well, still angry?" he said smiling. "I've given forty autographs today."

In Pyatigorsk I introduced him to an old Armenian woman, Auntie Nadya. She had worked hard all her life, never resting. At seventy, she was still helping her grown-up children. One day she said:

"I saw the film *Turkey's Head*."

She spoke little Russian, and it turned out that the film she had seen was *Iudushka Golovlyov* (there is a remote likeness between these words and "turkey's head" in Russian.— *Tr*.). One day the old woman was sitting by her house on a bench, and Volodya and myself sat down next to her.

"This is Auntie Nadya who has seen the film *Turkey's Head*. And this is Vysotsky. Do you know his songs? Do you like them?"

"I knows. I likes. They sing all the time. Must be good. Only hoarse, very."

Volodya burst out laughing. He talked to Auntie Nadya a little, and on the following day, as we were approaching Nalchik, about fifty miles away, he suddenly asked me:

"Did you notice her hands?"

"Whose?"

"Auntie Nadya's. Beautiful kind eyes and such work-coarsened hands."

In general, Vysotsky's attitude towards old men and women was touching. He liked to listen to them, or simply to look at them. A psychologist will probably say that he felt that he would not live to be an old man himself.

I cannot say as to that, but I know for certain, from

Vysotsky himself, that he valued Yuri Trifonov's *The Old Man* higher than his other works.

In the Caucasus, Volodya would stop his car and gaze a long time at an old woman with a cow, or a grey-haired mountaineer. In Siberia, in a hurry to catch a plane, he stopped his car to press the hand of a bulldozer driver he knew, a war veteran. To take leave of him. Later, he would remember that vet at one of his concerts in Moscow. He loved them, these common people marked by the war. That is the answer to the question of who were his idols.

He wrote with great feeling and understanding of the victims of the war — soldiers, officers, everyone who had had anything to do with it. People who ought to know say that Vysotsky's war songs are the summit of his creative effort. He handled the details of war with such skill that his uncle Alexei Vladimirovich, a former commander of division intelligence, was quite sure that *The Ballad of the Chap Who Did Not Shoot* was the story of his life. He must have been puzzled, and probably distressed, on learning that the nephew had invented it all.

"Amazing," said another retired colonel, "it's all about me."

I shall try to avoid appraisals. For myself, I only saw war in its isolated manifestations: horned mines by the ship's side, diving bombers, geysers of water rising before the ship's bows... I must admit, though, that his capacity for penetrating into other people's fates, living them out for himself, as it were, have remained a mystery to me. He never invited anyone into his "creative laboratory".

"I don't know, Vadim. It comes by itself." Or this: "A thought will drone like a busy bee, for days on end, sometimes... And then I write it down."

He wrote not only at night, and not necessarily at his desk.

In a well-known interview Vysotsky said:

"Each song wrings me out."

"This one, too?" He was asked after the first performance of the song *About the Vacha River*.

"It wasn't the easiest one."

It was a simple story of an unlucky gold-digger, with neither house nor home, just his last rouble in the pocket, "for a telegram". But I saw the way people listened to it, men who had been through the Kolyma, Dzhugdzhur,

Magadan, Yakutia, Bodaibo. They listened to it with a cheerful attention: it was part of their life, their past unfit for the newspapers. It was there, so why should they be ashamed of it?

Volodya wrote the song about the Vacha in Khomolkho, a god-forsaken settlement in the taiga of Bodaibo. There, Vysotsky sang for four hours for those who came to hear him from the most out-of-the-way taiga corners. As he sang, more and more people arrived. Pilots delayed their flights to be able to listen to their idol. They were passenger flights, so one can imagine the disciplinary consequences for the pilots. There was no standing room left in the canteen, so the window frames had to be removed so that everyone might hear. Vysotsky patiently waited for all the preparations to be over.

"I need these people more than they need me."

On that trip, his guitar was accidentally crushed. He did not turn a hair.

"What question would you like to ask yourself!" he was asked at the Pyatigorsk TV studio.

"How many years, months, weeks, days and hours of creative work I have left?"

On July 25, 1980, at twenty to four in the morning, the telephone rang at my flat. It was the doctor.

"Come... Volodya has died."

On that day, I answered hundreds of telephone calls at Vysotsky's flat. I remember a call from Grechko, the cosmonaut:

"Can I help in any way?.. Here's my telephone number, just in case."

Marina wanted to put an unusual wild stone on his grave.

"It needn't be beautiful, but it must express Volodya's image."

She asked me to find such a stone, and I did. It was a rare variety of troctolite, about 150 million years old, pushed up from the hot depths of the earth and — a real rarity — not crushed or covered with oxide. It was incredibly of a piece: when struck with a hammer, it rang like a church bell. But — another monument stands on Vysotsky's grave.

There is a great deal written about Volodya these days, a lot of arguments going on. I wouldn't like to get mixed up in the debate. There's one thing about him that I would like to say, though: he was a man of a tragic perception of the world. He wanted to live, but he was unafraid of death. In the words of his favourite poet, he could "remember at once the whole of the harsh and dear life, the strange and dear land". He died in sleep. He felt the coming of death, but did not invite it. Before he died, he just had time to write to his wife in Paris on a te-legraph form:

> *...I have a lot to sing to the Almighty.*
> *I have my songs to justify my life...*

Mikhail Shemyakin

ABOUT VOLODYA (The Last Years)

It's difficult for me to write about him. Too many memories rushing into my head all at once. He was too great a magnitude in my life. "Friendship with a great man is a gift of the gods," Corneille once said. Grieving over an irreparable loss, I thank God for letting me know this great and noble soul. The myths and fabrications about Vysotsky sometimes completely distorted the image of Vysotsky the man. All that was loose, rakish and reckless about many of his songs was taken for the essence of his soul. Few people knew that what Volodya loved more than anything else was quiet; he loved to sit behind his desk at night, and shunned crowds and parties. He collected autographs of old writers and poets, he was a great reader of books, he loved his friends warmly and sincerely, and often told me that friends were the most precious gift of life, sadly remarking that he had so few true friends. I knew how he cared for them, how tirelessly and endlessly he helped them, how he suffered for them in their illnesses or failures. I saw him cry when he went on a bout of hard drinking and, meeting some people, could not carry out some promise he had made them. (It had to do with some affairs of no great importance — some ballbearings for a car, wheels or tyres, something like that.)

What he loved to do more than anything else in life was sit in absolute quiet, digging among his stamps or reproductions. His whole work is that of one of the greatest analysts of the Russian land. He was no drunkard or rake — not by any means. He must be understood quite differently, if he is to be understood at all. It has been my great luck in life that I came to know him as a person, to know the depth of his soul, his sensitiveness and his suffering.

315

One day Marina called me: "Volodya is in a bad way, come please..." I took along the Russian painter Putilin, who adored Vysotsky and always imitated him in his songs, and we rushed to their place. Volodya was on the brink of going off into a world of his own. Marina had several lapdogs. I love animals, so I took up the dogs and hugged them. Volodya, who loved animals "at a distance", asked me, "Misha, what are you caressing them for?" And I replied, "Well, I love animals, without the beasts our souls would grow beastly..."

Suddenly I saw Volodya walk to a bureau, pull out some notebook and write down something, asking me again, "What was it you said? We'd grow beastly without the beasts?"

When Marina later gave me all of Volodya's diaries, his notebooks containing meditations, observations and notes for poems, I suddenly discovered an entry made in a very unsteady hand: "And without the beasts we would go beastly ourselves."

He liked to wear leather, and kept pestering me, "Mishka, you're a designer, will you design a costume for me?" One day I replied, "What costume are you talking about? What's all this nonsense? You are an image as you are." "No, I'm an actor," he objected. "You must design a costume for me in which the whole world will know me."

So I took him by the lapels of his yellow leather jacket and shook him: "Volodya, bethink yourself! Don't you know that you are a genius?" He looked at me, a sort of gloomy look, and said quite soberly: "I know."

There are moments that are remembered all one's life, for these moments are the truth. I will never forget his gloomy, cheerless look: "Of course I'm great! Another Napoleon." And suddenly he said it with such anguish: "I know." It was as if I had asked him: "Do you know that you are carrying a cross?" And this man suddenly answered me, instantly coming back, sobered, from his merry, drunken, Russian delirium: "Yes, I know..."

There was a reply for you! I believe that Volodya had an inner vision of what a genius is.

What made me take up my camera and take pictures of my friends? I had a feeling that this epoch would some day become history, and that the men, the artists and poets little-known then would become the history of Russia. From my father, a war historian, I must have inherited this passion for collecting historical materials, since, as it has turned out, I did not exaggerate the significance of these persons; I did not make a mistake about them. Of course I couldn't miss my chance when I encountered such an immense personality as Volodya Vysotsky. Naturally, I headed straight for the shops. Naturally, I bought the best tape-recorders. Naturally, I quickly learned the art of recording and said, "Volodya, let's work. Everything that you write must be recorded; you need it. Whether in a chronological order or not, but we must do it all in the best way we can." That was why the best microphones were bought, one for the guitar and one for the voice, to get the best quality of recording. And I began to goad him to start working. Talking would come later. Later we might sit down at the table, but work would come first. Afterwards, it became a habit with him. He would burst into my room, notebook in hand. He would put it on an easel and begin singing. He'd turn the sheets himself, and on many recordings you can hear the sound of rustling; and sometimes he would forget his spectacles: in the later years, Volodya's eyesight was pretty poor. That was the way the recording began. He would sing his latest songs, the ones he had just brought (to Paris.— *Tr.*). He felt that the result was something interesting, something historical. When IMCA Press published collections of Russian guitar poets (the quality of the records was awful, but at least the poems were collected), Volodya told me: "Look, let's record everything that I've written all over again, this time in the new versions." He felt himself that his soul had grown stronger, his voice and even his conception of his own work, had grown stronger. He began to sing — and how novel was the performance! It was the style of a real master, this time. He worked with great enthusiasm. You take such a song as *The River's Flowing*. "I have sung it many times," he said, "but now I would like to record it again, to sing it the way I understand it today." After that song, he couldn't sing anything, he was dripping sweat, he seemed quite spent after singing that song — which was not his song at all! I mean to say, he wasn't one of those singers who could only perform their own songs, as is sometimes the case. There are masters who find pleasure in copying other masters, they put their whole soul in the work and thus create something absolutely new. Thus Delacroix copied Rubens, creating paintings that sometimes surpassed that great master. In the same way, Volodya created a real masterpiece out of an ordinary song.

It was a strange evening — the evening when he sang *The River's Flowing*. An evening not unlike one in old St Petersburg — a sad, sad light. Summer, August, the French had all gone on leave, the whole of Paris was filled with sweet, aching sadness. Twilight fell. We were sitting at my place; a girl came over; her parents originally came out of Russia, and Volodya was a god to her. Volodya felt inspired, he felt strong, and suddenly, instead of singing one of his own songs, he decided to sing *The River*, for he heard in it the theme of love, of a loved girl, and a great many other ineffable things. He sang it, looking at the girl, sometimes shifting the gaze to me, askance — and how he sang! There was practically nothing left of the girl, and Volodya said, "Well, now for a little drink!"

That was no alcoholism or love of vodka, it's just that he felt spent, and everything within him was still boiling, so he had to relax, or he might go mad.

Rummaging in my archives, I came across an old photograph of an old Tibetan monk with a prayer rattle in his ancient withered hands. That was the teacher of the Dalai Lama himself, and exactly the same portrait hung in Vysotsky's flat in Paris... So I recalled the sad and merry story of our visit, Volodya's and mine, to the great Lama for the purpose of discussing the very problem that played such a considerable role in Volodya's departure for the other world.

In what light do I see the amazing insights of Volodya's work? They were moments of fantastic spiritual revelation, when the chest seemed to be torn open and one could see in it the blood-covered heart of man and poet. Those were moments of universal spiritual penetration and absorption. He could not live or sing without it, he could not exist without it. But each of those fantastic flights had to be paid for, in bundles of nake nerves, missing beats of an overworked heart, and drunken binges. As much as I could, I tried to help him to stop those sprees.

One day someone rang, late at night, at the door of my Paris flat. Russians' late visits are no surprise to anyone here. On the threshold stood Volodya and Marina. Their visit was no surprise either, only Volodya's appearance was somewhat unusual. Instead of his usual jeans he was wearing a well-fitting black suit, and with a tie, at that. Marina was also wearing black. I was puzzled and silent. "Birdie, dress yourself, and fast," Volodya said gloomily and seriously. (I must say that, despite his deliberate apparently rough manners, which were in keeping with his hoarse voice and general style, Volodya was always tender and sentimental towards me, and, although I was the taller of us, he obstinately called me "birdie", having once heard my wife call me that.) "Where — what on earth?" But they would not explain anything, and we were soon speeding towards some place in the suburbs of Paris, entirely relying on Volodya in the conviction that it was all necessary. "If my friend says I must, I will not ask him why..."

We stopped at an old mansion outside the city limits. When Marina moved off for a while, Volodya whispered to me: "We're going to be cured of alcoholism in a moment." "How? Who — ?" "Dalai Lama's Teacher!" Incredible! Slyly winking at me, Volodya pushed me towards an open door of the house, where I could see some strange figures in tall hats and yellow burnouses of some sort...

No sooner had we exchanged bows with a monk than we were asked to take off our footwear. Volodya had it easier, he had patent-leather shoes on (the first time I ever saw him wear anything of the sort), and I wore high boots, like always. OK, humility's the word. We walked on, bootless. Monks sitting in a vast hall, rattling their rattles and (Buddha forgive me!) mumbling something.

Volodya winked at me, cheerful and sly as always, but he looked fairly lost. No Marina in sight. She was somewhere in the upper regions. As we went up led by the hand by our yellow-faced brethren, Volodya confided in me that Marina's grandmother was a Chinese princess, and that was the only reason why we would be received by the Teacher of the Dalai Lama himself, who was stopping over here near Paris. He'd listen to us and help. "No drinking problem — it'll go as with a touch." Here, the mystical forces dozing within me came to life.

Which of us, the youngsters of the years of thaw, the legendary 1960s, was untouched by the Yoga craze! How many friends of ours had landed in mental homes after unsuccessful attempts to enter astral regions... My spirits rose. We entered a brightly lit hall where a tiny old man with roguish, cheerful eyes was sitting cross-legged in a corner under a bright-coloured silk canopy surrounded by narrow-eyed guards wearing exotic half-helmets, half-hoods. Frenchmen, all dressed in black, were kneeling before him in respectful postures, and in front of them all was Marina, her exquisite head bent low. The audience was drawing to a close. His face bored, the Lama was mouthing vague replies, all well-worn platitudes. Then it was our turn. The monk guard asked us what we had come for. Without raising her head, Marina translated the question into Russian. I looked at Volodya, Volodya looked at me. A slight confusion. The folks here were dealing in other-worldly affairs, purgatories, nirvanas, that sort of stuff, and we—Finally, Volodya said, "Marina, honey, tell him we have, um, a vodka problem, you know, fighting alcoholism —"

Marina translated, the Frenchmen who had not yet crawled out into the hall stopped and looked at us curiously. The effect on the old fellow was curious, too. He suddenly began to smile, and gestured with his withered hands for us to crawl closer to him. Although he clearly understood the question, he asked us to repeat it. Then, still smiling, he delivered an old parable, very similar to an Orthodox Russian one, to say that all sins came from alcohol. After that, he winked at us slyly and pointed to a small silver glass that stood on his left, on a shelf: it would seem that taking a glass of vodka once in a while was, after all, rather pleasing to the soul.

The audience was over. With his strong hands the Lama tore a silk kerchief into strips and tied them round Volodya's and my neck. "Go, I shall pray for you." The monks brought us photographs into the hall — gifts from the great Lama.

...Several months passed. Volodya was on location in Odessa, making a film. Whenever he phoned me in Paris, the first thing he would ask would be: "Well, old man, does it work? No drinking?" "No, how can I," I'd reply. "And you Vovchik? Does it work with you?" "Mishunya, the old man's great, just great! I'm fine! Completely dry!" It went on for quite a while.

So now I put on my favourite songs — Shulzhenko, Bernes, Utesov, I weep over them to my heart's content, I see this strip of silk and think: What is our old man doing these days?

I was always struck by Volodya's tact and his understanding of people. A man of great insights, he lived with his skin flayed. He was always afraid of making another soul suffer, even if it was by accident. He paid to fate an outrageous price for that gift. I always worshipped him as a person, I infinitely respected him as a creator. He was a great artist, a pastmaster. As for me, I'm only moving towards the goal I set myself in art, and I therefore often torment myself with doubts — was I worthy of his friendship?

Bella Akhmadulina

A WORD ABOUT VYSOTSKY

The unity of our thoughts and feeling consoles me, and inspires me with hope. It is fine to get together in admiration and adoration rather than for talking nonsense and for quarrelling. Although I am not, by the nature of my occupation, an entertainer of the public which I have always loved, I would still like to attenuate the stress of sadness that inevitably grips all our voices.

It's been many years since this burning pain dwelling somewhere near has remained inconsolable, and we shall hardly find a mint coolness which will some day lick this wound or comfort or anaesthetise this ever blazing spot. And yet, we have enough grounds for jubilation.

Mandelstam once said (I'm afraid that I will not reproduce his formula elegantly enough here) that a poet's death is an artistic act. That is to say, a poet's death is not an accident in the story of his artistic existence. So now, when we apply a sort of subjunctive mood to a fate that is completed, we err only on one point in our desire to comfort ourselves and each other. If we proceed from the truth that the crucial point about Vysotsky was that he was born a poet, that his was a poetic organism, we shall realise that the barriers and the perniciousness of insignificant and significant circumstances are nothing but trifles incidental to a great fate.

What could we have wished to the poet? Has any poet, ever, dwelled in prosperity? The answer is no. The subjunctive mood is not applicable to such people. Vysotsky was undoubtedly the leader of his fate. He was the ringleader of the whole story-line of his life.

I remember that I, too, had to bear the brunt of burning anger and insults for treating him as an independent man of letters. I know how his high and tidy pride had been stung (by the rejection of Vysotsky's application for the membership in the Writers' Union.— *Tr.*), but let us again take it that all this is vanity.

I believe Vysotsky's fate to be perfect, complete and happy, for it is impossible to make any revisions in it. He was undoubtedly guarded by a star of his own, and he faced it with a clear conscience. There is nothing that we can do about it — accidents are impossible here. Everything that accompanies the poet's noble, valiant and difficult existence is merely the necessary details; you see, one simply cannot do without them.

We know that there are editors and officials, but they are merely the necessary specks on the general picture of the poet's tragic life, you just can't do without them. It seems that is their only purpose.

And yet I would like to encompass you in the joy of knowing that that man has lived on this earth, irreparably and forever, and I believe that this is the only thought that can always console us and those that will come later.

He knew how well loved he was. This may have made his state of the mind even more difficult. But, accepting and never letting go of this pain, I shall still believe this fate to be absolutely accomplished and absolutely happy for mankind.

Mikhail Ulyanov

HE LIVED LIKE HE SANG...

He had a very rare gift — the gift of two voices. He had the voice of a dramatic actor, the kind that we all of us have, to some degree or other, a voice in which we express our thoughts and emotions. But he also had a unique talent: he had command of the song. This may well be the reason why his life was cut off so tragically early: he spent himself doubly, his two voices lashed out, and his two throats were rent.

People say that, strictly speaking, he was a much better singer than actor. I do not think so. The parts of Hamlet, Lopakhin, Khlopusha, and other roles in the theatre and the cinema were just as soul-shattering, they had the same fierce swing and intensity as the songs of that remarkable artist. But the songs are more democratic and more moving, they are more accessible and omnipresent, and that was why he was, of course, better known by his songs. But, as I recall his roles and songs, I see that it was an organic fusion, although in the songs he may have been more expressive — not because they were more fierce and temperamental but because he expressed in them the thoughts and ideas which were lacking in some of his roles, and which were more exactly expressed in his songs.

Vysotsky's songs. How are we to explain their phenomenal success? Everybody listened to them, everybody sang them, but only to oneself: no one could perform them. It is amazing, but no one has really sung, and will hardly ever sing, his songs. What is needed is his temperament, this strange, complex, cracked and seemingly dying voice in which he sang so many years without a single false note. No one could put the whole of himself into a song the way Vysotsky did, close to the fatal border; despite the frequently unimposing text and street melody, Vysotsky's

324

songs became a bitter, philosophical comment on life.

One of my favourite songs is *Unruly Horses*; here, he expressed so much and with such an incredible force that it would be enough for a lengthy treatise about life and death. It is a mistake to think that Vysotsky imitated a sort of pseudopopular rollicking style. Not at all. His songs, especially the last ones, were informed not only with feeling and emotion but also with fervent thought, thought that perceived the very essence of the world and man.

He died early. That is an awful tragedy, the more so that death carried him away at a time of a spectacular ascent: he was growing, expanding in all directions, and his promise was much greater than his achievement. He was a wealthy and happy man: his wealth was his talent, and his happiness lay in the years when everybody hung on his lips, listening avidly to his songs — the spring that slaked a thirst that could not be slaked by anyone else. What other artist can boast of such constant love of the public which he enjoyed?

Some of his songs were great, extraordinary; there were also those which were below his potential: artistic work is artistic work, some songs turned out well, others didn't, this is only natural. On the whole, though — why were his songs so appealing? Why were they loved so much? I will hardly be able to answer this question, but generally a song is sung when it touches the secret strings of the soul with a strong and warm hand, when it expresses and reflects the times. Why do the people, all of them, suddenly begin to sing a song? Why did the people sing *Katyusha*? I guess, a kind of dam bursts, and a poet's song finds a way to the people's heart. This is what happened to Vysotsky's songs. The people listened to these songs, they are still listening, and will yet listen to them for a long time. I have no doubt that I will express a general feeling if I say that it is necessary to collect, as soon as possible, all of his songs (and there are hundreds of them); and to make an album of LPs with his best songs (and there are dozens of these) as soon as possible, for his art is the art that "belongs to the people" (Lenin's words.— *Tr.*), or rather *must* belong to the people.

We were never close, I knew him the way all actors

know one another. Through his songs, though, he was close to all of us, even if his potential was not fully revealed yet. On one occasion, we were shooting a film on location, and I lived in a hotel where someone in the next room listened to a wonderful record made in France non-stop, day in, day out. I had to learn my part, and instead I learned all the songs, every single word and intonation. Later, I described all this to Vladimir. He smiled: "Well, I'm not to blame, am I."

He was the flower of our land, of our people and times. He was a flower that might not have looked exquisite but had stunning fragrance. He stuck like a thistle in the hearts of the people who were so much in need of literature, minstrels, actors, poets — like Vysotsky.

Alla Demidova

HE WROTE THE WAY HE LIVED...

The better one knows a person, the more difficult it is to speak of him. One is at a loss which angle to choose. Each of us, those who worked side by side with Vysotsky over 16 years at the Taganka Theatre could talk about him for hours — but writing is something different. At present, a great deal is written about him, thank God. Right after his death, though, all we could do, after a great deal of string-pulling, was publish a brief announcement in *Vechernyaya Moskva*. During his life, he sang:

> *Though my path was so long, and unstinting*
> *Was the praise people lavished on me —*
> *On my death, not one paper will print it,*
> *My brief, modest obituary.*
> *But I am not sorry...*

Still, all those who knew him, however slightly, must write memoirs about him, I believe. Let them merely be many-coloured pebbles for a future large-scale mosaic story of the poet's life, which will be written by a future artist of suitable stature. We know more about Pushkin now than his closest friend Sobolevsky did (who, incidentally, left no memoirs about him, although he probably knew Pushkin better than others): he had no access to the poet's correspondence and his journals, to all the archives which still keep surfacing, sheet after sheet, a hundred and fifty years later.

I do not want to draw any parallels or to compare anyone's fates; like Marina Tsvetaeva said, "the poet's job is to reveal and, having revealed, to hide."

And who or what is going to reveal things? It will be Time, apparently. If I recall Pushkin in speaking of Vysotsky, the reason lies in the similarity of the superhu-

327

man concentration of all the creative forces, in the powerful ability to absorb things and to give them away.

The perception of life as the highest duty. Uniting rather than dividing. Serving the great evolution of the soul and of life.

The perception of one's self in connection with the cosmic, highest spiritual element. High ideals and the light and warmth of moral emotions: every great poet must be able to kindle all this in other people. Like an Olympian god, the poet kindles the moral fire in the hearts of men.

...Vysotsky had a constant foreboding that the end was near, and that he would have no time to express his credo. The contradiction between high duty and real life crushed him. He knew no rest. His whole life was a rage of passions in the constant awareness that he could have done more.

He did not fully realise his potential. Hence his constant breakdowns and breaking off from friends: he never forgave the slightest betrayal. And the way he broke off with some people was cruel.

He himself described the duality of his personality very well in the poem *A Stupid Dream Lambasted Me...*

...So what am I to recall here? The day when Volodya came to our theatre in Taganka Square, only recently organised, having seen before that the graduation production of *The Good Woman of Sezuan*, and having decided (as he later said himself) to join this company and no other? He was then a young and completely unknown actor; he wore a grey tweed-like jacket frayed at the elbows; his face was not yet fully formed, slightly puffy. Or shall I remember his radiant eyes when he came to the theatre wearing a new synthetic leather brown coat with a fur collar? The way he gradually assumed his image: a medium-height broad-shouldered man in tight and always very tidy trousers (he preferred various shades of brown), in his favourite red short-sleeved silk shirt which fitted closely his biceps and breast muscles? The way the puffiness gradually disappeared and face assumed its characteristic set, his stubborn chin slightly pushed forward?

I do not know whose idea it was for Hamlet to wear jeans and a sweater. This happened, I guess, because we all of us dressed like that in those years. In the two years of rehearsing *Hamlet*, Volodya proved his right to wear the jeans and sweater, only in the play he wore black — black velveteen jeans and a black handmade sweater with a powerful open neck, which became broader with the years, stood out in relief, and was now like an instrument, an organ with pipe-like veins, especially when he sang. He was buried in a new pair of black trousers and a new black sweater which Marina brought over from Paris.

Generally speaking, he had a very special attitude towards costume, both onstage and in everyday life. Thus jackets did not suit him, and he did not wear them, except for the first tweed-like one. True, I remember one night when we celebrated someone's anniversary (or was it a first night?) and were all of us sitting in the upper canteen at tables; suddenly Vysotsky appeared in a fantastic club jacket, a blue blazer with gold buttons. We all groaned in amazement and delight. He had put it on to impress us. Well, he did. That was why I never saw him wear that blazer any more. The more surprising to me was his decision to play Lopakhin in a white suit, which did not suit him but, stressing a kind of isolation of Lopakhin from all the others, helped the actor onstage.

And his sudden, impetuous plasticity! One day, during our first years at the Taganka Theatre, we were sitting in an empty auditorium during a rehearsal on a tour in Leningrad. He whispered something into my ear (something frivolous enough). I replied sharply. He jumped up and walked towards the stage stepping over the rows of seats like a hurdle racer, to tame his fury. I did not hear a single curt word from him, although I often saw his eyes white with anger, and clenched teeth. I have kept a photograph of a rehearsal of *Hamlet* at which the director said something insulting and personal to me; I silently turned my back on him and walked towards the door never to return to the theatre. Volodya took me by the hand and spoke to the director, very stubbornly. The picture conveys the impression of this unflinching stubbornness: it was clear that, come what may, that man would have his way. I was always struck by this independence of his. I had the impression that he could do anything in moments like this. He merely awaited a lucky day when he would overcome all the hitches and do all the jobs that had piled up. He had an unerring nose for when such a lucky day would come, an animal feeling about it. I remember that after the rehearsal he took me home; he said he would have to drop in at Kolpachny Lane to get his passport. It was a summer day. I was waiting for him in the car. The lane was empty. Suddenly I saw Volodya walk down that humped lane, so elegant and radiant, he got into the car and said: "It's my lucky day, I can do anything I like, ask for anything you wish, I'll do it..."

One night, after playing in *Hamlet* in a stuffy auditorium in summer, we went to bathe to Serebryany Bor (a park in Moscow.— *Tr.*). We had neither swim-suits nor towels, and we dried ourselves on Volodya's shirt. Not far from where we were, some Frenchmen and women were sitting in comfortable folding chairs round a table covered with a red chequered cloth, wearing multi-coloured bath-robes and drinking Beaujolais. There was even a candle burning on the table! We laughed: we were in our own country, and yet we did everything in a hurry, off the cuff, while these French people were doing everything so thoroughly, as if they were at home. Several years later Volodya and myself went to a party of actors and writers, and we all of us went to someone's country house near Paris. When we came to the place, it transpired that the host had left the key to the house behind. We couldn't very well go back, could we? We made ourselves comfortable, as best we could, on the river bank, we bathed, and again we dried ourselves on someone's shirt. Nearby, a happy French family was picnicking in bourgeois comfort. Volodya and myself, we talked about this international trait of the creative intelligentsia, this complete lack of method and order, and remembered Serebryany Bor. On the other hand, whenever we went on tour, his hotel room would always be very tidy. He liked making tea, and he always had countless little jars with various kinds of tea. When he could afford to buy exotic wines, he would arrange a whole battery of beautiful bottles in elegant rows and never allowed anyone to touch it. Everybody cursed his miserliness, and then, one night, it would all be unpredictably thrown down the drain — no one knew why or with whom, all of a sudden...

So what am I to recall? How am I to tell it?

One day, after Vysotsky's death, there was a telephone call, and an excited man's voice said: "Don't put down the receiver, I've travelled here from afar. Tell me, did Vysotsky live the way he wrote?" I asked him, "Tell me, did Pushkin live the way he wrote?" Then I added — somewhat sharply, but only because I was not sure how to reply: "If you find an answer to this question — whether Pushkin lived the way he wrote — you will find the answer to the question about Vysotsky."

We receive endless letters with the same kind of questions. Endless declarations of love for him. People write to us, to those who knew him. I believe that a whole volume could be printed of poems entirely devoted to Vysotsky. I, for one, have hundreds of these...

People reproach us, those who worked with him, that we did not take care of him, that we forced him to appear on the stage although he was close to a heart attack. It is hard to justify oneself, but I sometimes wonder if it is possible to stop a plane during take-off with one's bare hands, even if one knows that it is heading for disaster in flight... He was carried along by a force that I cannot describe or name — was it fate? Predestination? Mission? I think — I'm certain — that he knew of his end, he knew that one day the heart would no longer be able to stand the inhuman strain and the mad tempo. But he could not stop.

He always looked strong and healthy. At one of his concerts he announced the title of the song he was going to sing: *My Funeral* — and there was laughter in the audience. And he started to sing: "I had a dream..."

The theme of life and death is the theme of *Hamlet*. In the Taganka production, the play begins with a scene in which the grave-diggers appeared on the stage and started digging, throwing real earth on the proscenium and unearthing the skull... It ended with the words of Hamlet/Vysotsky, who dies against the white backdrop:

> *Had I but time, as this fell sergeant, Death,*
> *Is strict in his arrest — O, I could tell you —*
> *...The rest is silence...*

On a tour abroad we saw Bergman's film *Gycklarnas afton*. There is a sequence there in which the actor plays death very naturally. As we walked towards our hotel after the film, we exchanged impressions, and I said that it was dangerous for an actor to play games like that — it was a bog that could suck one down... Vysotsky objected, saying that we were all of us mortal, that we would all die, simply each of us would die in his or her time. Some time later I read these lines in his poem *In Memory of Vasily Shukshin!*

> *Death goes for those of us in earnest*
> *Who play at death, and die in play...*

Incidentally, I often came across certain words and whole sentences in his poems and songs that originally cropped up in conversation, in verbal games, improvisations, and catchwords. Thus I heard "In my flight, sinews bursting, I hurtle..." in his account of how he played Khlopusha, and only later in his song. Familiar names often appeared in the songs, and not because they were about concrete individuals but simply because he liked the sound of the name. We had an actor at our theatre whose name was Butkeyev. Later he emerged in the line: "And, smashing my jaw, Butkeyev thought..." But that was not about our Butkeyev, for he was never a boxer and was generally a fairly peaceful person.

Songs that are sometimes seen as dedications to someone were originally impersonal, like *She Was in Paris...* or *Flowers in No-Man's Land...*

Generally speaking, as one reads his poems and songs now, one is struck by the great number of remarkable images and fine poetic lines which I, for one, previously missed because of the magic of the voice, of the manner in which he performed his songs.

And as for his presentiment of death — One day a literary analyst will trace the connections between such lines as: "How I will end, when I have sung my fill...", "I'm driving poison in my gullet...", "They are true poets, those who end their days in tragedy...".

Or you may remember these lines: "Our life expectancy has grown considerably of late —/Perhaps now poets also will last longer", "My heart's not mine — it is a distant frozen clot —/It's time I went where all there is, is *no* and *not*". Or this one, in *Katya-Katerina*:

"The funeral service is ahead..." Or: "No monument to me they will erect..." Not to mention his beautiful poem *The Memorial*, in which he described with absolute precision the monument which now stands over his grave in Vagankovo Cemetery.

When Volodya Vysotsky died, the theatre announced a competition among artists and sculptors in order to choose the best design for a monument. An exposition was arranged in the foyer. There were many interesting ideas there, but none was suitable for the place where Volodya was buried. He lived on a height open to all the winds, and he was buried right as you enter the cemetery, near the gates. At first, I was sorry that we had buried him in such a place, but I realise now that it would be hard to find a better place. There are many fine people lying in this unique Moscow cemetery. I often think that it would be nice for all of them to get together, to talk and sing. For they all of them were singing people — some sang with their throat, others with their heart. Yesenin, Shpalikov, Dahl, Dvorzhetsky, Vysotsky...

We, Volodya Vysotsky's friends, could not make up our minds about a design for a monument. During the sitting of the artistic council of our theatre, I recalled Yermolinsky's account of Mikhail Bulgakov's funeral. The writer's widow, Yelena Sergeyevna, did not know what kind of monument to erect. Somebody told her that a large stone from Gogol's old grave was lying near the gates of the Novodevichye Cemetery. No one needed the stone, because a new bust had recently been erected on the grave. Yelena Sergeyevna gave the workers some money, and they dragged the stone from the gates over to Bulgakov's grave. Those who know of that story, they just know it, and those who don't, well, they think that it's just a stone lying there, with the legend: "Mikhail Afanasyevich Bulgakov", and the dates of birth and death. Everybody liked the story and the idea of continuity it embodied. I don't remember who had the idea to find a chunk of a meteorite and place it on Vysotsky's grave, with an inscription in small letters at the foot: "Vladimir Semyonovich Vysotsky, 1938-1980". Anyone who would want to read the inscription would involuntarily have to bow — to the stone, to Vysotsky's grave, to the old church beyond the grave, and to the whole of the cemetery. Unfortunately, we were unable to put this idea into practice. For a while, the ebb and flow of time overtook and swamped us... As I attended, in the autumn of 1985, the opening of the bronze memorial, I recalled Vysotsky's poem *The Memorial* — and thought that here, too, he had proved clairvoyant.

Certainly he lived "along the chasm's edge, upon the precipice's brink", as he sang in his *Unruly Horses*. Certainly we were aware of it. And of course, the presentiment of inevitable misfortune seared our hearts when he was still alive. I remember that in May 1980 we were on tour in Poland, and a farewell banquet was given for us. We were all sitting at a great long table. Volodya and Daniel Olbrychski, with his wife, were sitting opposite me. As always, Volodya quickly ate what he had on the plate and then talked avidly. On that occasion, he spoke of a film they wanted to make — about three inmates escaping from a Nazi concentration camp. Of the three escapees one was a Russian, to be played by Volodya, another a Pole (Olbrychski) and a Frenchman (I forget the actor's name). They liked the idea and the story, but they could not find a director. For some reason, all the directors to whom the screenplay was offered refused. In the middle of the conversation Volodya suddenly looked at the watch, leaped to his feet and, without taking leave of anyone, rushed for the door. He was in a hurry to catch a plane to Paris. Olbrychski, amazed, jumped up, too, and hurriedly apologised to me for himself and for Volodya: "Today, I play the part of Vysotsky's driver, so you'll have to excuse me..." I only had time to say to his back: "Not a bad role, that..." At this moment Jan Lomnicki, who was in the chair, noticed Vysotsky going out of the door and shouted for all to hear: "Vysotsky's leaving us — a round of applause for Vysotsky!" This "Vysotsky's leaving us" suddenly sent shivers down my spine, a sort of chasm seemed to open, and, to smooth over the gaffe, I added, in the same tone: "Olbrychski's leaving us — a round of applause for Olbrychski!"

At the end of summer 1980 we, a group of Volodya's friends, sat around talking of the circumstances under which each of us learnt about Volodya's death. I remember well Ilya Averbakh's story [1]: "Me, Natasha and Tolya Romov were living at that time on Lake Valdai. Vegetating... I was lazily reading a script which Volodya had thrust on me before our departure; as I read it, I felt annoyed at the well-fed, well-to-do people suggesting that I make a film about victims of a famine... As I read it, I swore at their flats crammed with mahogany furniture (although I myself live in one), their Mercedeses, their endless trips abroad. During my angry monologue, I heard the announcement about Vysotsky's death on the radio. After the shock, after all the talk of the expected unexpectedness of this tragedy, I took up the script again and began reading it anew. I liked everything about it. I kept thinking what a wonderful film it might make with these unique actors, how absolutely right Vysotsky would be for this part..."

I often observed this sudden change in the minds and the attitude, both in myself and others. After Vysotsky's death, the whole country, which knew Vysotsky as a myth and a legend, wanted to know concrete facts from his life. And we, those who knew him well during his lifetime, were trying after his death to establish the roots of this legend and myth. As I think of Vysotsky now, his image is different from the one that I knew during his life. I learnt a great deal only afterwards: his poems, songs and prose unpublished during his life, stenographic records of the talks he gave before audiences.

All this may give them impression that we only began to appreciate him after his death, as often happens with persons we know but little. That is not so. Everyone at our theatre sensed the scope of his personality, his uniqueness — even if everyone sensed them in his or her own way. But we began all on the same level and lived on the same level, even if some of us spurted ahead. We never had a hierarchy. We knew all about him, and of his end. He, too, knew all about us, I believe.

I once read in Andrei Voznesensky that death pursued Vysotsky, and that a huge overhead-track hoist collapsed during a rehearsal of *Hamlet*, missing Vysotsky by a miracle. It was true that death had followed on the heels of our generation since the mid-1970s. Sociologists harshly call this "social deaths" accompanying a "change in the times". We lost our friends: Gennady Shpalikov, Vasily Shukshin, Larisa Shepitko, Ilya Averbakh... But others also died right next to us, in the theatre: Mila Voziyan, Oleg Kolokolnikov, Alexander Eibozhenko... The hoist collapsed when Vysotsky did not have to be onstage: we were rehearsing the scene of Ophelia's funeral. We were standing in the wings, the coffin of Ophelia on our shoulders, the whole retinue of Claudius and Gertrude. Our small amateur orchestra was playing the dead march, a few minutes before that, I scurried about in search of a piece of black cloth to indicate mourning... When we stepped on the stage, the ill-fated hoist (of which a stage-hand had said, "This thing looks clumsy, it must be unreliable.") did indeed fall on us. This ugly and bulky thing fell on top of us, covering us all with a knitted curtain. In the silence, we heard the director's calm voice, "Well, who has been killed?" On that occasion, we escaped with scratches... Vysotsky was sitting in the auditorium.

Now, all those questions — how come we couldn't control him, how come we made him act... I remember that during the 1978 tour of France, in Marseilles, Volodya went on a binge — kicked over the traces — disappeared. We looked for him all over the city, and found him at dawn. Marina flew over from Paris. She was the only person who had power over him in such a state. He was sleeping it off in his room having taken a dose of sleeping pills, while we were rehearsing a new ending of the play in case Volodya were to be unable to go onstage, in case the irreparable happened. The play began. Neither before nor after did Volodya play that part with such brilliance. He was a genius. It was not the state "along the chasm's edge, upon the precipice's brink" but one on a thin ray of light across a chasm. He was white as chalk. In the intervals between his scenes Volodya would run into my dressing-room, which was closest to the stage, and vomit clots of blood into the sink.

This kind of naturalistic detail is not usually acceptable in memoirs, as they can be disparaging to the bright image in our memory. One would prefer for the humdrum and the ordinary to go, and for memory, for the spirit, to remain. That's the way things usually are, but in an exceptional fate, everything is exceptional. Pushkin wrote to Vyazemsky: "We know enough about Byron. We have seen him on the throne of glory, we have seen his great soul tormented, we have seen him in his coffin in the midst of Greece born anew.— So you want to see him on a bed-pan. The mob avidly devours confessions, diaries, etc., for in its baseness it enjoys the humiliation of the high, the weaknesses of the mighty. Whenever some abomination is revealed, it is in raptures. *He is small as we are, he is disgusting as we are!* That's a lie, you rats: he is small and disgusting in a way different from yours."

He could die any second. We all of us knew it. His wife knew it. He himself knew it — and he went onstage. We never knew how the play would end, and when. On that night it ended fortunately — thank God.

Could we have cancelled the play, replaced it by another? We could. Could we have given it a miss in Poland? Not played it on July 13 and 18? We could. But we would have been different from the kind of people we were. Vysotsky would not have been the Vysotsky whose death brought many thousands to Taganka Square.

A long time has passed since his death. Now I remember him more often than I did during his lifetime. He is still giving me the gift of his friends, whose existence I had not even suspected. These days, I feel differently when I watch films in which he played, or listen to his records. Before evening performances, I very often listen to Vysotsky's songs — to absorb his energy, power, love of life... Summing up his brief life, I try to determine what the main thing about him was. What was his essence? And why did he, and no one else, find such a response in the hearts of dozens of millions of people? I am not a sociologist, but I believe that the feelings of protest, the self-revelation and self-realisation were expressed through art, and in this special case, in the 1960s theatre, through an outcry. There was a great deal that we could not express in words, but the cry of pain resounded. With his unique voice, Vysotsky sounded that note as no one else could.

As one reads his poems, one sees that some of them are far from perfect. But there is not a single line of lies there, there is no poetic floridness or flourishes with which our avant-garde poetry of that two decades sinned. The feeling — the word — the expressive means fused in his poetry. There was not a slit, no gap left for lies and rubbish. He wrote the way he lived...

Valery Zolotukhin

IT WAS LIKE I SAID, OR
A STUDY IN AN UNSTABLE VOWEL

I wouldn't like to pour any ointment on any flies or drop any flies in ointment, or rather a flow of hurried memoirs, indignations, visions and triumphs that now submerges Vysotsky's name, for the "rivalry at the coffin", as Thomas Mann put it, is sure to continue for some time, and I will apparently have time enough to take part in the competition, and to trumpet to the world what I have to say to glorify that name. And to reap the reward I deserve. Today, however, I was asked to produce an account of some particular case, example, episode or something like that of which I was the only eyewitness — without going too far in my analysis of the poet's verbal art or evaluation of his actor's ingenuity, without assessing the scope of the phenomenon, or attempting to exploit his feat for purposes of personal self-assertion. I gave my consent, for such a particular fact (the fact of a genuine case or the fantasy of the reporter) is in any case unverifiable: it was like I said...

So this how it was. I have an autograph: "To Valery Zolotukhin, accomplice in the making of *Bath-hut*, Siberian peasant * and writer, from Vladimir Vysotsky, with friendship." Let me decode this autograph.

It was a gift of fate that I was an eyewitness, an observant spy who was present when Vladimir Vysotsky wrote several of his most significant songs, including my favourite *Bath-hut*:

---

* The actual Russian word is *muzhik,* and the translation "peasant" now probably has historical relevance only. The root is *muzh-* "man" or "husband", but manliness accounts only for part of the semantic scope of the word. Other connotations are gumption, mother wit, hardiness, earthiness, and a host of other virtues, along with a few vices.— *Tr*.

Warm the bath-hut, my love, set it steaming,
I've been out in the cold for so long.
It still seems to me I must be dreaming...
Heady steam, it will loosen my tongue...

True, the word "song" is not a very good term to denote this kind of creations. Future generations will probably find a better one.

Well, now: *Bath-hut.* Summer of 1968. Shooting the film *Master of the Taiga.* Siberia, Krasnoyarsk Territory, Mana District, the village of Vyezhy Log. People said that during the Civil War, Admiral Kolchak had done some blood-letting here. We were billeted in the house of Anna Filippovna, or rather in the empty, abandoned house of her son who had left the whole of his homestead for his mother to sell, and headed for the big city, like so many of us. The Mosfilm Studios let us have two folding beds and the bedding; a guitar, when not in use, always lay on the orphaned iron bedstead which we covered with a cotton blanket, to please the eye. For some reason, this abandoned house without any curtains on the windows was lit by a huge electric bulb, about 500 watt strong. Who had left it there, and for whom? Who was going to enjoy its light? Vladimir later said that the bulb had been given us by the Mosfilm photographer. I don't remember the occasion, so the bulb must have been given to Vladimir. He worked during the night. In the daytime, he was on the lot. He would sometimes rouse me from sleep, that I might share the joy of an apt line. The apt lines were aplenty, so I was never bored in his company. The people, the Siberians, kept peering in the windows. The older ones stood about at some distance, smoking or cracking sunflower seeds, the younger ones were lying among the burdocks, very likely holding their breath: they were seeing Vysotsky in the flesh, they could even see him work. I just slept — I was sick and tired of having to drive them away, and there was nothing out of which to make curtains. I didn't take off the policeman's uniform in which I acted in the film — I had to get used to it as if it were my skin; the villagers, though, thought I was Vysotsky's guard. I'm not joking; in 1968, my phiz was literally unknown to anyone. The older boys (and the grownups with them — the latter would have been too shy to do it themselves) came and asked me, as his guard, to "show them Vysotsky in the flesh, and close". So I showed him. I would call Vladimir, joking: "Come out, sonny, show yourself to your people...". This happened once, and twice, and more — there was a constant stream of them, all wanting to see him in the flesh. So I called him, courteously, politely, often resorting to all kinds of ruses, of course. I thought I'd let them see him — that would be their chance in quite a long time, most likely... And then I thought (wasn't I the clever one, now?) why should I show him for NOTHING, when I can do the same for SOMETHING? The next time when visitors came, I said, "Look, lads, bring him some milk, and then I'll show him to you." So I got milk — by the ton. I got it every time somebody came to see him. I began to make cream and sour cream, keeping the surplus in the cellar or taking it to feed the colleagues; I even learnt to make curds, and was all set to start making butter when Vladimir Semyonovich put an end to my dairy efforts. "Look, Zolotukhin," he said, "you stop this dairy business. House full of jugs, one can't move. It's too much for us. You take it to the market-place on Sunday."

"What's the difference between a bath-hut the white way and a bath-hut the black way?" he asked me one day. I must say that he often used me as a consultant on peasant life, believing that as a native Siberian and a collective farmer I had to know the lexicon and the way of life in my native parts to a T (which was, of course, a great error). But I was in no hurry to dissuade him, playing my role of a born peasant willingly and to the end, sometimes lying till I was burning with shame. This time, though, I knew the answer to his question quite precisely, for my father used to rebuild our bath-hut every other day, white bath-hut to black bath-hut and the other way round, just as his soul and body craved. Now, a bath-hut the black way is a hut in which a small stove is built of boulders or stone slabs without any kind of chimney. The fire heats directly those stones on which water will later be splashed to make hot steam. The stove also heats the walls of the hut, you can hardly touch them. The smoke from the burning fire fills the whole hut, and it goes out through the door or any chink it can find. When a bath-hut like that is being warmed, it looks as if it is on fire. The walls and the ceiling are naturally covered with a layer of soot; it is, of course, swept away from time to time — but not all of it. This kind of bath-hut is easy to build but not so easy to warm. It's an art, sort of. You have to let out all the coal-gas and at the same time keep the heat. It's a whole ritual: some go in the first steam, others, in the second, the third, and so on. Then you take the birch-twig besoms for lashing yourself with. You have to warm them in the steam properly, otherwise the leaves will all fall off.

A bath-hut the white way is a more cultured establishment; it's clean within. The smoke goes out through the chimney into the wide world. Even the door of the stove is often outside. But there is something lacking about this kind of bath-hut, for me, at least; it's just like cooking fisherman's fish-soup on the gas range instead of over a fire by the riverside. Bath-hut the black way for me; although my brother and myself, we often came from the bath-hut with out behinds covered with soot, and would be sent to wash a second time, in a bath-hut that would be quite cold already...

That summer, Vladimir steamed himself in all kinds of bath-huts: there is no lack of these in Siberia yet. One night, he roused me from sleep and asked: "What did you say the shelf was called on which you steam yourself? *Polók*?" "Right, Volodya, *polók* it is..." "OK, sleep well, boy..." I don't remember if it was on that night or later that he roused me again, all worked up, guitar at the ready; and he sang *Bath-hut* in the hollow-sounding, abandoned house, milk jugs everywhere, lit by a 500 watt bulb:

> *Warm the bath-hut, my love, set it steaming,*
> *I will lash myself glowing red,*
> *On shelf somewhere near the ceiling*
> *I will squash all my doubts — kill them dead.*
>
> *I'll ease off to the point of brutality,*
> *Then a roll in the snow will feel good...*

Somewhere in the middle of the song I began humming the second part, carried away by the mood and the tune and the lyrics.

I hummed and I wept with the joy and happiness of

being an eyewitness. And when the first wave of adulation passed, I told Vladimir, in my pride of an accomplice, that it was wrong to say *na polóke* ("on the shelf"), the correct form was *na polké*. "Why?" "I don'know, you just can't say so."

"We in the Altai", "we in Siberia", "we common people", I swaggered, although the explanation was simple — unfortunately, it came too late. The vowel "o" in the word *polók* is an unstable vowel, and it is dropped in the oblique cases. But what did we care about that vowel? True, in the recordings of the later years one can hear clearly Vladimir generously allowing the "o" vowel to drop out, compensating for its absence by leaning on the rhythmical spring of the neighbouring "l": *na pol-l-l-ké...*

This my comment, which I could not explain, and the fact that we often later sang *Bath-hut* together, contains the whole of the secret of my autograph, and of my contribution, happy and fervent. Later still, it was beyond me to join in the singing, my voice sounded too puny when Volodya turned on such other-worldly, supernatural power that one even felt scared.

By way of an appendix, or an afterword, I'd like to say this. At one of my appearances before a live audience, I got this note: "Is it true, or is it gossip, that you envy Vladimir Vysotsky in a pure, disinterested way?" My answer to this query seemed to me not so much apt as sincere — almost.

"Yes, I envy Vladimir Vysotsky, and that envy is of the blackest kind there is. Dear audience, I beg that you understand me correctly: it is quite possible that I don't envy Pushkin himself the way I envy Vysotsky, precisely because I had the great honour and misfortune to be the latter's contemporary."

You may say that it's too bold and incongruous a statement. But there are many who hold the view, and even express it, like hitting one with an axe: "Vysotsky? We don't know of any such poet..."

The truth, now... Does it really exist outside our opinions, tastes, and definitions?

That's all about this episode.

Yuri Trifonov

A FEW LINES
ABOUT VLADIMIR VYSOTSKY

...Vladimir Vysotsky's creative life may rightly be said to be a biography of our times. True, a biography is something coherent and consistent, while Volodya's songs — most of his songs — covered, at different periods, very important and, if I may say so, very sore "points" of our history, of the life of our people. He responded to everything that concerned the people, and told us about it. He had songs and poems about war, about the difficult postwar times, when he was only a small boy yet felt and understood everything very well. He had songs about the great construction projects and the difficult time of 1937, about cosmonauts and sportsmen, mountain-climbers and frontier quards and poets, about everything — you name it. He covered a vast spectrum of our life, and that is the reason why his popularity was so great and perhaps, so unexpected to many. He went straight into the midst of the people as the most popular songsmith of our times. No wonder that he was close to so many.

Above all, I think he had a great talent for writing songs and poetry. If he had not had this great talent, he could not have become so popular a person. It is also very important that, far from fearing it, he aspired to reflect in his songs the most vital concerns of the people, the themes of the common people's thoughts and conversations. Another point is that he did not try to legalise his songs, to make them officially accepted and published. All that came later, and was quite a natural desire. At the beginning, though, he wrote and sang for the people around him, for the common listener. Not restricted by anything, he wrote of the most burning and difficult issues of our times and that was why his songs gradually penetrated into the very heart of the people. To many, it was unexpected. His songs were played in the flats of the most highbrow of intellectuals, he was loved by the young people, and is, of course, still loved — by students and schoolchildren. I myself was an eyewitness of that success. In spring, he gave a concert at a military club, and he invited me. It was the first time I saw him perform in public, and I was struck by the delight and understanding with which both soldiers and high-ranking officers listened to him. They accepted him as one of their own, for they all of them, to a man, had recordings of his songs. He also sang his new songs there, but on the whole they all knew him well. He entered the living rooms of all the people. His popularity was so universal that he was loved even by those who apparently couldn't possibly love him — by those whom he ridiculed. And there were so many whom he did ridicule. He was an acutely satirical poet and singer, he mocked at bureaucrats, high officials, lickspittles, fools and especially Philistines, the people who devoured well-being. He had very many malicious and extremely biting songs about this stratum of the urban population, and yet all these people loved him, as if they refused to understand that he jeered at them. To some extent, his vast popularity was mysterious, and I cannot explain it in two words.

In his human qualities and in his work he was a very *Russian* person. He expressed the quintessential Russian mentality probably better than anyone else. In this, he went into the very depths, sometimes going very far, even into the underworld, the criminal strata. All this was fused together: frontier guards, astronauts, officials, workers, the underworld — and all this was a picture of Russia.

Was there one main feature in his life and work? I don't know. I find it hard to single out one main feature, but I believe that Vysotsky expressed the daredevil spirit, the desperate and happy-go-lucky confusion of the Russian people and at the same time a breadth of the soul. All this taken together — it is hard to find a word for this quality — this poetic and at the same time mocking and wise attitude towards life lent his songs their vitality.

There were many people at his funeral. Even people who knew him very well did not expect that so many would come. Certain conclusions may be drawn from this. One of these concerns art itself. Volodya Vysotsky did not enjoy much official recognition, although he was an actor, he gave concerts and was an actor of the Taganka Theatre; considering his stature, though, he should have been given more scope. He was not often advertised in the media, but it turned out that he needed no official glorification at all: his talent did everything for him. That is indubitably an important lesson as far as art and life in art are concerned. Another sad lesson is that we do not appreciate people while they are alive. All of us who knew Vysotsky realised that he was a man of great stature, but no one actually realised just how great — not even those closest to him. That is a very bitter lesson but, like all the other lessons, it is of no benefit to mankind. Unfortunately, all this is going to continue, but each time this happens, one feels very bitter.

...There have always been a great many poets in Russia. Russia is in general a country of poets, it loves poetry. But love for Vysotsky, the nature and vastness of that love, is unique; one can only compare it, say, with the feelings of the people for Yesenin. People will probably reproach me for bias and exaggeration. Such personalities as Yesenin or Mayakovsky are colossal, despite all the differences in the people's attitude towards them; their death shook everyone. Vysotsky's death was also a shock. It shows that there is indeed a great love for true poetry in Russia: this is a feature inherent in the people. But I must be precise here: I am not speaking of love for poets in general but of love for our great poets, true poets. Alexander Tvardovsky's dacha is next to mine; I know that he enjoyed during his lifetime, and enjoys now, the people's great love. Or you take this: people come to the graves of Pushkin, Pasternak and Yesenin and read their poems; that is to say, they express a love for them which is unknown in other countries. The same will now happen to Vladimir Vysotsky.

...I did not meet Vysotsky very often, for we really became acquainted only in the last years of his life, when I began to write for the Taganka Theatre; and here we met. Still, I do remember some of Vysotsky's purely human traits. He had this desire to go away somewhere, to flee all of a sudden — especially in the later years. These flurries were sometimes inexplicable. He would suddenly up and say, "I'm flying for Alma Ata," or, "Tomorrow I'll have to fly to Sochi." The pretext was often very simple: he had to help someone, there was a friend waiting, something had to be done for him.

I remember the day on which *The House on the Embankment* would open in the Taganka Theatre — that would be the last première, to be followed by a banquet; in Krasnaya Pakhra, I met Volodya who was driving from his dacha to Moscow. Whenever he saw me on the road, he would stop the car, step out and kiss me very solemnly; that was a very touching custom of his — he could never simply ride past. This time he looked extremely worried and anxious. "Will you come for the banquet, Volodya?" I asked. He did not play in this production, but all the same I wanted him to come very much...

"No, Yuri Valentinovich, I'm sorry, but I'm leaving." "Where?" "To see some lumberjacks." It seemed he was going somewhere near Tyumen, in Western Siberia. I was amazed, of course: the theatre season was not over yet, what visits to lumberjacks was he talking about? We parted; on the following day, I flew somewhere myself. He did not fly to the lumberjacks, after all, it seems, but the episode just goes to show that in his last years he was constantly possessed by a desire to rush somewhere, to perform completely fantastic deeds.

We were together at the New Year's party of that year which proved fatal to him. I only remember that night because Volodya was there, and I saw proof of yet another character trait — his extraordinary modesty. This may sound trite, but then it may not... There was quite a big party here on the Pakhra. Volodya came with his wife Marina. He brought his guitar with him. It was a mixed crowd, I don't know what had brought them all together; no one asked him to sing during the whole night, although he had his guitar with him. And Volodya was very friendly towards everybody, asking them about their affairs, and offering his help; he even gave a lift to someone — no one else volunteered. When we were leaving some time towards morning, my wife told him, "Volodya, what a shame, we spent the whole night here, and you haven't sung anything, and we wanted so much to hear you, we even asked you to sing, and you wouldn't." And he said, "The others didn't want it, I could see it. Well, never mind, next time we will gather specially to do some singing."

That was an awfully absurd night, he was the only man in the whole crowd to have such popularity — a real star, as they say. But he behaved as a very modest, simple and tactful person whom everybody needed, and not as a star at all. I believe that this trait was natural to him, and thus all the more rare...

David Samoilov

MY ACQUAINTANCESHIP WITH VYSOTSKY

Living art cannot always be correctly appreciated by the contemporaries. They are often biased, one way or the other. However, the argument itself about an artist is an indication that the times need him. We do not know what the Greater Time's judgement on him will be. Vysotsky's fierce admirers and opponents would do well to remember this truism.

I first saw Vysotsky on the stage of the newly opened Taganka Theatre, in the very first plays. He was one of the leading actors of the company, along with Slavina, Gubenko, and Zolotukhin; their names were more and more often mentioned in the theatrical and literary circles of Moscow. Each enjoyed an almost equal share of fame.

The theatre soon invited me to take part in the making of *The Fallen and the Living*. That was how I made Vladimir's acquaintance. I often saw him during rehearsals, in Lyubimov's office (Yuri Lyubimov was the theatre's director.— *Tr.*), and during the company's meetings. It was a delight to see him during the rehearsals: he gave all of himself to his work. He marvellously recited poems by the war poets, in a style all his own, and sang to a guitar.

After a long rehearsal we would sometimes drink a glass of cognac at the theatre's refreshment room. Just to get us talking. The talking was all about the play, which was going from one official instance to another with the greatest difficulty. It is strange to recall the way in which that patriotic production was taken to pieces and maimed, considering that it later ran into more than a thousand performances to packed audiences. The affair was finally resolved at a sitting of the Board of the Ministry of Culture, where Furtseva [1] approved, at last, of one of the versions of the production — thoroughly emasculated. Vysotsky must have played some 700 times in the show.

In the summer of 1965, the Taganka Theatre went on a tour to Leningrad. The rehearsals of *The Fallen and the Living* continued there. Gribanov, one of the authors of the play, and me, we also went there, to polish the text. We and the actors all lived in the Oktyabrskaya.

One day Vysotsky came up to me after the rehearsal and asked, "Would you like to hear my songs?"

We gathered in the room where Gribanov and I lived. Vysotsky came with his guitar. He sang many songs, and we listened to him unwearingly. That was early Vysotsky. The broad public did not know him. He too, must have had only a vague idea about his mission, and the purpose of his creativity was not very clear to himself, I think.

Some critics condemn the "underworld flavour" of early Vysotsky. They explain this flavour by the desire of a boy coming from an intellectual Moscow environment to abandon the routine or ordinary life and to have a taste of the false romance of law-breakers. It can only be true to a very small degree. The point is that Vysotsky's early songs were not written by an adolescent, and only some of them were echoes of the legends of the Moscow streets, bearing the imprint of the substandard Russian he spoke then.

Vysotsky the writer of songs belonged to a different environment; he reflected the tastes of a definite period.

The need for nonconformist songs, which would replace the cheerful noises made on the radio and in variety shows, was felt in all the sections of our society in the mid-1950s. These songs did not appear all at once.

Home-made texts to loosely structured melodies were sung in various circles, large and small. Underworld songs, which reflected certain aspects of life, were also sung. Like Yevtushenko said, "Intellectuals sang criminal songs." Numerous stylisations appeared and songs to verse by contemporary poets came into being. At a different level of skill and popularity, this line was continued in the work of Sergei Nikitin.

The first to fully satisfy the social need for the new song was Bulat Okudzhava, whose work soon outgrew the confines of his "circle" and, with the spread of tape-recorders, was heard in all the corners of our land. He must rightly be regarded as the founder of the contemporary "author's song" (to use this term for lack of a better one). Okudzhava created a new style, a new intonation, a new range of themes, a new romantic mood and manner of performance.

I believe that this example made a great impact on the work of Vysotsky.

Vysotsky worked in the spirit and taste of the early guitar poets, reflecting one of the tendencies in the genre.

The image of the bard overshadowed that of Vysotsky the actor, although he had great talent. Some of Vysotsky's transfigurations in his songs reflected his gifts as an actor, but Vysotsky had to be seen on the stage. He developed into a theatrical phenomenon in his own right, and plays were produced in a "director's theatre" in which the artistic solution was subordinated to the actor's individuality.

In those times, the Taganka Theatre was one of the rallying points of the capital's cultural life. Writers, artists and scientists often gathered during the rehearsals and in the wings. These contacts raised the general tone of the theatre, creating an atmosphere favourable to the actors' work and communication. I was a member of the artistic council, and I had an opportunity to see all the stages of evolving the productions of Brecht's *Galileo* and Shakespeare's *Hamlet*, in which Vysotsky played the title roles.

I have known several actors in the role of Hamlet, and Vysotsky seems to me the most convincing of them. He undoubtedly occupies a prominent place among the Russian performers of Hamlet.

Vysotsky played Hamlet without the Hamletism which had grown round that image over the centuries, so that the image itself came to mean something different from what Shakespeare originally intended. Vysotsky recited the famous monologues without any emphasis, as comments on the search for actual solutions rather than as philosophical deliberations.

Vysotsky's partners — Alla Demidova and Veniamin Smekhov — were worthy of Vysotsky, implementing the same interpretation. The production was based on action rather than reflexion. In fact, the whole of Vysotsky's work was action, not reflexion. That was the way he prepared himself for the stage, and that was the way he sensed the effectiveness of the "feedback" of the artistic imagination. The reaction of the audience, its living perception, its demands were, I'm sure, necessary stimulants for his work.

I never attended any of Vysotsky's appearences before large audiences. It those years, his popularity was not as great as in the last decade of his life.

However, we regularly met at parties in a circle of close friends, birthday parties and the like. Here, the hit of the occasion was always Vysotsky's singing. He wrote many songs, and he sang generously. His early stylisations receded into the background. His friends boosted Vysotsky's confidence in the social necessity of his work. Serious discussion of various phenomena and events helped him to work out his worldview, and provided the subjects of his songs. It was no longer the "legends of the Moscow streets" that nourished his inspiration but a serious world outlook.

He had the gift of listening, and of absorbing what he needed. The range of the cultural traditions of Russian poetry and songs that he absorbed was constantly expanded.

An artist is someone who can absorb a great deal and transform it all into something entirely his own. Vladimir Vysotsky was an artist.

Vysotsky's opponents reproach him for breaking with the tradition. Some of his admirers are inclined to consider him to be a phenomenon of social life rather than art. The root system of his creative work has little been studied so far.

I believe that one of the more important causes of his popularity was the fact that he combined and realised several traditions that were close to the people's consciousness: Nekrasov, the "cruel" romance, the ballad verse of Soviet poetry in the 1920s, the soldiers' songs of World War II, and a great deal else. The theoreticians of poetry and songs have yet to study all this.

Vysotsky was interested not only in the ultimate result of his songs and in his own success. It was also important for him to find a place for himself in contemporary poetry, to know his own poetic quality. It was for this purpose that we once gathered — Mezhirov, Vysotsky and myself — at Slutsky's place [2].

This time, Vladimir recited his texts, he did not sing them. He was obviously excited. The three of us expressed our views on what he read, and decided whether it was fit for publication. We selected about a dozen poems. Boris Slutsky took them to *The Day of Poetry* [3]. If memory serves, only one text was published. This was the first and the last publication during his lifetime, it seems.

In the 1960s, I met Vysotsky in the theatre or at common acquaintances. One day in summer he came to my dacha in Opalikha near Moscow, with the poet Igor Kokhanovsky. He did not have his guitar with him on that occasion.

The popularity of his songs quickly grew. They spread throughout the country on tapes. I remember Mezhirov coming to me early in the morning one day; we spent the whole day listening to Vysotsky's songs. Mezhirov was then in raptures over them.

Since 1976, I never saw Volodya any more.

One summer day, the news of his death came unexpectedly. Yuli Kim, who was then holidaying in Pärnu in Estonia, told me about it. He rushed immediately to Moscow to pay his last respects to Vysotsky.

Kim was the author of a beautiful song, written before Vysotsky's death and dedicated to Okudzhava and Vysotsky.

Vysotsky's funeral showed the real stature of his personality.

Gennady Poloka

HE QUICKLY SHOOK OFF THE BURDEN
OF EACH DEFEAT...

I am sitting from morning till night in a cutting-room of the Lenfilm Studios, trying to restore the original version of *The Intervention.*

The film, which was shelved 19 yaers ago, has only been preserved in a compromise, much truncated form. The part of Brodsky, played by Vladimir Vysotsky, was especially mangled by the vigilant superiors and editors. Due to the noble efforts of Gosfilmofond workers, though, considerable sections of the materials which were then cut out have been preserved. So now G. N. Tanayeva and myself, we are rummaging in the half-forgotten sequences and listening to the "divine voice", as Lyudmila Gurchenko (popular Soviet film actress and singer. — *Tr.*) described the voice of Vysotsky. His unexpected and unique intonations, to which we once grew accustomed, now strike us as fresh as ever. We are drunk with joy, and our eyes are constantly watering. Still, our work is hard, and even tormenting: some sequences have been lost, and, most likely, lost irretrievably; part of the soundtrack has also been lost. The reason is that, after *The Intervention* was shelved, Stepanov, the other director, tried to put together, under the quidance of Kiselev, the executive director of the studio, a version of the picture that would be acceptable to the bosses of the film industry. Only after Lev Slavin and I made a statement withdrawing our names from the credits was all work on the film stopped. By that time, however, the materials of *The Intervention* were in a chaos, thanks to the efforts of Stepanov and Kiselev.

I first saw Vysotsky in the autumn of 1958. After graduation from the Cinema Institute, I worked with Boris Barnet, the outstanding Soviet film director. One day, the "male half" of the senior year of the Moscow Art Theatre's drama school came to our studio for screen tests. Our attention was immediately drawn to a tall, powerfully built chap with a thick mane of curly hair and a thundering voice; that was Yepifantsev, who, when still a student, had played Foma Gordeyev in the film by Mark Donskoi. But Barnet became interested in another student. Lower than medium height, not very imposing physique. He held aloof from his noisy comrades who did their best to impress Barnet. One could feel vast latent energy in that lad, under the apparent phlegm.

"We seem to be in luck!" Barnet whispered, eyes riveted to the puny student. "That's the chap to shoot..."

His disappointed assistants heatedly tried to dissuade Boris Vasilyevich. He had just had a heart attack, so he waved a tired hand at them:

"All right, all right! Calm yourselves... I won't..."

And, indeed, he took on another actor who pleased everyone.

This is the first episode which comes to mind as I think about the Vysotsky phenomenon and his dramatic fate. I realise, with growing bitterness, that he played very few roles in the films that would be worthy of his original, unique talent; in fact, it may well be that he played no such roles at all, although the list of the films in which he played is, at first sight, long enough.

At first, his looks — the short stature and the face, so unusual in our cinema — must have been in the way. The type casting in the Soviet cinema is different from that of the theatre, and Vysotsky did not fit into any of the types. Then there was his tendency — which made itself felt very early — towards plasticity and expressiveness, and the paradoxical quality of his artistic solutions. All this scared away the bulk of our film directors who were then in the grip of a belated "Soviet neorealism", and worked with the actors on the only principle: "Simpler! Simpler still! Absolutely simple, no acting! Now we can shoot it!" Still, he was invited, very cautiously, already in the 1960s to play adolescents, cheerful youngsters, second young leads. It may sound incredible now, but Vysotsky, with his unique voice, was dubbed in those days!

In January 1967, after *The Republic of ShKID* made such a hit, I was told to make a film after Lev Slavin's play *The Intervention*. Feeling mad at the clichés accumulated by the "official cinema" in films about the Civil War, I then gave a comprehensive interview, a sort of manifesto, calling for a restoration of the traditions of the theatre and the cinema of the first years of the revolution, the traditions of the show-booth, street-theatre performances. Actors eager to take part in the experiments began to crowd round me.

That's how it happened that the young actor Seva Abdulov appeared in my house. Straight away, he began telling me about Vysotsky and his acting at the Taganka Theatre. I hadn't been in Moscow for nearly two years, and I listened to him with great interest. Seva spoke mostly of Vysotsky's songs. Some of those songs I had heard before, only I hadn't listened attentively, so I was a bit mistrustful towards Seva's raptures. Soon Vysotsky himself appeared. He had changed a great deal. He was fully mature and strong-looking now, but still silent and reserved. There was the same old latent energy, though, about the way he listened tensely. It was clear to me from the start that he would play in *The Intervention*. Which part, though? When he began to sing, I thought of Brodsky. Indeed, here was an underground agitator from Odessa who kept playing roles one after another without respite — an interventionist officer, a tutor, a sailor, a boulevardier seducer, a White Guardsman; only in the end, on the threshold of death in prison would he become himself, and take a long-deferred rest. The tragicomic fireworks of play-acting that was the essence of Brodsky's role, was best suited to Vysotsky's creative personality — the personality of an actor, poet, the author and performer of songs that were a kind of stage miniatures. No wonder that that role seemed so interesting to Arkady Raikin himself: one day he told me about it, and even acted out several bits for me.

A many-stage battle for official approval of Vysotsky for the part began. I overcame the resistance of the artistic council and the studio directors rather easily. Their misgivings mainly had to do with Vysotsky's unusual looks, which did not conform with the prevailing notion of how a social hero should look in the cinema, and with his acting style, which they found too theatrical. I had to remind them of the conventional style of the future film, and in conclusion I stated that Vysotsky's acting style would in this case be a model for the other actors.

However, the higher we went up the ladder of the official hierarchy, the more problematic the approval became. In these days, Vysotsky was, in the eyes of the officialdom, above all, the author and performer of a certain cycle of songs — let us call them the *In Bolshoi Karetny* cycle. The first to get scared was the then head of the Lenfilm Studios Kiselev — who, incidentally, was very fond of singing criminal songs in a circle of close friends. And yet we managed to get Vysotsky approved — firstly, because there were several other leading roles in the film, but primarily because of the support of Grigory Kozintsev, the greatest artistic authority at Lenfilm in those days.

Without waiting for official approval, Vysotsky began to work. How he worked! As a rule, an actor feels he is a temporary roomer at the studio: his permanent home is the theatre. Vysotsky brought to our group a fervent and all-encompassing concern about the final result which one can ordinarily find only among young drama school students founding a new theatre. He was interested in everything, he studied the process of making sketches, he was worried about the choice of locations, he intervened warmly in my arguments with the composer, and even took part in getting the budget, which was mercilessly pared, approved.

One day he came with an absolutely lowering face: the editor had told him that Seva Abdulov's screen test for the part of Zhenka Ksidias had turned out bad. He asked my permission to take a look at the test. When he saw it, he grew even gloomier: he was very found of Seva.

"Seva is a fine actor!" he sighed. "This is just not his part."

His position was very difficult: after all, it was Abdulov who had brought him to me. But Vysotsky had already become part of the picture, he loved it, and at a tense moment like this he was ready to sacrifice his own part so that the screening might go on.

"This must be a Hamlet!" he said excitedly. "A grotesque one, of course! A tragicomic caricature of Hamlet!"

And he brought to me Valery Zolotukhin, very young then.

"Valera is exactly what you want!" he purred in my ear

insidiously. "And I'll talk to Seva myself, he'll understand..."

Vysotsky came over to Leningrad whenever he had a chance, whenever there was the smallest opening in his engagements at the theatre, even if he was not personally involved in the screening. He would appear smiling, feeling that he was a wonderful surprise for all those present. Then there was the ritual hugging, back-slapping, and kissing: we all got our share of his overflowing benevolence, including our universal pet, Tonya, in charge of the lights. To greet her, Vysotsky would climb on the scaffolding. He would then see the run-throughs. He would return red in the face, happy and moved, and silently hug me and Mikhail Shcheglov, the designer, with whom he became very close during the screening of *The Intervention*.

Let me repeat that he tried to be always present on the set, even if he was not in the scenes that we were shooting, and each time he became totally involved in the work. True, this attitude was normal among the actors during the screening of *The Intervention*, for most of them were volunteers who had read my manifesto/interview in the papers and came to the studio uninvited. Apart from Vysotsky, the unit included Yuri Tolubeyev, Yefim Kopelyan, Vladimir Tatosov and many other remarkable actors. All of them worked joyously and zealously, and, which was the most important thing, they overflowed with love, warmth and courteous tenderness for one another.

But Vysotsky stood out even among these high-powered individuals — first of all, because of the naturalness of his existence in the conventional medium of the cinema, and secondly, because of his creative generosity with his partners. He made countless suggestions, in the course of the screening, to Zolotukhin, Tatosov, Aroseva, and even Tolubeyev. And how selflessly and indefatigably he helped Kopelyan in the recording of the song *The Thunder Rumbled*! Before that, Kopelyan had never sung in the cinema, and he learnt from Vysotsky with hope and even some timidity.

How I wished that I had had such an actor in my previous films, with my love for clearcut expressiveness of form!

There were many things that I had in common with Vysotsky: fierce rejection of clichés, a penchant for paradoxes, for "movement in reverse", for challenging the audiences' well-established habits. Starting on *The Intervention* in 1967, Volodya and I were thinking of a musical in which there would be none, or almost none, of the usual song-and-dance routines interspersed with conversational bits; our film would be permeated with rhythm and music from within. Only somewhere closer to the end, in the climax — the scene in prison, could a full-length vocal piece be unfolded. That was how the idea of *The Ballad of Wooden Suits* emerged — and we had that idea almost simultaneously.

We had many other common plans and hopes. In 1967, we had years and years before us! Later, we worked together on songs for my films; there were infrequent previews of films we attended together, conversations that lasted days and nights, remarkable conversations — in Leningrad, in Odessa, in my mother's flat in Moscow, and then a whole summer I spent with him at his mother's flat where he gave refuge to me at a difficult period in my life. There was the fifth anniversary of the Taganka Theatre, followed by an argument over music that lasted late into the night... There were also preparations for his debut as a director, in which I was to have acted as his artistic adviser — and a great deal else... But never again did he appear in any of my films. Vysotsky and me, we did not inspire confidence in the gentlemen who until recently ruled the roost of the Soviet cinema.

During the screening, despite the measures that we took, countless friends of Vysotsky's invaded the set: scientists, pilots, engineers, soldiers, sailors, polar explorers; once we had a reindeer breeder from Chukotka. True, in 1967 Vysotsky's immense popularity was only beginning to spread throughout the country.

I will never forget a close July night in Odessa. It was my birthday. Vysotsky sang almost nonstop. There was a concert hall opposite our hotel, and the concert there was over. The respectable philharmonic public drifted outside and, hearing Vysotsky's singing, stopped in its tracks, flooding the pavement. It was past midnight, but the hotel management did not dare to interrupt the improvised concert. The last trolleybus rustled by, but the well-dressed crowd was still standing down there and, heads lifted, listened with bated breath.

Vysotsky was very fond of *The Intervention* and staked a great deal on his part of Brodsky; the news that the film was shelved was therefore a heavy blow to him. One of the main charges against *The Intervention* was "the presentation of the Bolshevik Brodsky in an impermissibly eccentric form".

He could not reconcile himself to this act and wrote a letter to the people in charge of the film industry. The letter was signed by all the actors who played in the film — all, with the exception of a certain actress. I still have a copy of that remarkable document. I have often had to write such letters, and, like my colleagues, I involuntarily resorted in these situations to the generally accepted clichés with demagogic phraseology. But Vysotsky remained true to himself even here: he wrote a sincere, emotional letter in his inimitable style, absolutely free from deference to high officialdom and newspaper clichés. The letter was entitled "A Plea".

Eight years later I managed to restore, unofficially, a copy of *The Intervention*. We saw it in an empty room, the two of us. He sat quietly, unlike his usual self, and continued to sit there, when the lights went up. His face, grown older, looked faded. Then he rose to his feet and pressed himself against me, still silent...

Only after the Fifth Congress of Film-Workers, eighteen years after the screening of the film and six years after Vladimir Vysotsky's death, was the decision passed to release the film.

In the spring of 1969, the Kinoaktyor group, a division of the Mosfilm Studios, invited me to screen the film *One of Us*, after a screenplay by A. Nagorny and G. Ryabov. I did not deliberate too long, for after *The Intervention* affair I was not likely to be permitted to implement any ideas of my own.

The screenplay was a spy thriller. I was not going to work in that genre, so it was necessary to adapt the script to my style of directing. I worked on the idea for the film together with Vysotsky. After *The Intervention*, we firmly decided to continue our collaboration. Our attitude towards spy thrillers was rather ironical — as clearly expressed in Vysotsky's song *Fear of Counterintelligence*.

Although the screenplay was based on actual events, the only thing we knew about its hero was that, unlike the heroes of other such films, he was not a professional intelligence agent. He found himself involved in a major operation of Soviet counterintelligence through a series of accidental events — hence the numerous unexpected turns, often comical ones, in the story of the future film. The main point was that this imposed no restraints on Vysotsky's and my own imagination as we created a hero completely new to the genre.

To begin with, we decided to turn to Russian folklore; we discovered that the most attractive figure in it was Ivan the Fool. He had neither the awesome strength of Ilya Muromets nor the cunning wiliness of Alyosha the Priest's Son. At the same time it was a unique figure without any analogues in other people's folklore.

Compared with, say, Khodzha Nasreddin, Ivan the Fool is simple-hearted and even naive. At the same time he has a remarcable capacity for putting to shame his powerful opponents.

This immortal and striking image became the basis of our work on the central character. The authors of the script viewed this with understanding.

In *One of Us*, I was going to use to the full Vysotsky's entire resources as an actor: his charm, his contagious temperament, and, of course, his musical gifts — his remarkable singing, also his amazing plasticity. Watching Vysotsky do a Spanish dance in one sequence, a leading dancer of the Leningrad Ballet said: "Give him a year's choreographic schooling, and he'll be an outstanding dancer."

In the summer of 1969, official attitudes towards Vysotsky were unchanged; besides, the aftermath of *The Intervention* did not help much, of course. Realising that at the Kinoaktyor group we would not have the influential support of Kozintsev, we decided to make a full-length screen test, quite different from the brief easy sequences that are commonly used in such cases. We chose a key scene, and a technically difficult one, requiring lengthy preparations — the kind that both directors and actors usually avoid at the beginning. Even after official confirmation, they are usually put off until the end of the shooting period, when the actor feels more confident about his part.

We chose the scene in which German agents recruit Biryukov, a reserve officer supplied by the Soviet counterintelligence.

Biryukov, as played by Vysotsky, turned the act of recruiting into an endless and absurd rigmarole agonising to the agents. According to their scenario, they were supposed to make him drunk, photograph him in the arms of a seductive lady agent, and then blackmail him. Time was running out, and the unmanageable Biryukov/Vysotsky still kept singing "cruel" romances, he did some virtuoso dancing, fervently wooed his "seductress", by now completely at a loss, showed a streak of fierce jealousy for the dazed, quite flummoxed agents, and finally drank them under the table. It was all a dazzling display of actor's skill, paradoxical invention, and musical and plastic expressiveness.

But Vysotsky's candidacy for the part was rejected by an absolute majority of the group's management and the artistic council consisting of the leading actors of the Soviet cinema, despite the emotionally charged arguments of Savva Kulish and Vladimir Motyl, who were, already in those times, well-known directors of considerable influence.

The view is widely current now that Vysotsky's life was made difficult by highly placed officials only. That is an error: his colleagues among actors, as well as we film-makers, were just as bad. Of course, Vysotsky's reputation gradually increased, and after he played the title role in Alexander Mitta's film *How Czar Peter Had His Blackamoor Married*, it became easier to have him approved for the leading roles. But an atmosphere of mistrust and even ironical condescension still clouded Vysotsky's work and personality even after the enormous success of the film *The Place of the Rendezvous Can't Be Changed*, in which Vysotsky played Captain Zheglov.

Let me insist that the intensity of the people's grief on Vysotsky death, as well as the present-day official interest of society for the artistic phenomenon called Vladimir Vysotsky, proved unexpected to most workers in the theatre, the cinema, and literature. Significantly, in these days, when we mark the 150th anniversary of Pushkin's death, the press pays just as much attention to our contemporary Vysotsky as to Pushkin.

After the defeat at the artistic council, I turned to the

top figures at the Committee for Cinematography. Their response was easy to predict. They were dead set against Vysotsky playing the hero, and after some deliberation they suggested that he should play one of the supporting roles — a Nazi spy.

The offer was obviously humiliating and unacceptable. By chance Vysotsky met the then First Deputy Chairman of the Committee. The latter firmly promised to get Vysotsky approved for the role of Biryukov, but that promise was not followed by any practical steps whatever. I then decided to give up the idea of making that film. It was Vysotsky who restrained me from that step.

"You have *The Intervention*, a black mark against you, as it is. If you refuse to do this one, they won't let you work at all." He drove me to Yumatov's place and introduced me to him. "Zhora will play Biryukov, and he will do it perfectly."

With the passing of years my impression from that act has become less acute, but then I was shaken. He was a complex and far from simple person, he could be weak and inconsistent in trifling matters, but the moral strength of his choices in decisive situations was striking.

Only an actor can understand what it means to voluntarily give up a part with which one has become closely identified and which one has practically evolved single-handed.

Moreover, Vysotsky wrote the songs for the film, and helped Yumatov, who had never sung in pictures before and was naturally very nervous; he helped him the way he had helped Kopelyan. In all the months when the film was being made, with great difficulties and long pauses, he was at our side; he came to recording sessions and run-throughs. He came to the opening night at the House of the Cinema, very solemn-looking, accompanied by Marina and her sister. After the première, he sang a great deal at the party I gave at my mother's house.

He loved the theatre. For a long time it was, in fact, the only field in which he could exercise his varied talents. But the theatre was never enough for him. Being a man of action he quickly shook off the burden of each defeat, and continued the fight for his art with the same old fervour.

After several years filled with vain hopes of appearing in some interesting film, he decided that he must no longer passively await propositions from directors that might never come.

One day during the shooting of *One of Us* he brought me a script set in Odessa recently seized by the Nazis. The only character in that script was a Red Navy sailor who barricaded himself in a tower on the roof of a high building. The tower was surrounded by the enemy; the hero's position was hopeless. In the last few hours before he died, the whole of his life passed before his eyes. At the same time he dreamed of the future which he would not have, he wrote poems on the walls of the tower, and sang songs... The script reminded me of the famous film of Marcel Carné, the French director, called *Le Jour se lève*, only it was quite different in intent and, besides, it was imbued with Vysotsky's unique intonation and the emotional charge characteristic of his songs. That script was never realised.

He offered me yet another of his ideas for a film, when we finished *One of Us*. One day he and scriptwriter Artur Makarov showed me a newspaper clipping — an extraordinary story of a merchant captain. Interrupting each other, Vysotsky and Makarov described to me its tempting dramatic possibilities. In general, Vysotsky had a particular fondness for men of the romantic professions: geologists, merchant captains, famous sportsmen, counterintelligence officers, mountain climbers, prospectors... I remember being quite interested in their suggestions. I went to the Mosfilm Studios, first approaching my immediate superiors and then the manager of the studios himself. I remember that Vysotsky and Makarov also went to the manager. But our attempts to get the management interested were not a success. Thus yet another of Vysotsky's cinematographic ideas fell through — and there were many more of these.

It is no secret that Vysotsky never gave a single officially approved concert. His performances were arranged by informal organisations, as we would call them now. And all the time he longed for a modest but officially recognised personal poster with his name on it, the kind a soloist at any of the most unprepossessing provincial philharmonic society had.

I remember that at the beginning of the "stagnant" 1970s, a deputy manager of the Bureau for the Propaganda of Soviet Film Art promised him a concert tour in Tallinn with an official standing and an official personal poster. On that occasion, Vysotsky, already a leading Soviet actor, was put through a humiliating examination and made to recite poems and fables on the school-required reading list. In the end, the already announced concerts were cancelled, money for the tickets was given back to the audiences, and Vysotsky never got the personal poster promised him.

At the same time, early in the 1970s, he got a chance to publish a collection of children's poems at the Detskaya Literatura (Children's Books) Publishers. Volodya was instantly carried away by the idea; he worked with great enthusiasm, almost nonstop. Finishing a poem, he would read it at once to his numerous friends. He recited them with great pleasure, mimicking the voices, very artistically — it was all uproariously funny. Everybody liked the verses, but the publishers' editors kept revising them for him. I remember artist Boris Diadorov, a friend of Vysotsky's at that time, taking Volodya to the publishers in his car. They returned tired and depressed. The collection was squashed; the rumour was that the move was initiated by the then head designer of the publishers.

Writing songs for the theatre and the cinema was the only kind of officially recognised literary work open to Vysotsky. Of course, even in this case things were much more difficult for him than for anyone else. Many, probably most, of his songs were rejected, and those that weren't were maimed beyond recognition or whittled down to nothing. For instance, they left about six lines of his wonderful song in *One of Us*, in the final version. The same thing happened to a superb tango parody in the same film. Incidentally, that tango was later recorded by Vysotsky and Marina for the Melodia firm, but the record never reached the shops.

Sensing the difficulty of his position, he worked harder than most, produced more variants of his verses, and was more exacting about the final versions of the songs.

I used Vysotsky as a song-writer for my films until his last day. In all these years, I never turned to any other poet; even when Vysotsky was very busy or went abroad with Marina, I tried to get hold of him, even if the time element in the making of a film became a problem. I could not act differently — not only because his participation in itself guaranteed most interesting results, or because he became my bosom friend from the very first meetings, but also because I knew at first hand how tragic his life was, having been sentenced to twenty years of silence after *The Intervention*.

During the thirteen years of our joint work, I witnessed the process of the formation of his method of working on songs for films. For his first films, he himself determined, quite on his own, regardless of the director's wishes, the number of songs, their content and place in the film. In this, he was guided purely by emotion and intuition and, as I have mentioned, he worked very generously, sometimes writing twice or three times as many songs as could be squeezed into the final product. For instance, when we were making *The Intervention*, I failed to find room for the song he suggested — *There Was a Sense of Measure Once Upon a Time*. The song *Monte-Carlo* sounded in the background, almost inaudibly, in the sequence showing Zhenka's room. Still, these songs became popular, because Vysotsky performed them at his concerts. But the song of Sanka, *A Lass Lived Near the Harbour*, was written especially for the actress Gelena Ivlieva, and was never sung by Vysotsky himself; it is therefore still unknown to the public. Unfortunately, the melody of that song was lost. I only remember that it was written in the tradition of the Odessa port folklore, and the pointed lines were reminiscent of the satirical sketches of Odessa's variety actors. Generally speaking, characteristic features of Vysotsky's individuality as song-writer were a striking sense of style, his confidence in handling extremely diverse manners of expression, deep knowledge of folklore, and constant skillful use of its traditions; however, this never conflicted with his strikingly original artistic essence, which can be sensed in all his songs. But all this should be discussed separately.

Many of his songs, written for various films, were never used in them; the reasons were, at first, his inexperience, his failure to establish contact with the directors, and his creative generosity or "poetic fertility", if one may say so. But the main reason was the editors' sabotage, and the abuse of power on the part of the then bosses of the cinema. We can therefore expect to discover unknown songs and poems of Vysotsky.

All this will also have to be discussed separately, and I hope that I shall have occasion to recur to this theme. For the present, I would like to finish these notes with Vysotsky's song *A Lass Lived Near the Harbour*.

A lass lived near the harbour
Where sailors and landlubbers
Would saunter, seldom sober —
Sailors from distant lands,
From far, mysterious lands.
But they were really careless,
Those handsome sturdy fellows,
They never saw that baby —
There was a reason, maybe:
They all ignored the lass
Thirsting for a glass.

Her friend — a pretty face —
Lived near the market-place
In sin and in disgrace:
A party every night,
And every night a fight.
The quiet girl, however,
Could sing and dance, but never
Went at the blonde one's prancing,
She had no time for dancing,
And parties and success
Were not for this good lass.

Good manners and low bows,
Cold smiles and fervent vows,
And fops and noisy rows —
For all of that she had no time,
For all of that she had no time,
She had no time to loiter,
She fought against exploiters —
The fat men of the world.
She'd beat them, take my word,
And then all would be fine,
And then all would be fine.

Joseph Heifitz

TWO FILMS WITH VYSOTSKY

Just as many other people, I heard Vysotsky's songs, before I heard anything about him. That was at the end of the 1960s. On a filming trip to the Crimea, I heard them every day as I walked towards the location past a Yalta shooting-range. The songs were played to attract crowds of people towards the plywood pavilion, drowning out the reports of the pneumatic rifles. There were no records of his songs in those days: instead, there were records "on the ribs" — old X-ray pictures which Vysotsky's admirers somehow got hold of and used for recording purposes. The pictures of chest bones, grooved by the recording needle, were fully as good as LPs, although they added more wheezing to the performer's already muted voice.

The first Vysotsky song that I heard was also recorded "on the ribs"; it was, if I'm not mistaken, this one:

> He drank with us, and seemed to be as gay,
> We met him like a brother, we were merry...
> And he — he ratted on the following day.
> Forgive me, brothers, it was all my error.

The crowd listened, spellbound, and I remember being touched immediately by this voice that was yelling rather than singing. It was as if someone's strong hands were squeezing the singer's throat, and he did all he could to sing the song to the end, to make himself heard. I asked who it was. That's Volodya Vysotsky, people answered, amazed at my ignorance.

Hearing him sing, I imagined him to be a powerfully built man, a kind of superman. That was why I thought of him when early in 1972 I began to look for an actor for the part of von Koren, the zoologist, in my film version of Chekhov's *A Duel*. Chekhov's von Koren is a broad-shouldered swarthy man, his figure produces an impression of great power, he is an embodiment of arrogance and coldness. But the man who came over from Moscow for an interview was not tall at all; he was puny, one might even say. A big head sitting handsomely on the shoulders emphasised a certain lack of proportions in the figure. I was struck by the discrepance between voice and appearance.

At first I was rather disappointed, frankly speaking. But soon I was attracted by the sense of great inner strength emanating from that man. I knew from experience that during their first interview with a director actors usually wanted to find out which of their traits to hide and which to stress; because of this, they behaved unnaturally, as if trying to play several badly rehearsed roles at once. From the very first moment of our acquaintanceship I had the impression that we had known each other for a long time, that Volodya was a close friend. This immediately attracted me to him.

Let me make this clear: I do not call him Volodya in the spirit of familiarity at all. That was the usual way of addressing him. I have never heard anyone address him as Vladimir Semyonovich (that is, using the patronymic.— *Tr.*) under any circumstances. He was Volodya to everyone from the studio's carpenter to the director. Andrei Voznesensky put it very aptly when he called Vysotsky "Volodya of the whole people." *

So I looked at him and wondered: he seemed so small next to Oleg Dahl, invited for the role of Laevsky; yet I could not give up the idea of using him in the film. The more I observed him during our interview, the stronger I felt that we must slightly revise Chekhov's description of von Koren's appearance. After all, that "despot in the first place, and zoologist in the second", could have looked exactly like this — short and puny. Despite his looks (and

---

* "Volodya" is a more informal mode of address than the proper first name "Vladimir", which sounds rather stiff. One has to bear in mind that Russian has a dozen or more forms of a person's name expressive of varying degrees of formality, familiarity, tenderness, contempt, etc.—*Tr.*

most likely because of them), he was "a king and an eagle, he ruled the population with an iron hand and made them bow to his authority". I plucked up courage and spoke of this to Volodya. And I immediately found an ally in him.

"Indeed," he recalled, "so many tyrants and despots were short, and they tried to make up for the defect by aspiring for power and superiority."

We quickly reviewed the history of character and found a key to the part of von Koren. An enthusiasm for Nietzschean philosophy, certainly. Rightness founded on wrongness, of course. Distant intimations of maturing fascism, sure. But, apart from all that, a complex of physical inferiority corroding his soul, a smouldering hatred towards men like Laevsky and his lover, the most beautiful woman in town.

That was the way Volodya played von Koren, rising on tiptoe to seem taller, and speaking softly (his speech, curt like military orders, had to be listened to attentively, not just heard). I believe that Volodya's open hatred for tyranny and despotism helped him to play that part. In the film, he aimed that hatred in the opposite direction — at the people around him, at the characters of *A Duel*, whom he called "macaques".

But let us go back to the beginning of our acquaintance-ship. I noticed that the deeper he went into his part, the more successful his preparations for screen tests, the more often he predicted his failure, obviously feeling depressed about something. "They are not going to okay me for this role anyway," he told me one day. "And for any other role, either. Your screen test is not the first one; all the previous ones failed. Someone has decided not to let me appear on the screen at all costs."

After the screen test, which confirmed the formula which we accepted, and which showed the complexity of the character even in a short sequence, Volodya took me aside and said: "Our only hope is a letter from the cos-monauts to the proper authorities. I gave a concert before them, and they asked me why I didn't appear in films... They promised to put a word in my favour."

The cosmonauts' letter must have reached those they wrote to. Volodya was confirmed for the role, and we went to Yevpatoria for the shooting.

I was already aware of Volodya's immense popularity, and the things that happened on one of the first days on location confirmed it. But the episode was markedly different from the usual razzmatazz and cheap publicity stunts accompanying the appearance in public of film stars dispensing autographs and smiles. Love for Volodya was respectful and tender, it expressed itself more like concern and solicitude as would be shown by relatives towards one of their own.

We were shooting on the beach. Von Koren was doing his daily exercises, while Deacon Pobedov watched him, laughing loudly as usual.

Suddenly a large launch with tourists on board approached the beach, and the young guide drew their attention to some sightseeing must, most likely. Although the launch was about a hundred yards away, it interfered with the shooting, and we made a short break. I noticed that the tourists paid no attention to the guide whatever, staring at our group, leaning all of them against the railing on one side, so that the launch listed noticeably. When the guide finished his talk, the launch stayed where it was. The captain, a mere boy, leaped on the beach and headed for our group, or rather for Volodya, who was smoking somewhat apart from the others. In his embarrassment the boy did not even say hello and, stopping at a respectable distance, froze like a private before a general; he invited Volodya to go on board and have a drink of cold beer, adding thoughtfully that it was Czech beer. Volodya declined politely, saying that he was working. The captain grew even more embarrassed; he stood at attention for a while, then asked Volodya's permission to send a case of Czech beer to the group. When this was rejected, too, he smiled sadly and went back to the launch. Unwilling to waste precious time, we resumed the rehearsal. No sooner had we begun, though, than a sailor with a large netbag of apples appeared and, gazing with fond eyes at his idol, naked to the waist, dumb-bells in hands, held out the bag.

"Have some apples."

We explained to the sailor that this attention interfered with our work, touching as it was. Volodya roared something to the same effect. The chap did not know where to look and what to do; he kept glancing back at the launch, as if for support; in the end, he slowly walked back with his present, looking crestfallen.

We continued to work. The scene included some dialogue, and the sound operator was glad that there was silence at last. After it stood there for about half an hour, the launch pulled away from the beach, slowly, as if against its will. Suddenly the loudspeakers on the roof of the wheel-house blared out:

> *The ladies fell in love with me.*
> *Where they all came from I can't say...*
> *I knew they loved me dearly,*
> *But I ignored them anyway.*

The song rumbled over the sea as their gift to Volodya, like the beer and apples, as a gesture of love and gratitude. The wind was blowing towards us, the hoarse voice went on and on, the song was a long one, and the loudspeakers were very powerful indeed. The tourists were waving their handkerchiefs and, I believed, joined in the singing...

The critics were appreciative of Vysotsky's acting in the film. They referred to the part of von Koren as his undoubted success. At an international film festival in Taormina, Sicily, I learnt that in 1978 Volodya was awarded the prize for the best male role. This country had never taken part in that festival before, so that no one, Volodya included, knew anything about that prize. When I returned to Moscow, I wanted to pass the good news on to Volodya, but he was away on a trip. And later it was I who was away, so I couldn't let him know of that fact, and kept putting it off. And then it was too late — to my everlasting regret. But I am running ahead of the story.

Some two years after *A Duel* we met again. I saw him in the refreshment room of the Lenfilm Studios, we hugged each other, and he said — in his usual manner, without beating about the bush or anything — that it would be a good idea to work together again. I was then working on Pavel Nilin's novella *Stupidity* (the script had the title *The Only One*), and had not yet begun the casting, but promised on the spot to invite Volodya to play one of the parts.

It was soon clear which part he would play: the man in

charge of an amateur singing group, a genius that never was, a failure with a mystery which broke up his life. Undoubtedly a very capable man who gained neither fame nor success. There was no future for him at all — while his friends, sheer mediocrities, had become variety stars, constantly on tour abroad. All he had in his life now was his tiredness and envy: fine soil for a failure complex to grow on. Again we had a complex, an affinity with the zoologist from *A Duel*, though very distant and transposed onto a different soil and different times.

Naturally, Volodya knew nothing then about the success in Italy, but he treated the role of von Koren as marking a stage in his career, probably because it legalised him as a film actor. He immediately liked the idea of playing a provincial failure and victim of envy. He was a very intelligent actor, so he did not go for the externals, for striking effects: he was attracted by the inner content, the multidimensionality and mystery of a character, the strangeness and inexplicability of actions. He was even somewhat distressed on learning that there would be an episode in which he would have to sing.

"All the spectators will think that if Vysotsky is in the film, it's to do the singing."

He soon realised, though, that the song he would sing would be no hit but rather an "anti-hit", that he would sing as a man who never came close to becoming a variety show idol, a man in a well-worn suit, with a netbag in hand with nothing in it but a bottle of *kefir* and a packet of tea; so he agreed, and sang his *Chase*, somewhat changing his usual style.

Although it was not a leading role, he treated it in a very responsible and disciplined manner. Let me give an illustration. Before leaving on a tour abroad, Volodya had a single day free from evening performances and rehearsals. The theatre was preparing for the tour, and there were no days off. So we scheduled the shooting of a very important scene for that single day in Leningrad. With the greatest difficulty, we got all the other actors to play in that scene — some for the whole day, others, for just a few hours. As luck would have it, the evening performance in Moscow ended very late, and Volodya would not be able to catch the night express. We agreed that he would fly over by the morning plane on the day of the shooting. It was easy to imagine the tenseness of the whole unit. If the shooting fell through for some reason or other, we would not be able to get everyone together in less than a month. And that would create a major snag.

According to the law of the sandwich, which always falls with the buttered side down, there was a snowblizzard blowing on that ill-fated morning. The Leningrad airport was closed, they only extended a weak hope that the weather might improve in the afternoon. But, even if we went all out, we would not be able to shoot the scene in half a day.

We were all sitting in the pavilion with glum faces, cursing the weather and unable to find a way out. Suddenly (thank God for this saving "suddenly") Volodya burst in, putting on costume as he was walking, followed at a run by the wardrobe people, the makeup man, the property-man with a thermos of hot tea.

"Volodya, dear! By what miracle? The airport people said no hope!"

"I asked the military. They fly in any weather. Fortunately, there was a plane going this way. We got here in forty minutes!"

Yes, he was a favourite of the whole people, "Volodya of the whole people". No one could refuse to help him: taxi-drivers, waiters, shop assistants, pilots, they were all eager to help. For he was their soul.

As we parted, we swore to get together again to make another film. Time passed, but there was no part that Volodya could play.

One day I was walking home from some conference along Vorovsky Street. It was a gloomy spring day, the pavements all covered with slush. I heard a car driving close to the pavement overtake me. I looked back and stepped aside, to avoid being splashed on. A grey Mercedes, plastered with mud to the rooftop, braked abruptly. Volodya leaped out of the car and, after the greetings, I told him: "Talk of the devil! Volodya, I have an idea for screening Babel's *Sunset* and *Odessa Stories*. And you will play Benya Krik the gangster." He grinned hugely and, without a moment's hesitation, went down on his knees where he stood, in the slush and all...

That was our last meeting. My idea came to nothing, and I had to change my plans.

Then there was that trunk call, the persistent and alarming ringing. I snatched the receiver and heard someone crying, unable to start speaking. I waited, growing pale. Through the sobbing came Iya Savina's familiar voice: "Volodya has died... Has died..." Nothing more, just the sobbing.

I cried, too, like thousands of people on that morning...

NOTES ABOUT VLADIMIR VYSOTSKY

Almost every day we hear announcers say in level tones: "Mayak Radio Station broadcasting Vysotsky's songs. Performed by the author."

Right: there's nothing unusual about it. Although it *is* remarkable: Vysotsky's poems in magazines, his records on sale in shops, his films on TV and in the cinema. Songs on the radio.

We quickly get accustomed to all good things. We are already accustomed to hearing Vysotsky's songs every day on radio and TV. Ordinary programmes, which somehow seem precious nevertheless.

Several years ago, all we could do was dream about it. As did Vysotsky — while he lived.

As long as he lived, there was hope in his heart. It wasn't as if he hankered for more fame: the many millions of home-made copies of his tape-recordings far outnumbered the discs of the most famous singers, of the brightest variety stars; thousands of people queued to get tickets for plays with Vysotsky at the Taganka Theatre; at his concerts, there were people hanging from chandeliers, almost literally....

He knew all about it, and he liked it. It was only natural; he was proud of it all.

But he disliked being an underground singer constantly on tour. Deeply embittered, he often wondered why it was that the authorities stopped him from reaching the greater audiences, raising insurmountable barriers between him and his listeners, spectators and readers. What was gained by counting him among dissidents and even anti-Sovieteers, when in actual fact he was part and parcel of his people, expressing the spirit, ideas, emotions, and the humour of that people by the very nature of his gift?

We often discussed this "mysterious phenomenon"

with him, although, come to think of it, there was nothing mysterious about it: the obstacles in Vysotsky's path were raised by those same people who roused his honest civic anger, multiplied a thousand times by his hard-hitting sarcasm and devastating humour. Their hatred for the unmanageable bard, multiplied by officials' caution — fear that a simple word of truth might have unpredictable consequences — cut off the poet, singer, and actor beloved by the whole people from all the mass media for a long time.

So we got together and talked it over, and on the following day one of those top officials who implacably "closed Vysotsky down" would pull all the strings he could to get Vysotsky come to his flat or his status-symbol of a dacha, where he would talk in a highly liberal strain with his folks at home, turning a benevolent ear to Vysotsky's singing.

Later, Volodya would smile bitterly: "Well, it seems we're quits... I mustn't get huffy with them..." And he went on with his work.

Truth to say, it was not without certain deep-seated doubts that we made up our minds to write these notes. Of course, after Vysotsky's death, spurred on by the avid interest of Vysotsky's admirers, we reminisced about him at our meetings with spectators and readers, before various Vysotsky clubs, in particular the Leningrad one. There was no question, however, of publication of any sort at first.

But then the fresh wind of the new times began to blow. Vysotsky was "rehabilitated", and side by side with his true friends and old associates, numerous "friends" began to sprout like mushrooms after a summer rain or, better to say, like basilisks crawling from abandoned wells — from completely unknown actors to respectable poets, prose-writers and musicians of nationwide fame. Vysotsky himself would have been infinitely amazed at the appearance of these "friends": during his lifetime, some of these highly placed members of writers and musicians' unions humiliated him, others he just did not know, never met them even. And here it has turned out that friendship or mere acquaintanceship with Vysotsky could be prestigious, that these things could lend them weight and stature — so why not tell the world all about their great friendship with the late lamented Volodya, after all, he could no longer protest...

Alas, we cannot boast that we were Vysotsky's friends. We were his acquaintances over many years, we worked together on the film *The Place of the Rendezvous Can't Be Changed,* we exchanged visits, we argued and consulted with each other. We loved everything that Vysotsky did. He said that he liked our books.

Still, we do not dare call our relationship friendship — he had too high ideas about that notion. Volodya once said jokingly, "Nowadays only people who work together can be friends. Or people who live together. There simply is no time for all the others."

If it was a joke, there was too much truth in it.

Our family album settled our doubts. In it, we found the snapshots of the last few years: our friends, colleagues, actors, chessplayers, cosmonauts... And almost no snapshots of Volodya... We were all so young, there was so much time before us, that it did not even enter our heads that we should take those pictures: time enough for that! An eternity before us!

And then there was no time at all.

People from newspapers, magazines and almanacs kept writing to us: send us some photographs of Vysotsky, you're sure to have a few. Send us some unknown poems by Vysotsky: you must have them. He dedicated two songs to you: let us have the texts of these songs. And please write your memoirs...

It is unbearably sad to write memoirs about Vysotsky: this remarkable man died so young! But the people are interested in all things connected with his name. So we must find time to do this, if nothing else...

It so happened that we first became acquainted with Volodya's father, Semyon Vladimirovich. This strong-looking man of great vitality produced a very fine impression on us. We said, quite sincerely, that we envied him so much: what luck it was to have such a son! Semyon Vladimirovich said jokingly: "A chip off the old block!" We could feel, though, that deep at heart he was proud of his son — and that was in the days when Volodya's records were regarded as almost criminal; besides, they were ascribed to all sorts of people, including real criminals.

We asked Semyon Vladimirovich to give our best

regards to his son, to tell him that we were admirers of his work. Vysotsky the elder was obviously flattered, and promised that he would tell Volodya all about it by all means. He was as good as his word: several days later Volodya phoned us, and we met. That was the beginning of our acquaintanceship.

Fast-moving, well-built, very lively — though without any fussiness — Vysotsky literally radiated charm. It will probably be no exaggeration to say that this charm was his principal feature as a human personality. Over the years that followed we had numerous occasions to find that literally all people who had the great luck to know him personally succumbed to that charm: it was apparently impossible not to fall in love with him forever, once one came to know him!

And it was not an actor's charm, the desire and ability to *look* attractive; it was a natural quality of his soul. When we discussed the principles which Gleb Zheglov (the main character in *The Place of the Rendezvous Can't Be Changed.— Tr.*) followed in his life ("When you talk to people, smile more often, people like it; listen to a person carefully, and try to steer the conversation towards himself; to do that, find a subject that is close and interesting to him; and you can only do it if you show genuine interest for that person..."), Volodya laughed uproariously, repeating: "Isn't it great, I never thought about this, never formulated it like this, and yet all my life I have behaved precisely along these lines... No I'm really the spitting image of Gleb Zheglov!"

Unfortunately, our meetings were not all that frequent; there would usually be some important occasion for getting together: either a new publication of ours, or Vysotsky's new part. But he would also sometimes drop in out of the blue with his new poems or songs, invariably with his red guitar which we dubbed Stradivari. Then a fest for the soul would begin: Volodya tuned his guitar and started to sing. He sang everything — lyrical songs; ballads, humorous songs, everything that he had written between our meetings. Also his previous songs, for an encore. We were mostly delighted with his new works, but sometimes there would be cause for criticism: after all, he worked very much, and there is sure to be waste in the workshop of even the greatest of artists. Vysotsky's attitude towards criticism was striking: he listened with great curiosity, with an acute and good-natured interest, mostly without comment. He would sometimes agree, and only rarely argue. In the final versions of the songs, however, those which he took to the wider audiences, we saw every once in a while revisions prompted by our remarks, and that pleased us, since it indicated a trust in our taste.

Of course, the main thing about our acquaintanceship was the conversations. There were discussions, mostly very heated ones, of a great number of varied problems ranging from politics to literature, to purely everyday matters. Vysotsky was an excellent conversationalist, he at once charged the discussion with the high energy of his interest in the subject.

Particularly interesting were the conversations about politics, mostly domestic politics. People often believe, out of a kind of inertia, that Vysotsky was an extreme left-winger, and a left-winger of a pro-Western orientation, at that. As far as we can say, that was not quite so. First and foremost, he was a great patriot in the best sense of the word: he loved his land, the people and his city sincerely and simply, he sensed acutely the links between his creative work and the native roots, his dependence on the native audiences. This did not interfere, of course, with his lively interest in everything that happened in the West, especially in politics and culture (he was always very well informed); on the personal plane, he was highly pleased with the appearance of his LPs abroad, and generally with his growing popularity there. For instance, Volodya told us, not without pride, that a certain pirating firm recorded illegally, by bribing the sound operator, one of his concerts in New York (or it may have been some other city in the USA, it's hard to remember now), and several days later sold like pancakes his records without labels, with the inscription "Vysotsky Sings"; so he had to buy his own disc — a very expensive one.

But all this was mere byplay, purely human weaknesses. His real listeners and admirers lived here in his native land, and it was for them that he wrote and sang. He sang the truth about our life and the people, the truth about the good things and the bad. It was this simple truth that irked those whom he called the "grey bureaucratic scum", against whom he fought every day of his life.

But even in his most bitingly satirical and devastatingly grotesque pieces he remained a kind person; he did not want to, and obviously could not, by his very nature, charge his poems with the poison of malice. There was no malice in him even in the hardest times. And the fury with which he spoke of the "grey scum" was sad rather than angry...

In 1976, our novel *The Era of Mercy* appeared. Following a long-established tradition, we invited ten closest friends, colleagues and relatives to celebrate the birth of our brain-child — according to the number of the free copies of the novel provided by the publishers. Volodya Vysotsky, too, came to the Central House of Journalists for the occasion. We presented each guest with a copy of the novel, with tender inscriptions, and the celebration, accompanied by the libations permissible in those times, began. That evening, Volodya was out of sorts, he did not drink at all. He soon rose to his feet, said something censorious about the pleasures of the table being an idle waste of time, and declared that he was going home to read the book. We were awfully distressed, of course, but there was nothing we could do.

On the following morning we were woken up early by a ringing at the door. It was Volodya.

"Congratulations, brothers, you've written a remarkable novel!" he announced from the threshold. "I spent all night reading it!"

"Thanks," we mumbled, with unconcealed amazement. "So you got up so early in the morning to —"

"Of course! In general, I'm not a lazy lad," he quoted Zheglov. "But that's not the point."

"Well, what is?"

He slashed at the air.

"I've come to stake out a claim for Zheglov!"

"Stake out a —" We were dumbfounded. "What do you mean?"

"What do you mean, 'what do you mean'? Your *Era*... is great cinema stuff! And no one is going to play Zheglov the way I shall play him!"

"Really?" one of us said maliciously. "And what's wrong with, say, Sergei Shakurov as Zheglov?"

For a moment, Volodya was taken aback. It is appropriate to remember here that he was uncommonly scrupulous about his judgements on other actors — exceptionally honest in his attitude towards them. He thought a bit, biting his lips, shook his head, and said slowly:

"Shakurov... Well, why not? Manly, handsome... Yes, Shakurov could do it. Perhaps as good as myself."

We should have been content with that, but we were carried away by the game, so we asked:

"And what about Gubenko? Won't Gubenko cope with Zheglov?"

Who doesn't know Gubenko — intelligent, charming, manly-looking, and full of plasticity? Volodya froze as if struck by thunder. He frowned, obviously confused. He stalked about the room, mumbling something to himself. Then he stopped and said resolutely:

"How could I have forgotten about him? Ye-es... Let me tell you: Nikolai Gubenko will play the part *better than me!*" He stared at us, a hard, strict scrutiny.

It was our turn to feel taken aback: we hadn't expected an admission like that. Volodya stood for several seconds staring at us severely, then he bent his head to one side, exactly as Zheglov would, lifted an eyebrow, and repeated emphatically:

"He will *play better than me...*" He was silent for a while, then smiled and added: "Only you don't need anyone *better!* What you need is the way *I* will play Zheglov!"

We all burst out laughing. The game was a game, but we realised, we felt it in our bones, we were confident that Gleb Zheglov would have to be played by Vysotsky, with his absolute knowledge of the Zheglov material, the environment, the lexicon, and with his ability to express it all not only through the outward pattern of the performance but also through his unique mode of speach unrivalled in its wealth of intonation.

In short, he staked out his claim. Preparations for producing "great cinema stuff" began.

The first thing to do was to reach an understanding with the TV, the more so that the Odessa Film Studios was ready to start working on the film immediately.

Together with Alexei Batalov, the prospective director of the film, we wrote an application for a TV serial in seven parts; that was exactly the length of the film which, in our view as well as Vysotsky's, was needed to cover the whole of the literary material.

The TV people looked very favourably on the project, but they only allowed five parts. "They are sure that the authors always ask for more than they need," Volodya laughed. "You should have asked for ten parts — and you would have got seven!"

Incidentally, the footage ran into seven parts exactly. But there were only five parts in the plan, so the problem was solved very simply: we were told to take up the scissors and cut out the extra footage — keep it as a souvenir. It never entered anyone's head to revise the plan instead...

But it was not the size of the future film that was the main problem we discussed with Vysotsky. There were two pressing issues that had to be settled at once.

First, there was the question of Vysotsky's playing in the film. The TV people gave us to understand, quite plainly, that there was no hope of Vysotsky being allowed to play in the film, not even some supporting role: "The view prevails that it is *not expedient* to use Vysotsky..." And that was exactly what we could not accept! The word we gave Volodya was not the only reason: like himself, we were absolutely certain that no one would be able to play Zheglov the way he would do it.

We were indignant about that attitude towards Vysotsky — not only the injustice but also the blind senselessness of it revealed in numerous episodes of that period. Digressing somewhat from the story line, we can recall one day when Volodya came to us with a draft letter he wanted to send to Kosygin, the then Chairman of the Council of Ministers. Volodya wrote that the covered stadium at Luzhniki stood empty on dozens of nights, and he suggested that he could give concerts there on such nights. He stressed that he would "stick closely to the approved programme, without improvisation", that is to say, he guaranteed that he would only perform those songs that were loyal to the regime, loyal even by the standards of those days. He rightly predicted that the vast auditorium would always be full. "Everyone will profit by the scheme," wrote Vysotsky. "The spectators will get a good concert, I will get creative satisfaction, and the state will be able to build another power station with the money gained in just one season..."

These days, there is no need to prove the plain common sense of that approach: it was a normal approach of an intelligent man of our times. In those times, though, they didn't even bother to answer Vysotsky's letter.

But let us go back, to the second problem of the future film. The circumstances changed, and Alexei Batalov could not start to work on the film at that time, he had another job in hand. But neither the TV nor the Odessa Studios could wait: planned targets were planned targets. So another director had to be found.

Those were the circumstances in which we had to fight our "strategic battles" — and we had to do it together with the director.

But we still could not pick our director, although we had a gentlemen's agreement with the Odessa Studios that we had the right to do so.

One day Volodya, who was terribly anxious about his future part, and kept continually in touch, phoned to invite us to lunch at the Central House of Writers. We accepted the invitation with pleasure, and met him early in the afternoon on the verandah of the House.

"I want to introduce you to a friend of mine," Volodya said during lunch. "He is a director of the Odessa Studios, Slava Govorukhin. I played in several of his films. He loves *The Era of Mercy*, he's positively dreaming of screening it. Would you like to meet him? Maybe you'll like him."

We said we'd meet him.

At that time we knew nothing about Govorukhin, we had not seen any of his films, but when he came and began speaking of our novel, we simply melted. That feeling must be familiar to many writers: he quoted the *Era*... by the page, he knew it by heart, and he favoured the same principles of cinematographic treatment of the material as we did. In the end Slava suggested, with some embarrassment, quite understandable in this situation, that we choose him, swearing not to change a single word in our script without our consent (incidentally, the principal stumbling-block in our dealings with directors).

Vysotsky warmly supported Govorukhin.

"You know," he said, "there are directors who are struck by brilliant ideas on the set, so they start maiming the script right there and then..."

"We know," we sighed bitterly.

"Now, I can give you my word that Slava is not one of these, he's a serious chap!"

As God is our witness, we could appreciate Volodya's recommendation; besides, we could see for ourselves that Govorukhin was a serious person.

The alliance took shape, and we began acting together with the director now. Our persistence, all kinds of military ruses, and the support of the consultants of the film, Generals Nikitin and Samokhvalov, who were then Deputy Minister and Chief of Staff of the USSR Interior Ministry respectively, carried the day: Vladimir Vysotsky was confirmed as Gleb Zheglov.

At the time when the screening began, we had already written scripts for quite a few films, but we had never seen anyone work *so much and so hard* as did Vysotsky. Generally speaking, it has been observed that the higher an actor's creative standard, the more conscientiously he works. Vysotsky's diligence both on the set and between the shooting periods was amazing. He kept searching and thinking — not only about his part but also about the film as a whole. We don't think that the only cause for that was his love for *his* Zheglov and for the story of the film. It was rather professionalism of the highest order, the professionalism of an actor and a true man of letters.

During the shooting, he kept spouting new ideas, sharing them with the director and ourselves. He never went a huff when these ideas were rejected, and he was radiant, when they were accepted.

We recall our search for an organic cinematographic solution of the episode in the cellar. The gangsters took Sharapov along as a hostage, and we were absolutely at a loss how to get him out of the fix. In the novel, Zheglov simply "heard the cry of Sharapov's soul": the only place where Sharapov could hide from the gangsters was the small closet with a thick door. In prose, this kind of "heuristic insight" is quite possible. In the cinema, we had to find a visual solution. Vysotsky and ourselves, we spent hours in search for a way out, until the idea came to pin a picture of Sharapov's beloved on the door of the closet, as a sign that the hiding place was there.

And there were quite a few of these joint quests and solutions.

People often ask us why Zheglov in the film was gentler and more human than Zheglov in the novel. The answer is quite simple: despite his love for the character of the novel, Volodya simply could not be a photographic image of that character; he breathed his own personality into that character; hence the gentleness and the humanity. Thus, when we discussed the plan of one of the last episodes of the film — Levchenko's escape attempt — Vysotsky said bitterly:

"I just can't shoot a man in cold blood at five paces — and with a mischievous grin, yet, as you have it in the novel... There must be something that will force me to do it... Let's think."

And it was he who made the suggestion.

"Supposing Levchenko's escape is real... Supposing he can disappear in another second — then my shooting will be somehow justified. Otherwise, I will look just like the 'chap from Vologda' in my own song: 'A step aside is an escape, the guards will shoot without warning...'"

So we played the episode like Volodya suggested.

It takes a long time to screen a serial. Imperceptibly, Volodya became the heart and soul of the whole unit. All those long months when people get tired, when they inevitably get sick and tired of each other, Volodya always found a way to diffuse the tensest of situations. He would joke, he would try to cheer the people by telling a good joke (incidentally, he never told any bad ones). If that did not help, he took up his guitar, and sang one of his songs, most often a funny one, and the people's faces lit up with a smile, the stresses disappeared, and we could go on working.

That Volodya knew his part to a T went without saying. The remarkable thing was that he knew by heart, to the "tiniest note", as he put it, the roles of his partners and of all the other characters. He spared neither time nor effort rehearsing again and again the episodes in which Konkin/Sharapov had to pose as a gangster among gangsters in their den, teaching him the criminal lexicon

386

and the intonations, which he knew as good as the authors.

It was a pleasure to see the way Vysotsky treated the other actors — respectfully, patiently, and with the greatest goodwill, despite his fame that was by that time enormous. That fame did not spoil him at all, and he treated any actor, even someone totally unknown, as his equal. Everyone paid him back with fond admiration: it had to be seen, the tenderness with which everyone in the unit, from the director and the leads down to the most modest lights operator, looked at Volodya. And he just worked along with all the others — simply and cheerfully, patiently and perseveringly.

He had it tougher than most of the others. For one thing, his part was a long one, and not too simple, either; and then he could not drop his work at the theatre, or his concerts — he had his hands full, as he put it. Very often, right after the end of the day's shooting at the Odessa Film Studios, the studio gates would open, and a police car, its siren going, would rush Vysotsky to the last plane for Moscow. About an hour or so later, another police car would pick him up in Vnukovo (we should mention that the USSR Interior Ministry helped him with a will), lights blinking, it would tear towards and through Moscow to the Taganka Theatre, while Police Captain Gleb Zheglov was transformed into Hamlet, Prince of Denmark, before the pedestrians' eyes, with the aid of the makeup woman...

When the play was over, he had to hurry back to the studio; no time to tarry, but the regular flight had already taken off for Odessa. A transport plane would do just as well, or an Air Force anything, not to wreck the next day's shooting...

...Vysotsky's songs in films. Many people were amazed that *The Place of the Rendezvous...*, a long TV film in which Vysotsky played the lead, had not one single song for him to sing.

It was like this. Originally, all of us — the authors, the director, Vysotsky himself — would not dream of letting the film appear without a few new songs from Volodya.

So he began writing them, he made a few rough notes

(it was assumed that there would be one song for each of the five parts), but one day, as we were walking in the morning through the large park of the Odessa Studios before the day's shooting, Volodya said:

"Boys, I have some awful doubts... About the songs..."

We did not quite see what he was driving at, at first.

"Look, the action is set in the last months of 1945," Volodya continued. "It's all about detective Zheglov and his group. It's easy for me to turn into Zheglov, I just become Zheglov, believe me... I guess the audiences will also see no one but Zheglov before them. Imagine, though, that I'm taking up my guitar, that I start singing... Aren't you afraid that we'll destroy the image? I'm afraid that the people may see it as a Vysotsky concert number, and my character will split into two. Do we want that?"

After a turbulent discussion we had to admit that he was right, though we were awfully sorry, having got accustomed to the idea of having a few of Vysotsky's songs connected with our film. Alas, he was dead right; however great his love for the new brain-child might be, Volodya always retained a sober professional view of the proportion between the necessary and the redundant in a film.

It is no accident that we stress here his love for his work, for the Zheglov character; Volodya did not merely reveal his enthusiasm during the shooting of the film — he proved the strength of that enthusiasm later.

When we were halfway through the shooting period, Volodya suddenly said to us:

"Look here, brothers, you have absolutely no right to abandon Gleb Zheglov..."

At first, we did not see what he meant. It turned out that he was nursing an idea for a sequel to *The Place of the Rendezvous*... in which the main character would, of course, be Zheglov played by himself. He even had certain ideas for the story line, which he immediately outlined to us. The ideas were interesting, but we could not accept his suggestion, not at that time, at any rate, for we had other plans and other obligations: a great deal of work would have to be done on a new novel that we had embarked upon. Without rejecting the idea, we therefore tried to put off its realisation. But we reckoned without Vysotsky. He resolutely rejected our tepid objections, proving to us that we simply had to "give to the people what belonged to them in all justice — Zheglov and his story". Having begun in this vein, Vysotsky returned to the subject again and again whenever we met, each time finding new arguments. "I'll persuade you whatever it may cost me," he said. "We must go on with Zheglov."

The more stubborn we got, the more varied were Volodya's methods of attack; he used both the carrot and the stick, now taking us to task, now praising us immoderately. We still stuck to our guns, although on the quiet we were beginning to think out the literary aspects of his idea.

One day he came to our place with a guitar and said, "I've written some new songs. Would you like to hear them?" Who would refuse to listen to Vysotsky? And Volodya started to sing.

> *Arkady and Georgi Vainer,*
> *Salaam to you, you and your art.*
> *I guess there can be nothing finer —*
> *You know the Penal Code by heart...*

And so on and so forth, the whole of the long and funny song about the Vainer brothers, so widely known now. Naturally we listened to it with the greatest pleasure and immediately recorded it. Volodya sang the other one, too and it was also about us. Volodya even called it *The Song about Vainerism.*

Thus we found out how pleasant it was when people wrote a song about one. It was doubly pleasant when there were two songs. And absolutely delightful when they were written and performed by Vladimir Vysotsky...

There was one thing we could do: write a song about Zheglov. So we surrendered.

We settled the details on that same day, and soon we began work on a script for a six-part TV serial, a sequel to *The Place of the Rendezvous...,* the whole to be called *The Era of Mercy.*

Alas, that work would never be completed: we were halfway through when the terrible news of Volodya's death came.

Of course, we could not imagine any other Zheglov, than Zheglov/Vysotsky. We couldn't and we would not.

He was totally of this world. Incredibly curious, he could not be indifferent to anything in the world, he was interested in everything — the world of things and the world of processes: the design of the Mercedes and the organisation of medical care in the state of New York, hypotheses of cosmogony and the price of sausage. He travelled a great deal and he saw a great deal, both in this country and abroad. He was never a mere observer but always a participant, even if it was sometimes in his mind only. He brought back innumerable impressions from his trips, and many of these were later forged into poetic lines. He spent just a few days in the Urals, and when he came back, he was full of stories about the interesting life of gold-diggers, and some time later he produced the amazing *About the Vacha River,* awfully funny, very musical, and in its own way very touching.

He was an uncommonly communicative man, he greedily absorbed the impressions of his new acquaintances, he willingly talked with them, argued with them, but never slapped them down: despite his incredible popularity, he retained his natural simplicity, and the virus of stardom missed him.

The only thing that Volodya did about his fame was ridicule it.

"So I'm sitting quietly in a corner of the restaurant, having lunch. Now this chap comes up to my table — young, good-looking, built as a safe. He looks at me suspiciously, then, bingo! he gives me one big bear hug, lifts me with my chair, practically, and kisses me most warmly: 'Volodechka, dearest, isn't it great, meeting you like this...' So we sit down and talk awhile, and then I pluck up my courage and say, 'Look, mate, I can't remember for the moment, just where it was that we met first?' The chap is honestly amazed: 'How could you have forgotten? You came to Kemerovo, right? You gave a concert at the House of Culture, remember?' 'Well, yes, I do —'. 'So who was it in the third row, next to the aisle? Me, that's who... I clapped louder than anyone else!...'"

Well, that was the reverse side of popularity. But there was also the good side.

One day, as we talked in Peredelkino with Chinghiz

Aitmatov, a very fine and interesting conversationalist in his own right, we mentioned in passing that Marina Vlady and Vysotsky would soon be visiting with us. Chinghiz was fired with the idea of meeting Vysotsky: "Boys, introduce me please! I've heard so much about him, I like ever so much what he does, and I have never met him."

We introduced them to each other with the greatest pleasure, of course, and everybody profited from that acquaintanceship, the party was even more interesting than usual, for their opposite temperaments clashed: quick and explosive Volodya against the slow-moving, even somewhat heavy, solid Chinghiz. This difference in a conversation between very honest and very intelligent men is always fruitful. I remember that Chinghiz started an argument about the cycle of Vysotsky's underworld songs, expressing the view that the criminals in those songs were too ennobled and idealised. "A criminal is always a rat," said Aitmatov with total conviction "He knows neither shame nor conscience, he can betray his best friend. And in your songs they are sometimes — well, almost chivalrous."

Volodya argued that there were examples of true friendship even among the worst criminals, but in the end he gave in: "You see, Chinghiz, you mustn't take all this too literally. 'Criminal' songs — that's a whole genre; it's sentimental, melodramatic, but very sincere. Whatever you might say, my songs are stylisations. It's a form in which, I hope, I was able to convey very simple and very sincere human feelings, characters and conflicts. In a 'serious' song, the things I talk about might sound, well, a bit false," Volodya smiled here. "And these songs are parables or, to put it even plainer, fairytales, simple and honest..."

They spent a long time talking and arguing, to the accompaniment of the tooting of the toy car which Marina's youngest son drove around the flat all the evening; from time to time he would stop to talk to Volodya in French, tenderly hugging him.

Later Volodya sang. Really, even as we listen to the recording these days, we have the impression that he had never sung so well, with such abandon, emotion and pleasure. *Apples of Paradise*, *The Old House*, *Customs*

House, A Trip Abroad. Honestly, we believed that at our flat Volodya sang better than anywhere else, he felt more relaxed and cheerful, and enjoyed himself more. We cannot really insist on this of course, for, as the Russian proverb has it, every sandpiper praises its own marsh.

At parting, Volodya said very sincerely: "Arkasha, Zhora, thank you so much for Chinghiz. It was your gift to me today — I have wanted so much to meet him for a long time... Now we'll all be friends together..."

Alas, this too proved to be a dream that never came true.

It's terribly sad when dreams, especially dreams that could easily become true, are not realised. Vladimir Vysotsky lived through a great many happy moments, but he must have known more bitterness than happiness. He had certain sore spots, and one of them was his great desire, probably a naive one, to become a member of the Writers' Union. What's another hecatomb to Zeus, one would have thought? What's formal membership in the literary union to Vysotsky who was crowned with the laurels of the whole people's admiration — laurels which, incidentally, very few writers can boast of?

Of course, it would be useful to recall here what Vysotky was *in formal terms*: he had no rewards and no titles, he was an ordinary actor of an ordinary, though highly popular, theatre; he was at the very bottom of the theatrical hierarchy, an actor with a pitiful salary, "not a member of anything", as Volodya put it, smiling bitterly.

His desire may have been somewhat childish: to the very end, there was a wonderful air of boyishness about that serious and intelligent man, a real man.

It may also be that the entire environment in which he lived induced a certain lack of confidence in his own poetic talent — who knows? This is quite possible. We were present at a conversation between Vysotsky and a very prominent poet — and a very talented one, in our view — who condescendingly explained, from his Olympian heights, the difference between *verse* and *texts of songs*, even if they were the very best *texts*. Volodya listened to him, teeth clenched; he did not argue, he did not make a single objection, he simply put his poems back in the folder. But *we* couldn't stand it, we blew up, and although we are no poets at all, we told the great master just where he got off, with his snobbishness and arrogance. But our intervention was not professional, and the poet merely patted our shoulders condescendingly, as he had Volodya's.

His authority did not convince us, though; we believed then, as we believe now, that literary critics and historians, and poets themselves, will yet put in a professional word in defence of the remarkable and unique master whose work marked, in our view, a whole epoch in contemporary Russian Soviet poetry.

Everybody is speaking about it now. No one wanted to, then. Not even the famous poets who now turn out to have been Volodya's best friends... He did not live to win his more respectable brethren's recognition; only millions of people at his funeral, and his tomb that stands like a hill of ever blooming flowers, forced them to pay attention to, and recognise, his remarkable gift. It was already after his death that Vysotsky was awarded the prize for the best male role in the TV serial *The Place of the Rendezvous Can't Be Changed* at the All-Union Festival in Baku; it was also posthumously that his first book of poems was published — and even that one did not include some of his best works; it was also posthumously that the first normal-size LP of Vysotsky's songs was issued, a planet was called by his name, and the USSR State Prize for the part of Zheglov, awarded him; this book will also appear post-humously.

All this should have happened during his life.

This may prove a lesson to all of us. Indeed, what does a genius need for happiness? Only love, and a little human gratitude...

We had so many conversations with Volodya, so many arguments and heart to heart talks; there were quite a few personal nuances in our relationship, and episodes from our personal life involving him. All this must of course be interesting to his admirers.

But there must be a sense of proportion about any

reminiscences about the people who are no longer with us. As Vysotsky himself wrote:

> *I hate when people peer over my shoulder*
> *And crane their necks to try to read my mail.*

So we shall stop here, too, having paid the tribute of our love and respect to this remarkable artist — poet, musician, singer, actor — whose principal talent was, and will eternally be, the talent of being human.

Vladimir Vysotsky giving a concert

Vysotsky, his father and step-mother. Germany, 1948

Vysotsky in Eberswalde. 1948

Vladimir Vysotsky and his mother, Nina Maximovna.

1941

Vysotsky in the village of Valentinovka.
1951

Vysotsky and his friends at the
Exhibition of the Achievements of the
National Economy. 1954. On the left :
Vladimir Akimov

Vysotsky and his wife Iza. 1957

Vysotsky as Galileo in Bertolt Brecht's
Life of Galileo

Vysotsky and Valery Zolotukhin. The
first years of the Taganka Theatre

Vysotsky as Khlopusha in *Pugachov*
after Sergei Yesenin

Vysotsky as Kerensky in John Reed's *Ten Days That Shook the World*

Vysotsky as Svidrigailov in Dostoyevsky's *Crime and Punishment*.

Vysotsky as Hamlet

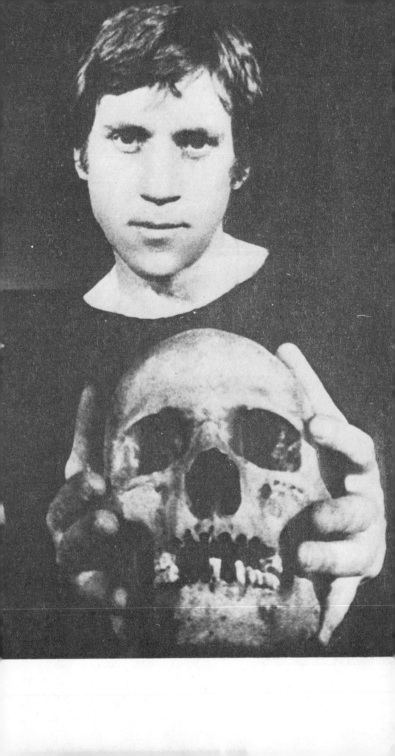

Vysotsky and Yuri Lyubimov

Vysotsky as Lopakhin in *Cherry Orchard* after Anton Chekhov

After a performance

Vladimir Vysotsky in the films:

713 Requests Permission to Land

Leave of Absence

Two Buddies Served

How Czar Peter Had His Blackamoor Married

Little Tragedies

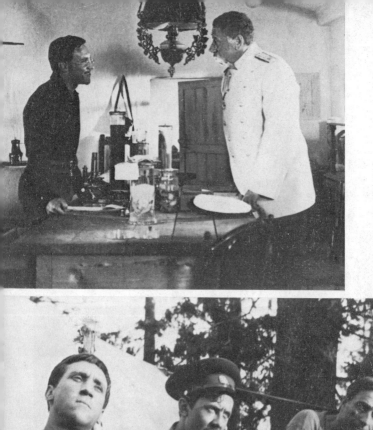

The Bad Good Man

Master of the Taiga

The Place of the Rendezvous Can't Be Changed

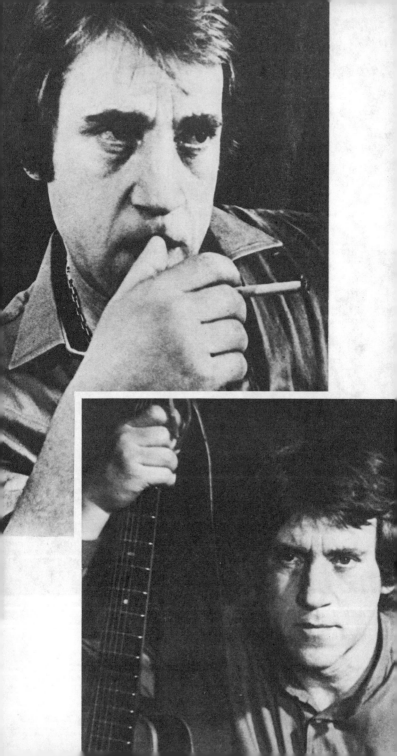

Vysotsky and Bulat Okudzava

Vysotsky and artist Mikhail Shemyakin

In Mexico

In the gold fields. Visiting with Vadim
Tumanov

A housewarming party in Malaya
Gruzinskaya. 1975

Vysotsky and Marina Vlady

Brief Notes on the Authors

Bella Akhmadulina — Soviet poet; at one time, a member of the artistic council of the Taganka Theatre of Drama and Comedy.

Vladimir Akimov (b. 1937) — scriptwriter; a friend of Vladimir Vysotsky.

Vladimir Beekman (b. 1929) — Soviet Estonian writer.

Andrei Dementyev (b. 1928) — Soviet poet; editor-in-chief of the *Yunost* magazine.

Alla Demidova — theatre and film actress; Vysotsky's partner over many years in Taganka productions.

Alexander Gorodnitsky (b. 1933) — Dr. Sc. (Geology and Mineralogy); one of the originators of the genre of the Soviet "author's song".

Joseph Heifitz (b. 1905) — Soviet film director; he made the films *One of Us* (1975) and *The Bad Good Man* (1973) in which Vysotsky played.

Igor Kokhanovsky (b. 1938) — Soviet poet, a friend of Vysotsky in his youth.

Lyubomir Levchev (b. 1935) — Bulgarian poet, head of the Writers' Union of Bulgaria.

Bulat Okudzhava (b. 1924) — Soviet writer and poet; one of the founders of the genre of "author's song" in the Soviet Union; at one time a member of the artistic council of the Taganka Theatre.

Gennady Poloka (b. 1930) — Soviet film director; in 1967, he directed the film *The Intervention* in which Vladimir Vysotsky played.

David Samoilov (b. 1920) — Soviet poet, one of the authors of the scenic composition *The Fallen and the Living* in which Vysotsky appeared more than 700 times. Samoilov was a member of the artistic council of the Taganka Theatre.

Mikhail Shemyakin (b. 1940) — Russian artist; since 1971, he has lived first in France, then in the USA; a close friend of Vysotsky's last years.

Yuri Trifonov (1925-1981) — Soviet writer.

Vadim Tumanov (b. 1927) — head of a gold-diggers' team; a close friend of Vysotsky.

Mikhail Ulyanov (b. 1927) — film and theatre actor.

Arkady (b. 1931) and Georgi (b. 1938) Vainer — Soviet writers, authors of the screenplay for the TV serial *The Place of the Rendezvous Can't Be Changed* (1979).

Andrei Voznesensky (b. 1933) — Soviet poet; author of a number of scenic compositions for the Taganka Theatre.

Iza Vysotskaya — the poet's first wife; a theatre actress.

Yevgeny Yevtushenko (b. 1933) — Soviet poet.

Valery Zolotukhin (b. 1941) — theatre and film actor, Vysotsky's partner in many films and drama productions.

Notes

The texts of the poems published here are the result of A. Ye. Krylov's work on all the sources available at this date (January 1988): the author's MSS and tape-recordings, publications during his lifetime, and so on. As a rule, they are final variants approved by the author, and reflect most fully the author's will.

On My Song Writing
[1] The text was written by Vysotsky in the early 1970s as notes for a talk.

N. M. Vysotskaya, "Kindness Was His Main Character Trait"
Ogonyok, 1986, No. 38.

S. V. Vysotsky, "That's What My Son Was Like"
Argumenty i fakty, 1987, No. 3.

Iza Vysotskaya, "Life Was Wonderful When Volodya Was Alive"
Studenchesky meridian, 1987, No. 12.
[1] *Foma Gordeyev* (1899) — a novel by Maxim Gorky (1868-1936).
[2] Oleg Borisov (b. 1929) — Soviet actor.
[3] *Uncle Vanya* (1897) — a play by Anton Chekhov (1860-1904).

The Father Through the Eyes of the Son. An Interview with N. Vysotsky
Argumenty i fakty, 1987, No. 51.

Marina Vlady, "I'm Living Thanks to You..."
Ogonyok, 1987, No. 47.

Vladimir Akimov, Volodya (The Years of His Youth)
Written in 1987 for the present collection.
[1] Works by Fyodor Dostoyevsky (1821-1881).
[2] A novel by Mikhail Sholokhov (1905-1984).
[3] A novel by Alexei Tolstoy (1882/83-1945).
[4] A novel by Alexander Stepanov, a Russian Soviet writer (1892-1965).
[5] A novel by the Russian Soviet writer Vyacheslav Shishkov (1873-1945).
[6] A sci-fi novel by Alexei Tolstoy.

[7] Mikhail Shchepkin (1788-1863) — Russian actor, founder of realism in Russian scenic art, reformer of the Russian theatre.

[8] Maria Yermolova (1853-1928) — Russian actress, a major figure in Russian theatrical art.

Igor Kokhanovsky, The Beginning
Written in 1987 for the present collection. Abridged.

Vadim Tumanov, Life Without Lying
Ogonyok, 1987, No. 4. Expanded for the present collection.

[1] Nikolai Nekrasov (1821-1877/78) — Russian poet. In 1847-1866, editor and publisher of *Sovremennik*, a magazine which spread revolutionary and democratic ideas and realistic aesthetics.

[2] A literary-artistic and socio-political monthly.

Mikhail Shemyakin, About Volodya (The Last Years)
Written in 1987 for the present collection.

Bella Akhmadulina, A Word about Vysotsky
Sovetsky ekran, 1987, No. 10.

Mikhail Ulyanov, "He Lived Like He Sang..."
Teatr, 1987, No. 5.

Alla Demidova, "He Wrote the Way He Lived..."
Literaturnoye obozreniye, 1987, No. 1.

[1] Ilya Averbakh (1934-1986) — Soviet director, and scriptwriter

Valery Zolotukhin, "It Was Like I Said, or A Study in an Unstable Vowel"
Ogonyok, 1986, No. 28.

Yuri Trifonov, A Few Lines about Vladimir Vysotsky
The reminiscences were written in 1980; they were discovered in the writer's archives after his death.

David Samoilov, My Acquaintanceship with Vysotsky
Written for the present collection in 1987.

[1] Yekaterina Furtseva (1910-1974) — the then Minister of Culture.

[2] Boris Slutsky (1919-1986) and Alexander Mezhirov (b. 1923) — Soviet poets.

[3] *The Day of Poetry* — a yearbook of verse.

Gennady Poloka, "He Quickly Shook Off the Burden of Each Defeat..."
Avrora, 1987, No. 8. The memoirs were expanded for the present collection.

Joseph Heifitz, Two Films with Vysotsky
Written in 1987 for the present collection.

The Vainer Brothers, Notes about Vladimir Vysotsky
Written in 1987 for the present. collection.

Общественно-политическая литература

Серия «Мемуары и биографии»

Владимир ВЫСОЦКИЙ.
ЧЕЛОВЕК. ПОЭТ. АКТЕР.

Составитель *Юрий Андреевич Андреев*

На английском языке

ИБ № 17552

Редактор русского текста *Г. И. Дзюбенко*

Редактор английского текста *Л. А. Романова*

Художник *Б. А. Казаков*

Художественный редактор *Ф. Б. Денисов*

Технический редактор *Е. В. Антонова*

Сдано в набор 20.07.89. Подписано в печать 26.03.90.
Формат 84×100^1/$_{32}$. Бумага офсетная № 1. Гарнитура тип. таймс. Печать офсетная. Условн. печ. л. 20,67.
Усл. кр.-отт. 41,63. Уч.-изд. л. 21,22. Тираж 16770 экз.
Заказ № 985. Цена 2 р. 80 к. Изд. № 46558.

Ордена Трудового Красного Знамени издательство
"Прогресс" Государственного комитета СССР по
печати. 119847, ГСП, Москва, Г-21, Зубовский
бульвар, 17.

Можайский полиграфкомбинат В/О "Совэкспорткнига" Государственного комитета СССР по печати.
143200, Можайск, ул. Мира, 93.